MR. SPEAKER

MR. SPEAKER

THE
BIOGRAPHY
OF
TOM
MURPHY

By Richard Hyatt

MERCER UNIVERSITY PRESS

1979   1999

TWENTY YEARS OF PUBLISHING EXCELLENCE

ISBN 0-86554-607-X
MUP/H458

© 1999 Mercer University Press
6316 Peake Road
Macon, Georgia 31210-3960

First Edition.

Library of Congress Cataloging-in-Publication Data

Hyatt, Richard, 1944–
     Mr. Speaker: the biography of Tom Murphy
          p. cm.
     Includes bibliographical references and index.
     ISBN 0-86554-607-X
     1. Murphy, Thomas Bailey, 1924– 2. Legislators — Biography.
3. Georgia. General Assembly. House of Representatives — Speaker — Biography.
4. Georgia — Politics and government — 1951– I. Title: Mister Speaker. II. Title.

CONTENTS

*To Johnny Mitchell, a friend who can unlock doors
you didn't even know were there.*

PROLOGUE

HIS

BROTHER

THE

HERO

JAMES MURPHY TURNS his back to the top of the stairs at the rear of the courthouse. He looks down at his brother who is there to catch him if he falls. A crutch is under each arm. He takes a breath, then reaches up and plants one of the crutches on the step behind him, pulling a lifeless leg up beside it. Then the other crutch, and the other leg. Determination covers his face, not pain, though he's forcing his body to do things it never expected to do. Between steps, he rests. Then he does it again. One more time. One step at a time.

Every morning when court is in session, Tom Murphy picks his older brother up in Bremen, seven miles away. They drive to the courthouse in Buchanan with a heavy and cumbersome steel wheelchair tied to the top of the car. Tom parks as close to the back door of the two-story building as he can. It's early, long before court, long before there would be an audience for their tedious climb to the second floor. He helps James up to the backdoor, then the two of them, together, start up those rickety wooden stairs.

One crutch. One leg. One step.

Most folks use the front stairs, twenty-eight steps that wind through a cupola 110 feet above the ground. The courtroom is divided by a center aisle with two sections of broad benches. If this were a house of God instead of law, you would call them pews. Tall windows on either side of the room reach almost to the top of the ageless oaks outside. Even when the windows are open it gets Georgia-hot in there, so people bring fans with them, funeral home fans with pictures on the front of Jesus knocking at the door or of the scene at the Last Supper. People need the fans to keep cool and to knock away gnats that come inside and make themselves at home.

Jurors sit in a fenced off section, their backs to the spectators, their eyes on the judge. The judge sits on a throne that looks out on the room as if the people sitting there are his subjects, reminding all who come that he is the judge and when he swings his gavel this is his one-room kingdom. This is where the Murphys, James and Tom, make their living. But first they have to get there, one step at a time.

They reach the top. James is tired but says nothing. He slowly goes into the courtroom, while Tom goes down for the wheelchair. Chair in hand, he muscles his way back up the stairs, setting it up for his brother and helping him into it. It will be a long day as they wait for their cases to be called. When lunchtime comes, Tom Murphy goes out to the town square and buys lunch. He takes his brother's food back to the courtroom. Twice a day up and down those stairs is enough for both of them.

The courthouse is the centerpiece of the town square in Buchanan, Georgia, the Haralson County seat. At the square is the intersection of US 27 and Georgia 120. Highway 27 is a lively road. For in the days before sterile interstates it was the major route coming and going from Florida. Court convenes twice a year and it's an event. When a talked-about case is on the docket, justice is a spectator sport and seats are scarce. Latecomers sit on the windowsills, if there's room.

Sometimes, Tom's stair-step children, Mike, Martha, and Lynn, come along. He gives them a nickel each and they wander the square looking for five-cent treasures. Coming to work with their Daddy and Uncle James is a treat. They stretch the money to the four corners, waiting for lunch and their Daddy.

The court is James Murphy's arena. His legs don't work, but his mind does. He and his brother are law partners. He had another partner who died during World War II and Tom joined him after the Navy in the Pacific and law school at the University of Georgia. James is among the county's more able lawyers and some times other lawyers ask him about a point of law.

"Look it up," he advises. "You'll remember it better if you look it up."

During a recess, the judge sometimes casually wanders out and whispers a question to James. He has a keen legal mind, which means he not only knows the law, he understands it. When their cases are being heard, James shuffles the papers and Tom argues and closes, for he is known for his fire and brimstone delivery and how well he thinks on his feet. James's feet dangle out of a wheel chair.

When court is over, the lawyers pat their clients on the back and finish their paperwork. By then, the courtroom is nearly empty. James climbs out of his wheelchair and sits on a bench while Tom refolds the chair and takes it down to the car. Then, slowly, one crutch and one step at a time, they repeat the morning routine. James Murphy turns his back to the top of the stairs. His face looks down at his brother who is there to catch him if he falls.

Neither of the brothers knew it at the time. How could they? But over the years the memory of James has been there to catch Tom Murphy when *he* has been about to fall.

1

BREMEN'S

BAD

BOY

TROUBLE FOLLOWED TOM and Carl like a lonesome dog. Not that the Murphy boy or Carl McPherson were bad. They weren't criminals or delinquents, just what folks used to call live wires. In those days, if there was a commotion anywhere around Bremen, folks didn't ask who did it, rather where was Tom and his buddy Carl.

They were farm boys. But so were all the young guys in Haralson County. They rode their bicycles everywhere, even places they weren't supposed to go. They rode to the swimming pool if they had a nickel to get in—which wasn't often—or they pedaled out to the creek to swim in the wash hole. If the fish were biting, they went fishing, watching the cork bob up and down on top of the water, not knowing what a rod and reel was.

Life wasn't all play for Tom Murphy or his friends. There were animals to feed—cows, hogs, and chickens. And when they were old enough, Tom and his older brother James had to work in the garden. It was work, too. If their garden didn't prosper, there would not be red ripe tomatoes on their plates or peas to put up or corn to grind for meal. The Murphy garden had to stand their Daddy's inspection, too. In their garden, there was no room for Morning Glories. It had to be as clean as their dinner table. But there was always time for some trouble.

Such as a day at school when a boy who sat behind him brought a homemade model airplane to class. Tom Murphy sat on the front row. Always did. Teachers wanted him up front so they could keep an eye on him. When the other boy dropped his little plane, Tom picked it up and slammed it on a table. Sixty something years later, he gives a blow-by-blow of what happened. "He had on one of those aviator caps, the ones with goggles. He yanked it off and hit me. Didn't have the goggles on but there were these snaps and buckles. He hit me across the head and it hurt. I came up out of that desk and went after him. We liked to have tore that room up. Fast as he'd get up, I'd hit him again."

The two boys were sent to the principal's office and the other fellow went in first. Murphy sat outside, and he could hear his classmate's testimony. He said Tom started it all, that he hadn't done anything. The principal listened. Then he called in the rawboned Tom to hear his side of it.

"I just told the plain facts," Murphy says.

The principal left the two boys in his office and went back to their class to ask some of the girls what had happened. When he came back, he took the other boy into his office and as Murphy remembers it, "liked to have beat that other boy to death." Now it was Tom's turn, which he still tells with the passion of an adolescent. "'Tommy,' he said (he always called me Tommy and I despised it) 'Tommy, you know you ought not to be fighting in school. I know what happened, but you know I gotta whip you.' Then he hit me two licks."

As soon as the afternoon bell rang, Tom Murphy headed for the door, bounded down to the street and started running. Ahead of him, running for his young life, was the boy with the aviator cap. "He knew I'd be coming after him and he got himself a running start. I chased him all the way to his house. He ran inside and his Mama wouldn't let him come out. I finally went on home."

When Murphy's Daddy got home that evening, he already knew what had happened at school. Towns like Bremen didn't need CNN or cell phones. Daddies just had a way of finding out things, especially bad things. Murphy knew that the whipping he was about to get would be far worse than the one he was given at school.

It wasn't the only whipping he ever got, at home or at school. So why the vivid details and why the raw emotions after all these years? "I remember that one," he says, "Because I didn't think I deserved that one." Big thoughts for a kid and a way of life for the man he became.

For Thomas Bailey Murphy, this was a simple world, one that extended only as far as the county line. He was born 10 March 1924, in a house near Bremen High School. His father, Willliam Harvey Murphy, was a telegrapher and agent for the Central of Georgia Railroad, a job he held for forty-four years. On weekends, he was an ordained Primitive Baptist preacher, "a foot-washing Baptist," his son will tell you. He was also one of the few men in the county who was a member of organized labor. His mother, Leta Jones Murphy, ran the house and, when she was needed, she worked beside the men out in the field. Even when her boys were little, she pulled a heavy sack up and down the rows of cotton.

The Murphys had been around that West Georgia county since before the Civil War, coming there from South Carolina. His grandfather, Bailey Murphy, was ramrod straight with a flowing white mustache. When Tom was just a boy, his grandfather enraptured him with colorful stories of the elder's childhood such as hearing the cannons in the Battle of

New Hope Church in Paulding County, the battle in which his own father was shot and killed.

On Sundays, the family would often go out and visit his grandparents, piling into an old Model A. His grandmother always hid homemade cookies in a lard bucket, knowing the boys would find them. "But we always stood there and waited until she said it was all right to eat them. Best cookies I ever had," Murphy recalls. With grandmother's cookies they wanted milk and they had to pull it up from the well on the back porch. More was kept cold in the nearby creek. So was butter. They didn't have an icebox. Not that it would have done them any good since they lived at the end of a country road, a dusty path that no ice truck would have ventured down.

Five years after Tom Murphy was born, the country was hit by the Great Depression. In the beginning, he noticed few changes around Bremen, where the only stock a young boy worried about was grazing in the pasture. But as time passed, even a free-spirited boy on his bike began to sense something was going on.

Men gathered in his father's office at the Central of Georgia every day at noon to watch the ticker for stock prices. News was not good for William Murphy. He lost everything he had dealing with cotton futures. Sometimes, Tom would go down to the Central of Georgia office where his father worked. Five trains came through there every day so it was a busy place to be. For Murphy, it seemed to be the center of the universe watching people buying tickets for a ride to Birmingham or Atlanta or some other faraway spot. There was freight to be moved to the dock and mail to get ready. But soon there were other sights.

"I'd be there with my Daddy and see whole families riding on flat-beds or coal cars, going somewhere hoping to find a job. I can remember their faces," he says. "Then folks started coming up to our back door, good folks, wanting to know if they could cut wood, anything for a hot meal."

There was talk of the local bank failing. His father was a director at the Farmers & Merchants Bank and when it went under he had to pay his share of the assessment. For his son, it was even more personal. What about his savings?

"I lost $13 and some two cents," he says. "But I didn't worry much. I knew Pop would take care of it. Still have that bank book, too, in the vault."

The bank book is a reminder of a time that was both childlike and sobering, an era that would shape him in ways he wouldn't understand until many years later. For around the dinner table he began to hear about Herbert Hoover and the Republicans and the shape they had gotten the world into. Later, he heard even more about Mr. Roosevelt, how the Democrats and the New Deal were going to help straighten things out.

Across the county was a CCC Camp. As a young person, Murphy didn't know that it stood for Civilian Conservation Corps, that it was a program President Roosevelt had created to put men back to work, to return to them a slice of dignity that they had lost. All Murphy knew was that sometimes on Saturdays guys from that camp were around town, all wearing green uniforms.

Roy and Warren Sewell came to town about this same time from Atlanta and their presence would forever change the face of Bremen and the counties around it. They could make suits in Atlanta but not money, so the Sewells had been shopping for a new home for their burgeoning company. Nine years before, they quit their jobs as drummers sharing a dream that one day they would sell clothing they made instead of suits that had been manufactured up North. Their first venture was in Atlanta. There were few paved roads and no trucking lines to move their goods so, needing to be near the railroad, they had set up shop near Terminal and Union stations, first on Mitchell Street and then on Forsyth Street.

Rent in Atlanta proved costly. People who worked for them couldn't afford to live there and the Sewells couldn't afford to raise wages. So for months they had been looking for a new location. Everywhere they looked there was some kind of drawback. That was on their mind one afternoon when on an Atlanta street they ran into a friend who knew about their dilemma. He was from Bremen, Georgia, a town of three or four hundred people that was cut in half by the Southern Railroad—ninety minutes out of Atlanta and three and a half hours from Birmingham.

"And right there in Bremen, the Southern crosses the Central of Georgia," he added.

The Sewells were intrigued enough to pay Bremen a visit. They soon met J. J. Mangham, a former state senator, who had founded the Bank of Bremen in 1903. He was glad to do business with the two brothers from down the road in Graham, Alabama. What transpired between him and the Sewells is not clear, but a deal was struck. Some say he loaned them $100,000, an unlikely amount for a small town bank in those years. But Mangham was also mayor, and before it was over the Bremen City Council had given Sewell Manufacturing Company the city-owned light plant on a lot right next to the rail line. They opened for business in 1928, the first of many clothing manufacturers who would do business in that part of Georgia over the years. The newcomers would provide jobs and leadership and years later be friends to a young struggling lawyer.

The Sewells liked to say they sewed suits for the common man, "the Ford of clothing," they claimed. And as they advertised for workers in Haralson County, Warren Sewell offered his foreman a single piece of advice: "If the print of the hoe handle is in their hand, hire them."

Around Bremen, that wasn't difficult. Folks there were born with a hoe in their hand. From the day Haralson became Georgia's 112th county in 1856, it was an area not afraid of work. Surveyors took a little bit out of Carroll and a little bit of Polk to outline its 185,000 acres. Like so many other counties in the state, it was created so that farmers would be home by sundown when they hauled their crops to town and so that a person wouldn't have to stay overnight if they went to the courthouse to serve on a jury or pay their taxes.

Its land was carved out of old Indian territory bartered from General William McIntosh and the Lower Creeks in 1825. The land obtained in the purchase eventually became the Georgia counties of Carroll, Coweta, Lee, Muscogee, Troup, Polk, and Haralson. It was named for Hugh Haralson of LaGrange, a major general in the Georgia Militia and a one-time member of both the Georgia General Assembly and the United States Congress.

Buchanan became the county seat, but there were other settlements scattered around the county. Villages with the colorful names of Possum Snout and Wolf Pen sprang up in 1830, just after gold was discovered in the area. Possum Snout became Tallapoosa, site of Georgia's first free school in 1888 and the eventual home of Tallapoosa Mill and the American Thread Company — plants that were a boon to area cotton farmers.

Wolf Pen became an incoporated town in 1883, changing its name to Kramer, after a German immigrant. His vineyard was near what is now the center of Bremen — the name he suggested to honor his hometown in Germany. Built around the railroad tracks which were laid in the 1890s, the original city government could not collect taxes exceeding three-tenths of one percent. People who didn't pay their taxes were put to work on city streets.

For youngsters like Murphy, it was a wonderful place to be a boy. But his father had plans that extended beyond baseball, basketball, and all the activities his son and his friends enjoyed. William Harvey Murphy had only a fourth grade education, but he intended for his sons to do better than he did. When Tom talked about being a fireman or an engineer and working for the railroad, his father would remind him that people needed an education if they were going to be somebody.

His brother James was an outstanding student and Tom was better than he likes to admit. "Just decent," he claims. But at Bremen High, there was a rule in those days that if a student made above a certain average in a class, they didn't have to take the final exam in that course. Tom Murphy took only one final—in geometry. And like his memory of the school room fight, this one gets his Irish up.

"I had the average in geometry," he explains to anyone who'll listen. "But the school superintendent taught that course himself and he decided that no matter what your average was, you had to take the final exam."

More than school, there was baseball.

On the school team, he was the catcher and Red Cruze was the pitcher, all six-foot-four, 230 pounds of him. "When he threw, it looked like a marble coming up there. That big old leg would come and there it was," he remembers.

Even as a teen-ager, he played for the town team, in a lineup that included mostly grownups. The mills had teams and so did most of the nearby towns. There was plenty of competition, some of it not so friendly such as the day Murphy's unpredictable mouth almost cost him his health, if not his life.

One of the guys on the other team had been hit by a wild throw. Not just anywhere, but in an area of the male anatomy that pains a man just to think about it. The boy was rolling around on the ground, holding his groin. He was hollering and he was rolling. Murphy—his teammates called him "Cotton"—stood over the fallen baserunner, a wad of chewing tobacco in his cheek the size of a golf ball. Everybody there saw him spew a stream of tobacco juice on the fellow. "Aw, hell, he's dead," Murphy said. "Let's get on with the game."

Seeing what he had done, outraged fans ran from the dusty sidelines and chased Murphy off the diamond. But to

Murphy, that's the way you're supposed to play the game and live your life: spikes high, belly to the ground. There was a little bit of Ty Cobb in him, and still is. If he could, he'd wear spikes all the time and he'd keep them sharpened. "I never was good at taking anything from nobody," he says.

Except his Daddy. Tom Murphy worshipped him as much as anybody in his life except his older brother James. Both of them were steadying influences on the sometime tempestuous youth. "Son, you're plain spoken sometimes," his Daddy would tell him. "You're too plain spoken."

He also talked to him about his need for revenge. "Son," he said. "I don't understand you. If you owe somebody a dollar, you pay it. If somebody does you a favor, you return it. But if somebody does you a bad turn, you can't wait to give that back either—and you weren't raised that way."

THE MURPHYS WERE reared in the Primitive Baptist Church, a hard-shell group that follows the King James Bible—to the comma and to the period. There are no musical instruments, because the New Testament church had no instruments. There is no Sunday School and no missionaries because that's the way the early church was set up. There is no seminary for the preachers. They learn from each other, delivering sermons in a rhythmic patter. They believe in the humble sacrament of foot washing, because Jesus did and because the Bible describes the ancient rite.

William Murphy was a Primitive Baptist preacher, an elder in their terminology. He walked the walk and he wanted his children to follow him. "We went to church Sunday and most Saturdays," Tom Murphy says. "We went there a whole lot more Saturdays than I really wanted to go in those days. But we went. No 'ifs.' No 'ands.'"

It was a close-knit family, a trait that an older Tom Murphy also cherishes. They might bicker and quarrel, but if somebody bothered one of them, they locked arms. And it was a family that had its own law and the law was William Murphy.

"I never sassed my Mama or my Daddy as long as they lived," he says. "They were the law, and all of us knew it and respected it. Of course, I did things when I was out of sight that I shouldn't have done, but their word was law."

He admits to rebelling against only one of his Daddy's rules. "When you had company in those days, the grownups ate first and we kids ate last. I always said to myself that when I had a family it wouldn't be that way. That's the way it's been, too. The little ones eat first, then the older people. That's one policy of my Daddy's that I've changed."

Because he admired his Daddy so much and because of the stability he had seen in his railroad job during the Depression years, Tom Murphy decided that when he got out of Bremen High School in 1941 he was going to get himself a railroad job. His older son James was already in school at West Georgia College, and William Murphy intended for his younger son to get more education, too. He had already enrolled him at North Georgia College, a spit-and-polish military school in the mountains of Dahlonega, Georgia.

Tom had ideas of his own. He was going to get a job with the Central of Georgia Railroad just like his Daddy. Only he was going to hop aboard one of those trains and see the world. It was more than his childlike dream of being a train engineer. He was serious now, and changing Tom Murphy's mind has always been like trying to reason with a South Georgia mule—only the mule will sometimes listen to you.

"I wanted to start making money," Murphy explains. "I took all the tests to be a railroad fireman. They sent me up to Cedartown to this old doctor who was a friend of my Daddy's. I passed the physical. No problem. Then he was going to test my eyes. He got out this little shoe box filled with twine and had me tell him the colors of each string. And he declared me to be color blind."

Railroad men had to be able to identify colors, so they could read signals and signs along the tracks at a glance. It was a rule, a safety rule. So Tom Murphy was turned down. "I always accused my Daddy of fixing that test. He wouldn't admit it—but he wouldn't deny it either."

Like it or not, Tom Murphy was going to North Georgia College. He would also see the world—but not from the back of a train.

2

MARCHING

TO

CLASS

AND

WAR

REVEILLE WAS THEIR wakeup call and taps was their lullaby. For a high-spirited country boy from Bremen, this was a new kind of life. Up at 6:30 A.M. Stand formation. Go to PT. Put on your military uniform before you march to breakfast. Stand at parade rest while the blessing is said. Only after the Lord has been duly thanked, are you given permission to sit. When your plate is cleared and your breakfast is done, you snap to attention and are given orders to march to class. In step, of course. "It was good for me. It gave me the regimen I needed," Tom Murphy says.

High school in Georgia covered only eleven grades then so Murphy was just sixteen years old when he first arrived in

Dahlonega from Haralson County. He really didn't want to be there, but quitting wasn't in him.

North Georgia College was a two-year school in the fall of 1941. It would not become a four-year school for several years. It was all male and all military. Discipline was a required course, just like math and English.

Murphy adapted readily to the military side of the school. He was used to discipline, hard work and following rules. His Daddy had seen to that. Class work was another matter. During those first few months, academics proved a major challenge for him as it did for many of the young men who had come to North Georgia from small rural high schools. "The boys from Lanier down in Macon or Tech High in Atlanta or the Columbus schools, they had taken all the stuff we were doing at North Georgia back in high school. It was new to me, and that freshman year liked to have killed me," he says.

College campuses today are often ghost towns by Friday afternoon as students hop in their cars and head home for the weekend. North Georgia College in 1941 was another matter. Nobody had a car, and it wouldn't matter if they did for the roads in and out of there were coiled snakes and the valleys beside them didn't have a bottom.

Bremen might as well have been a foreign country and Murphy didn't make it home until Thanksgiving that year. "When I went home the first time, I wore my uniform everywhere," he says. "I was proud."

Education at North Georgia didn't stop on weekends. When they were on campus, there were Sunday formations to stand. On one of those Sundays, not long after they got back there from Thanksgiving, news circulated through the ranks that would chart new maps for everyone of those young men's lives. It was 7 December 1941.

On radio that afternoon, President Franklin Delano Roosevelt told Americans that this would be a day that would live in infamy. For those young men lined up on the parade grounds, it was a day when the military training they were being given there in the mountains took on a far different meaning.

"The battalion was waiting to march in our regular Sunday parade. Then we heard that the Japanese had attacked Pearl Harbor. All I remember after that is that they dismissed us. We didn't have that parade," Murphy says.

They were just kids. Now they knew they were about to become men whether they were ready to or not. This wasn't a worldly bunch. There was no television to make their world smaller. They hadn't traveled and they hadn't lived. Geography to them was Rome, Georgia, not Rome, Italy. They knew about Augusta, Macon, and Columbus. Most of them didn't know where Pearl Harbor was, and they had yet to learn about faraway places such as Correigidor or Leyte or Normandy Beach. Those lessons would come later. Before those lessons were learned, there were the faces of the classmates who were changing from the uniform they wore at school into other uniforms.

"We not only lost classmates, we lost some of our professors. One of our military science professors, Sergeant McConnell, left and later on, when I was in the Pacific, I read a story about him in Yank Magazine. He was a colonel somewhere in Italy," Murphy recalls.

In 1942, during his second year at North Georgia, Murphy knew he would soon face a crucial decision. He was still just seventeen years old. He could get his two-year degree, go on to the University of Georgia and then, with a bachelor's degree, he could become an officer. But he had no desire to be an officer and no desire to spend another day in a classroom. "I was young and I was stubborn," he says. "I was afraid we'd lose that dad blame war if I didn't get in there soon. When I told my Daddy that, he said, 'Yeah, you want to go now. But you are going to repent in sack cloth and ashes before this is over.' Truer words were never spoken, I guarantee you."

Every week from the beginning of the war until the end, The *Bremen Gateway* published long lists of the young men who were enlisting and those who were being drafted. There were also stories about county boys who would never make it back. A subtle message was being sent to those who stayed home, for this was an era when the young men who stayed in college and received student deferments were not very popular. Not when neighbors and loved ones had enlisted. Not when they were somewhere overseas. And Murphy admits it would have killed him for folks to talk about him that way. It was a far different attitude about service and the draft than future young men would have about another war.

Not only did Murphy want to go—he wanted to be a United States Marine. He let the local draft board know of his desire and they invited him in for a physical. Just as it was when he took the exam for the railroad, they told him he was color blind. And, strangely, those are the only times doctors have ever told him that. When the Marines wouldn't accept him, he enlisted in the Navy.

Nine days after graduating from college, he reported for duty. At North Georgia, students had received a daily dose of Navy Pre-Flight training so when he reported to boot camp he knew what to expect. "It was a breeze," he admits. "North Georgia College had made a man out of this seventeen year old boy. We were ready. We had been going through those obstacle courses every day. We knew what to expect."

Boot camp was a breeze for Murphy, but not for some of his classmates. "There was this poor fellow from Sandusky, Ohio who was working in the bakery. He was real fat with this roll around his belly. We helped him all we could. He made it, too, and at the end of boot camp he had gone from 180 pounds all the way down to 135."

For Murphy, it was a learning experience. "There was a lot of understanding that came during World War II. Us country folks were in pretty good shape and we took care of the others. We also found that we could get along with each other whether we were from Georgia or Ohio. We learned a lot. We found that underneath we were all the same," he says.

Life was also changing back in Bremen. The *Bremen Gateway* sponsored a recycling campaign that the newspaper called "Slap a Jap with Scrap." Recruiters at the Bremen Hotel came looking for men making less than $65 a week, offering defense jobs around the country. Coffee was rationed—one pound every three weeks for persons over the age of fifteen. Sewell Manufacturing and Hubbard Slacks Company sent about 200,000 cigarettes a month to soldiers overseas and Sewell's made Eisenhower Jackets for the Army instead of men's suits. The Bremen Theater where Tom Murphy ushered for a dollar a week upped the price of a ticket to thirty-five cents for grownups but it was twenty-five cents for soldiers. School kids were let out of class to pick cotton because so many pickers were in uniform.

Change for Tom Murphy was more dramatic. After boot camp, he was sent to the South Pacific, assigned to the 4th Marine Division, a unit of the Seabees in the Pontoon Division. His tour in the Pacific was a grueling one. His construction unit was among the first Americans tabbed to be in the invasion of Japanese-mandated territory in the Marshall Islands. A country boy who had never been too far from home before celebrated his nineteenth and twentieth birthdays there, and started for home a few days before his twenty-first.

Like many soldiers from that war, Murphy has never talked very much about what he did or what he saw, much less what he felt other than to say bullies in a courtroom or on the floor of the House chamber can't scare him, not after all those months he spent on nameless South Pacific islands. "We were somewhere in the Marshall Islands and I remember laying there on the beach watching those big guns fire at one of those little islands. I guess we would have shot anything that moved," he says.

He was on Guam when one of those planes that would carry the atom bomb to the Japanese mainland landed on a tiny airstrip there. "They wouldn't let us get close to the plane," he says, also making it clear that he is not one who would criticize President Harry Truman for deciding to use the deadly new weapon. "How I can I? I was one of those young men waiting to go into Japan."

Even years later, he's still critical of the way the military computed the point system that determined how long men would serve in combat areas. "I was out there all those years and guys who were married got to come home sooner—and they hadn't been out there as long as fellows like me. It wasn't fair. But I'm still thankful. So many fellows had it worse than me. All I got was a little piece of shrapnel and I put some sulfur on it and went right on."

He will only talk about the more severe memories in short choppy sentences, and only if prodded. He carefully chooses his words, leaving out more than he puts in. What he doesn't say is as graphic as what he does. "I don't want to talk about it and I won't," he says. "When you see innocent young boys blown right out of the water, it ain't pretty."

War did give him time to think about himself and about his life, time to decide that North Georgia College had prepared him well, giving him enough military to take care of himself, to survive. Looking back, he is very grateful to the school, bragging that North Georgia College had more general officers in Desert Storm than the military academies.

Those months in the Pacific also gave Murphy time to realize that he really did need that education his father had lectured him and his brothers about for as long as he could remember. He promised himself that one day he would get it. And he did, paying for it with the GI Bill he had more than earned in the Pacific.

Back in the United States, his unit was sent to South Carolina to prepare for discharge. But they were still in the Navy and there were still procedures to be followed. The drill called for a lecture by a chaplain who would give the men the needed paperwork and a final government check for $400.

There was a logjam at the Naval Air Station in Charleston, however. "The chaplain, a Catholic priest, called us all together and explained that all of the buildings on post were full, that it was going to be the next morning before there would be a place for us to get our discharge."

That news and the red tape it was wrapped in did not set very well at all with those grizzled Navy veterans — including the boy from Georgia who legally became a man somewhere around the world. "We got him to go under this big old tree and give us our lecture and our papers," he says. "All because we wanted to get home."

The war was over. He was a half-inch more than six-feet tall and he was a red-haired skeleton, weighing just 128 pounds, nearly twenty pounds less than he had carried when left home. But at last, he was going back to Georgia. Back home.

Only at home, Tom Murphy would learn of another kind of war: a life and death battle that he did not know was being fought — one that still makes him cry.

3

A

SHOCK

BACK

HOME

WHILE HIS RAMBUNCTIOUS little brother was trying to find a ball game or trying to avoid trouble, James Murphy was trying to find a way to find a way to the courthouse. It was miles away in Buchanan, but for him it was worth the trip. Even as a child, he enjoyed sitting on the benches watching the lawyers at work, wondering what it would be like to be up there talking to the judge and pleading to the jury.

Among the four Murphy boys, James was the family scholar and Tom was the unpredictable one. As boys, four years apart in age, they picked cotton together and planted and picked the family garden. Even then, James knew he wanted to be a lawyer. He was never as robust as his younger brother. He never played baseball or basketball like

Tom, but he could do all right on a tennis court. He shined at school, while his brother coasted.

Both brothers worked at the Bremen Theater along the way and their cousin, Harold Murphy, remembers when James was an usher there. "It seemed like everybody who came in there knew him," he says. "Everybody liked James. He was just that kind of young man."

James finished at nearby West Georgia College then went on to law school at the University of Georgia. He passed the Georgia Bar in his junior year and never finished his degree—a mistake he later would not allow his brother to repeat. He came back home and started to practice law in Haralson County.

James was always sickly and frail, but after Tom left for the Navy in 1943 things got worse. At first, doctors didn't know what was wrong. Finally, a somber diagnosis was delivered. James had rheumatoid arthritis. Slowly, his joints began to solidify. His walk became an uneasy shuffle. Then he needed crutches and finally a wheelchair.

Harold Murphy, now a federal judge in Rome, remembers the abrupt change in the way James got around. "I remember seeing him walking across to the courthouse in Buchanan one day. He was walking pretty briskly. Then, a few weeks later, I saw him again. He could hardly get along," he recalls.

Tom was somewhere in the South Pacific and would be there for three years. He was on an island, but no one at home knew exactly which one. Letters were going back and forth, but no one told him about James' condition. It was the family's way of saying that the only subjects Tom needed to dwell on were surviving and coming home.

When Tom Murphy did get home in 1946, he was not greeted by the same big brother he had left behind. For him it was a shock that still brings tears to his eyes. "His head was drawn and his mouth was crooked. He was on crutches. But James still worked every day. It's in us all to work, I guess."

James Murphy had not allowed the progression of the arthritis to deter him, however. He had built a good law practice, going into partnership with another lawyer who left the small firm during the war. William Murphy had always been interested in politics, state and local, serving as a member of the school board and as mayor of Bremen. In 1944, the arthritis hadn't completely taken hold and James thought running for some kind of public office might be good for him and his career. Time was running out for qualifying so he had to make a decision. He decided to run against a well-known incumbent with sixteen years in the Georgia House.

He never planned on winning. He just thought it would be good to get his name out before the public. Three or four weeks before the election things changed. He realized that he might get elected. Deciding there was a chance, he worked harder, knocking on doors and shaking hands.

On 7 April 1944, James Murphy became the newest member of the Georgia House of Representatives. He defeated W.O. Strickland, the entrenched incumbent, by eighty-eight votes. Other than the race for sheriff that year, which was decided by a mere twelve votes, his was the closest race on the Haralson County ballot.

No one would have imagined it at the time, but his election to that seat was making history for the family and for the state. He became the first of three Murphys—James, then Harold and then Tom—to represent that area in the Georgia House. Only an obscure legislator named Charles Smith would break that string and then for only a single term. "Public service was just in our blood," Harold Murphy says.

James Murphy was already a member of the House in 1946 when Tom was discharged from the Navy. Tom even spent a few days in Atlanta with him, carrying him into the state capitol a few times. He stayed and watched the proceedings a few days, but nothing about it impressed him.

He even shared an elevator ride with the former governor's son, Herman Talmadge. Tom, still wearing his Navy uniform, recognized the younger Talmadge, but he wasn't impressed. His own daddy had never been a disciple of Gene Talmadge. But before that legislative session was over, the Talmadges would get to know Tom's brother James.

James Murphy went to the General Assembly for the first time in 1945. By then, he was spending more and more time in a wheelchair so serving in the House would be a challenge. He checked in at the Ansley Hotel and hired someone to help him take care of himself. This took up most of his $14.00 per diem. He wasn't alone at the Ansley. Secretary of State Ben Fortson, also delegated to a wheelchair, had a room there as well. They developed a lasting friendship, riding to the state capitol each day in a covered truck. At the state house, Big Charlie, a longtime state porter, would carry the two men up the steps into the capitol building.

For any freshman legislator, the session of 1945 would be a challenge. Gov. Ellis Arnall, whom James Murphy admired greatly, was proposing a new State Constitution. The old one had been amended and amended again. It needed streamlining. It wasn't glamorous work, but they were creating a document that would affect the way Georgia did business for years to come. Among the new items included in that Constitution was the office of lieutenant governor. This person could be a stand-in for the chief executive and would preside over the State Senate. And he would, the document spelled out, become governor in the event the governor died. It was a section of the Constitution that would be used sooner than anyone expected.

Gene Talmadge, to the surprise of everyone, was elected governor of Georgia in 1945. It was the fourth time, but he never served a day. On 20 December 1945, with several weeks to go before his inauguration, he died in an Atlanta hospital. The state didn't know what his death would mean. Who would be the governor and who would choose that person? Eyes focused on that new Constitution and on the General Assembly.

For Georgia, it was an embarrassing time. Over the weeks to come, Ellis Arnall said he wouldn't relinquish the governor's office. Herman Talmadge claimed the post, citing the write-in votes he had received. Former educator M.E. Thompson, the new lieutenant governor, said he thought he should be sworn in as governor even though he had not yet taken the oath of office for the second slot. It was political chaos. The national media were having a field day, reporting the outrageous events that led up to January and the 1946 General Assembly.

Among that group of legislators was James Murphy.

Lower courts had ruled that the General Assembly should elect the governor and when they convened January 13th, the galleries upstairs were packed with boisterous people — most of them supporting Gene's boy Herman. Red suspenders, a Talmadge symbol, were everywhere. The first order of business was a resolution calling for a joint session of the House and Senate to validate the election returns. That passed and the following morning at 10:30 A.M., both bodies gathered in the crowded House chamber. No one could maintain order and they finally recessed until 2:00 P.M.

Again the hall was packed, many of the people drunk on moonshine imported for that occasion. Representative J. Robert Elliott of Columbus, the Talmadge floor leader, moved that they elect a governor. His motion ultimately carried and tabulating started about 4:00 P.M., going on for more than five hours. The write-in votes were vital since the legislators had been told they would only be able to consider the top two vote-getters on the ballot. At first, Talmadge ran third, but at the last moment additional ballots from Telfair County were presented. His home county vaulted Talmadge to the top with 675 votes.

Nearing 2:00 A.M. on 15 January Elliott made the motion and the General Assembly elected Herman Talmadge governor. He received 161 votes. By voting "present," eighty-seven members voted against him. One of them, was James Murphy, even though his county had voted for Eugene Talmadge.

The scene that followed that night was the worst of all. Fist fights were breaking out, some involving state officials. Intoxicated people were running wild through the capitol. Talmadge went to Arnall and asked that he yield the governor's office to him. Arnall refused, calling the other man a "pretender" to the office.

Nothing was settled, however. Law suits soon were filed and it would be months before the State Supreme Court ruled that Thompson, the lieutenant governor, was the legal governor of Georgia. Meanwhile, Talmadge was in control. During a wild sixty-three days, he appointed department heads and he appointed committee chairs.

James Murphy, despite the fact he supported Thompson, was given chairmanship of one of the House's two education committees. But for the Talmadges there was more work to be done. He and his supporters wanted the General Assembly to, by law, create an all-white primary in the state.

In 1944, a black preacher in Columbus was turned away at a Muscogee County polling place. The Rev. Primus King, a barber by trade, joined by a number of other black people, filed a federal law suit alleging that his right to vote had been abridged. A federal court in Macon ruled in his favor and in 1945 the all-white Democratic Party primary was abolished. Keeping black voters from voting in the primary effectively meant they had no voice in statewide elections since Georgia was a one-party state.

The white primary issue had inspired Gene Talmadge to leap into the 1946 race and a year later, the Talmadge forces—led by former Speaker of the House Roy Harris of Augusta—wanted to reinstall the old system. With Herman Talmadge in the governor's office, now was the time to act, they concluded.

Emotions were still high on 27 January just two weeks after the General Assembly had elected the governor. Now Talmadge was asking the Georgia House to consider a bill recreating the all-white primary, this time carrying the power of law. Elliott told the House that the White Primary Bill would turn the Democratic Party into a private club with the ability to limit membership to white persons in sympathy with its policies. As a private club, it would be outside of federal jurisdiction.

Critics claimed the move would turn the party over to Talmadge and Harris, who Augusta voters had put out of office the year before. And in a 27 January column in the *Atlanta Constitution*, political editor M. L. St. John said the move would lead to the destruction of the primary system and put white voters under control of machine politics. St. John described openly the racial motives of that conclave.

As the House convened that morning, many members wanted to avoid the issue, which already had passed out of committee. There was a move to adjourn until April, assuming the courts would have by then ruled on who the legal governor would be. For a number of reasons, others disagreed, including James Murphy.

"I favor adjournment, but not the way the resolution was put," he said, indicating he would appear to be against a white primary if he voted for adjournment.

His stance was reported on the front page of the Constitution and so were his remarks the following day when the House vote on the White Primary Bill finally came. Balanced on his crutches, Murphy explained his position. "All that is within me cries 'no' on this bill," he told the House. "But Eugene Talmadge told the people what he would do to restore the white primary and the people of my county and the state approved it. This bill will give the people a white Democratic primary, but there is fear in my mind what else it will give them. I see a decade of fraud and corruption. Fulfilling the duties imposed upon me, yet expressing my own opposition, I hereby cast my vote in favor of the bill."

The House easily passed the White Primary Bill that day and the Senate followed suit. But those decisions and all others adopted during Herman Talmadge's brief reign were declared null and void by the Georgia Supreme Court when it ruled Talmadge had no claim on the governor's office.

Strange how things work out.

J. Robert Elliott went on to become a federal judge, appointed by John F. Kennedy and recommended by Herman Talmadge, by then a United States Senator. Elliott is still on the bench in Georgia, though he took a leave of absence in the summer of 1999. He is the oldest sitting federal judge in the country. James Murphy did not run for reelection. He could have kept his views quiet, cast his vote, gone home and survived to return again. On that vote, his decision meant nothing to either side.

Yet, he chose a route that for him was political suicide and he knew it. He voted with his county, but he listened to his conscience, and courageously told the voters back home they were wrong, that their view would lead to destruction. That was his final term in the House and observers say he probably wouldn't have been elected had he run again. He would later run for district solicitor and be defeated.

"He was a liberal for this county and that time," says Harold Murphy, who two years later succeeded his cousin in the House. Forget the political descriptions. To his brother, James Murphy will always be a hero.

"He was the smartest man I ever knew," Tom says. "He and I were as close as brothers could get. If he had fifty cents, I had a quarter and if I had fifty cents, he had a quarter. Everything I am I owe to him and my father."

ROBBIE RIVERS, NOW clerk of the Georgia House, was a boy growing up down the street from Tom Murphy in Bremen. As a young child playing out in his yard, he remembers the vivid picture of seeing one strong man lift another man out of an automobile and carry him into the house.

" Who was that?" he asked his mother.

"That's Mr. Murphy and his brother," she said.

It was a poignant scene the boy never forgot.

They were brothers and they became law partners, but their relationship went deeper. Everybody around Bremen knew that. So did anyone who ever saw the tender way Tom Murphy treated his big brother.

Tom Murphy's oldest children remember going with their father to nearby hot springs, hoping the tepid water would loosen their Uncle James' tightened joints. They remember going with them to doctors, praying something could be done for Uncle James. They remember the hopeful excitement they shared when doctors at Emory University Hospital suggested a new drug known as cortisone.

Harold Murphy saw him soon after that treatment began.

"It was helping to loosen his joints and he was so thrilled. Then he had to get off it and the joints started solidifying again. I went to see him after that. He was staying with his mother and father and he was in great pain. It was terrible. But a few weeks later, I saw him at the courthouse again as if nothing had happened. He never stopped trying."

Their brother-to-brother relationship still impresses Harold Murphy. "I know what people do for their children or their parents, but you don't often see that kind of bond between brothers. When you help people who are handicapped over a long period of time, you either love them or you grow to hate them. Tom never complained. He loved him even more."

James Murphy died in 1966. He was forty-six, still young and still working. In Bremen, right next to the railroad tracks, is the office of Murphy & Murphy, the office of James and Tom. In the lobby is a portrait of James Murphy, alongside a photo-montage of the Georgia House. He was among the members. There is a photo of him with Governor Carl Sanders. He's standing on crutches. There is also a plaque in his memory.

His was a relatively short life, but his impact lingers. His life and the way he lived it toned down his tempestuous brother and gave him a focus he had never had before. James Murphy never was able to finish the things he started, but his brother has. Tom Murphy practices law and fifteen years after his brother left the Georgia House, he took his old seat. And the memories of his big brother have shaped the motives and the career of Tom Murphy, even his politics.

Not long ago, Mike Murphy was looking through some family keepsakes. He is the oldest of Tom's four children, a former member of the family law firm and now a Superior Court judge in the Talapoosa District.

In that collection of family souvenirs, he found old letters his Uncle James had written to Georgia governors over the years, sharing his personal and pointed views on particular issues. The letters they wrote back to him were there, too. There were also two books that his uncle had signed in the front—both political biographies. One was on Tom Watson. The other on Gene Talmadge.

A few days after Mike Murphy found those old books, Roy Barnes stopped by Bremen on his way to Birmingham where his daughter was going to college. Barnes was a law school classmate of Mike's and he is also governor of Georgia. "I showed him those books and said he ought to read them," Mike recalls. "He said he had already read them both."

They were the last two books his Uncle James had read. Now his nephew was reading them, embarrassed that it had taken him fifty-two years to get around to them. He carried them with him to the judge's chambers, in a new county courthouse down the hill from that old one in Buchanan.

They don't try cases in the old courthouse anymore. It's a museum now. Only a few ornamental law books are left in the courtroom, just for show. The old back stairway those two brothers climbed so very slowly is roped off now. It's too dangerous. But folks around there still remember the last trial held in that second-floor courtroom.

One of the lawyers in that final case was Thomas Bailey Murphy.

4

Miss Agnes

and

the Law

A LOT HAD HAPPENED to Tom Murphy and a lot had happened to Bremen since he left there in 1943. He had been to war and, in a way, so had the folks back home. He had seen young men die and they had seen them buried.

When he was at North Georgia College, he thought about teaching physical education, maybe coaching. But the war sent his mind in other directions. So did the condition of his brother James and the shock of seeing him in that wheelchair. Murphy began thinking about law school and being a lawyer. Hearing that, his brother talked about bringing him into his law firm. But there was also the matter of living.

One of his friends said he had a date that Friday night and offered to find one for Murphy who didn't know that many girls in Bremen after being away so long. Randall Williamson, who went on to become a prominent Methodist preacher, had a date with Agnes Bennett and that night he introduced Murphy to the young woman who would be his date. "I didn't like her," he says. "Me and her didn't see eye-to-eye on nothing."

But there was something he did like about Randall's date.

"Before that night was over with, I had me a date with Agnes for the next night and I never dated another woman," he says. "Six months later, on July 22, 1946, we got married. I was twenty-two and she was eighteen."

Agnes Bennett had never met Murphy before their double date that night in January. She was born in Cleburne County, Alabama and had moved to Talapoosa, Georgia when she was five. Her family moved across the county to Bremen five years later. She was four years younger than her future husband, so he was away in college and the Navy by the time she became a hot-shot basketball player at Bremen High, one of the best the school had produced to that point.

That fall, the newlyweds moved to Athens where he had been accepted at the University of Georgia's Lumpkin School of Law. For the next three years, they would live on the GI Bill and the savings account Murphy's mother had opened for him. While he was in the Navy, he sent her money on her birthday, on Mother's Day and at Christmas. She had put that money in the bank in his name. For the last two years he had been in the Pacific Theater, he had been far away from the pay line. So with that back pay in his pocket when he was discharged, his pocket was full of cash. Tom and Agnes would need that savings because the GI Bill paid them just $90 a month, soon to rise to $105 a month. It went all the way up to $120 each month when Mike, the first of their four children, was born in 1947.

Never a motivated student before, a more mature Murphy applied himself to the new surroundings in Athens. It was a small class, around 100 students. There were only three classrooms and classes met from 8:00 A.M. to noon. His cousin Harold Murphy was one of his classmates and the two of them had every class together for their entire three years of law school.

There was still time for fun, however. He had followed University of Georgia sports from a distance but during those years the Bulldogs became a lasting passion. "Me and Mama watched Georgia play football religiously," he says. He still gets excited talking about Frankie Sinkwich and Charlie Trippi, two of the greatest stars of that era. "I can still see Sinkwich coming through the line with those big old long arms. They were so long they made him look like a three-legged animal out there. And Trippi, he'd run all around the field, thirty or forty yards, then gain ten yards after scaring you to death," he says, getting more animated with every word.

Like his brother James, he passed the Georgia Bar exam before he graduated from law school. With a young family to support, he was ready to hurry home and join his brother's law firm. But there was one problem: James wouldn't let him. "He said he had made that mistake and there was no way he was going to let me do the same thing," he remembers. So in 1949, Tom got his law school degree. It was a proud day for him, for his brother and for his father—the man with a fourth grade education who wanted so much more for his youngest sons.

As for as achievements in law school, Murphy laughs and calls himself the "black sheep" of the family. Four Murphys—James, Harold, Tom and Mike—have received their legal education at the University of Georgia. James, Harold and Mike were on the Honor Court and were Chief Justice of the law school. "I was the only one who didn't make it," Tom says. "But I had a wife and child. All I wanted to do was study and get home."

Harold Murphy has gone on to a distinguished legal career. In 1971, he was Governor Jimmy Carter's first judicial appointment, naming him to Superior Court in the Talapoosa District. In 1977, when Carter was president, he appointed Murphy to a seat on the Northern District of Georgia federal court, a position he still holds. Mike Murphy is a Superior Court judge in the same Tallapoosa District where his cousin once served. He was appointed by Governor Zell Miller in 1998.

As Tom Murphy graduated from law school in 1949, his brother followed through on his offer, bringing him into his law firm in Bremen. After that first year, it was going to be an equal partnership. For the first twelve months, they were each going to draw $25 a week then at the end of the year divide the profits—with James getting two-thirds and Tom a third.

For the first term of court that year, Tom did little but sit at the table and watch while James prepared and presented the cases. By the second term, Tom was handling the cases. He argued five and won five, learning that you can't just study the law, you have to practice it. After that fifth victory, the two of them left the courthouse in Buchanan late one Friday afternoon and were on their way home. "Son," James said, looking over at his brother. "I see you can pull your part of the load, so right now we'll start splitting things 50-50." For Tom, it was a moment to remember. Not because of the raise in pay for it was insignificant, but because his hero had just given him the praise he needed so much.

As a lawyer, Tom Murphy's reputation began to grow around the West Georgia legal community. His legal batting average was high. He even defended the first black man accused of killing a Haralson County white man— and the black man was acquitted.

Everybody said that Murphy could "flat talk" in front of a jury. That's why he usually did the openings and closings instead of James. "But we were trying this murder case one time and he said he'd make the opening argument for me. Gosh, it was the greatest speech I ever heard in any case in my whole life. When he sat down, I was so mad I could chew a ten-penny nail. I turned to him and said, 'Why didn't you tell me you wanted to make a speech?' "

As most lawyers will tell you, however, you make your reputation in criminal cases but you make your living in civil court. That was true for Murphy & Murphy. For in 1951 they had a major civil case in Tallapoosa that involved a will and the Methodist Church. The night before the trial was to begin, Tom Murphy found out he would be the lead attorney. His side prevailed and the payoff was around a quarter of a million dollars. "With that money, I finished paying for my house and bought my first new car and TV. From that day on, good things started happening for us," he says.

The business people around Bremen were also noticing the firm of Murphy & Murphy, including Warren Sewell, one of the brothers who had founded Sewell Manufacturing Company. They were the largest employers in the area, having plants in several West Georgia communities.

Warren Sewell had been watching Tom since as a boy he came to the plant with other youngsters, asking for contributions to their baseball team. As he noticed him growing as a lawyer, he called him on the phone and said he'd like to come over and see him.

Murphy insisted that he'd come to Sewell. The main Sewell plant was within sight of his law office and he offered to cross the railroad tracks right then. He was curious what the Old Gentleman, as he respectfully called him, had to say. Once he got there, Sewell didn't make him wait. He got to the point as soon as the young lawyer was seated.

"I want to hire you," he said. "What would it cost?"

Murphy didn't think for long. He threw out an amount of money, but first he wanted to know what kind of relationship Warren Sewell had in mind and just what kind of legal cases he would be handling.

Sewell, to Murphy's shock, said he didn't want him to try many cases. "Tom, I just don't want you to be agin' me."

As he left that day, Tom Murphy was the legal counsel for Warren Sewell Clothing Company. He did handle a few matters over the years, but not many. Murphy says the Old Gentleman never asked him for a political favor and Sewell—a Republican—never once gave him a political contribution. The only contributions he ever sought from the Sewells were for Ben Fortson. When Fortson would be running for Secretary of State, he would come to Bremen and Murphy would be allowed to push his wheelchair through the Sewell plants, never forgetting the popular Fortson's friendship with his brother James.

Not long after Murphy began practicing in Bremen, he became involved in one of the most headlined cases ever to occur in Haralson County and it also involved the Sewells. It started in broad daylight on the Friday of Labor Day weekend 1949.

It was just after 9:00 A.M. and it was payday. Three of Sewell's employees were on their way back to the plant from the bank when a 1949 Ford swung alongside the payroll truck. Three bandits, waving a submachine and two pistols, ordered the driver, Bill Gallman, and payroll clerks Irma Schell and Sarah Davis to get out of the truck. While one of the men held a gun on the three in the truck, a second man waved a gun and told people on the sidewalk to get out of the way.

The frightened Schell tried to run with part of the payroll money but she either fell or was tripped by one of the gunmen. "Please don't shoot her," Gallman pleaded. "You can have the money."

Wearing sunglasses and handkerchiefs over their faces, the men got away in their gray Ford. A two-state dragnet was put out for the armed trio. All three were arrested and charged. One of them, Joe Lee Bishop, had gotten all the way to Temple, Texas. When the leader of the group, John Carrigan—alias John Valor—was apprehended, he had $6,000 of the Sewell payroll in his possession.

They were taken back to Atlanta for trial and Bishop tried to break out of the old Fulton County Tower. Guards found six hacksaw blades in his second-floor cell and later authorities foiled a plan to smuggle him a pistol. Carrigan was equally dangerous and before he was going to be tried on the Sewell case, there was the matter of Beatrice Samples, the mother of three school-age children. Carrigan was accused of murdering the Atlanta woman, who had threatened to turn him in to police for his part in a car thief ring. Carrigan was convicted and sentenced to death. During the trial he had rushed the witness stand, threatened the prosecutor and berated the judge.

With that case out of the way, John Carrigan was to face another trial for his part in the Sewell robbery along with the other two masked men. Carrigan's court-appointed attorney was Tom Murphy.

Fifty years later, Murphy still talks about the security. When James and Tom went to talk to Carrigan at the Fulton County Tower, they were surrounded by Atlanta detectives and deputy sheriffs. Every one of them had two guns in their pockets. It was a setting that wouldn't be legal under today's system. Feeling the pressure, Tom Murphy looked at the defendant and said he had one request.

"John, if you're gonna run, give me thirty seconds."

The unpredictable Carrigan asked why.

"Because I want to be over there under that desk. They'll fill you so full of lead that if they put a water hose in your mouth you'll look like a shower."

Carrigan just grinned.

That was Murphy's only trip into the old tower that was only a few blocks from the state capitol in Atlanta. "Man, you go in there and they're locking those big doors behind," he remembers "I made myself a promise that I'd never go in it again. And I didn't either."

Murphy was young, probably too inexperienced to be trying such a case, but that didn't keep him from being aggressive and bold. Sizing him up, the over-confident prosecutor figured he could run over this small-town lawyer. Early in the trial, he was shocked when Murphy rose to object, citing a rule of evidence that required a lawyer to physically produce such evidence. "You mean if Sewell Manufacturing Company was the highest and best evidence that I would have to bring it up here?" the prosecutor asked.

"Yes sir," snapped Murphy. "I would require you to tear it down brick by brick and bring it up here."

Gaining respect for each other along the way, the two lawyers settled down and continued the case. Finally, the case was winding down. It was late in the afternoon. The prosecutor suggested they should wait and finish the next morning. A brash Murphy wasn't agreeable with that idea and said so.

Hearing that, the prosecutor slammed a law book down on the table and blurted out, "Then let's finish the goddamn thing tonight." The judge heard him. So did the jury and everyone in the courtroom. And that's what they did—finish it.

Murphy had little defense to offer, so throughout the trial he was forced to turn his full attention to the Atlanta police and how they had handled the case. He attacked them at every turn. The police officers in the courtroom heard every word and they didn't forget them. As for John Carrigan, he was found guilty. Later, he would be executed.

Soon after the verdict was read, the Murphys and the other lawyers began to gather up their papers, stuffing them into fat brief cases. Tom carried James down the back stairs and went back up to the courtroom for his things. When he started back out, several Atlanta police detectives were waiting on him in the stairwell. One of them started yelling at him. There were three or four of them and he didn't know what they were going to do. By chance, a friend of Murphy's from Haralson County had been there for the trial. He had his two sons with them. When they appeared, the lawmen disappeared down the stairs.

Murphy & Murphy was doing well, only to be saddened by James Murphy's death in 1966, though he continues to be listed as the senior partner in that fifty-year-plus-old firm. Like most small-town firms, the cases they take cover the law from the front of the book to the back.

Except one type of case. "I've never defended a drug dealer and never will either," Tom Murphy says. "There was this one case over at West Georgia College. This fellow came in and wanted to hire us. I said, 'Whoa! I won't take your case 'cause I have children and grand-children and if you ever got one of them hooked on that stuff, you wouldn't have to worry about the sheriff or no lawyer. I'd come get you and I'd kill you with my bare hands.' I guess word spread 'cause they quit coming to see me."

In the 1950s and 1960s, life was also falling into place for Tom and Agnes. Their family was growing: Mike was born in 1947, Martha in 1949, Lynn in 1950, and Mary in 1956. They were rearing their children as they had been reared, passing on the same brand of small-town values. They were parents involved in any activity that helped their kids. Tom coached American Legion baseball—proud that Mike became a power-hitting catcher just like his Daddy had been. He was president of the school PTA and the first president of the Bremen Rotary Club.

To the kids in town, Mrs. Murphy was simply "Mama Agnes." Around Bremen, her old Plymouth station wagon was usually so full of kids that another one couldn't have squeezed in if he had tried. She would haul kids to school and back. If somebody needed a child picked up somewhere, they'd call "Mama Agnes." Most of the time, the Murphy yard looked like a playground full of kids and if it was time for lunch, the children came inside and joined Mike, Lynn, Martha, and little Mary.

Remembering how involved his own father had always been in the community, Tom Murphy began to voice his opinions on local politics, whether people wanted to hear them or not. He was an active school board member and became chairman of the school board in 1960.

But that would not be the only election he was involved in that year. Since 1944, there had been only two years that Haralson County wasn't represented in the Georgia House of Representatives by a Murphy—first James then Harold. Maybe it was time for a third.

One-year-old Tom sits besides big brother James.

In 1941, Murphy was a freshman at North Georgia College.

Not long after this relaxing moment, Murphy was in the
South Pacific.

As a young lawyer, Tom joined brother
James' firm in Bremen.

The Murphy family gathered for granddaughter Lauren's debutante ball in 1996. Left to right are Murphy, Mary Murphy Oxendine, Martha Murphy Long, Chad Long, Holly Long, David McBrayer, Lynn Murphy McAdams, Lyndsey McAdams, Kenneth McAdams, Lauren Murphy, Carol Murphy and Mike Murphy.

Around Bremen, he's Mr. Tom.

Like most items, Murphy buys his Stetsons in Haralson
County.

Fishing and gardening are Murphy's
great escapes.

A big Bulldog fan, Murphy helps auction off
Herschel Walker's jersey.

Joining neighbors at the Bremen Town Festival, Murphy is his
community's biggest supporter.

The Murphys are a close-knit Irish clan. Here he is flanked by
grandchildren: Chad Long, Holly Long and Lauren Murphy.
That's Lyndsey McAdams in his arms.

Agnes and Tom were married 36 years before her
death in 1982. He still calls her Mama.

When Mike and Carol were married in 1970, Murphy was decked out in tails.

5

GOING

TO

THE

HOUSE

IF GEORGE T. SMITH had been packing a gun that day, he'd have shot Tom Murphy dead—right there in front of God Almighty and the House of Representatives. Rising from his seat, Murphy had asked for the floor on a point of personal privilege. When the Speaker granted his request the young legislator slowly started down the aisle for his long walk to the well of the House. The closer he got, the quieter the noisy chamber became. You could have heard a pin bounce off the carpet as Murphy moved one step at a time.

Smith just glared. He had been around there long enough to figure out what Murphy was about to do. Most of the House members had drawn their own conclusions. That was on everyone's mind as the lanky country lawyer milked every step.

Just a few days before, the governor had fired the second-term Democrat as a committee chairman. Carl Sanders didn't strip him of his rank and ribbons in person either. Murphy had to read about it in the morning newspaper. Two other representatives who were also busted had already made their anger heard. Frank Branch had taken his case to the hallways of the capitol, telling anybody who would listen his side of the issue. Don Ballard had talked about it in the newspapers, making headlines as he unloaded his feelings. Murphy had been silent. Now the chamber was silent as he was about to speak. You could almost hear the ticking of the six-foot-tall time bomb they figured was about to explode.

"Mr. Speaker," Murphy said, arriving at the podium.

Again, George T. Smith had to formally recognize the gentleman from Bremen.

House members in the halls hurried back to their seats. Nobody wanted to miss the explosion. They watched the faces of the two men who stood there in front of them. First Murphy. Then back at the Speaker. Then Murphy again. A floor below, huddled around the squawk box, the governor's staff was also waiting for the opening salvo.

"*Miiiiiissssterrrr Speeeeaker,*" Murphy began, stretching out every syllable. "Mister Speaker, there comes a time in everybody's life that a man has to do...and say...things that he doesn't want to do...."

He paused...here it comes, people thought.

Then he grinned.

"But this is neither that time, nor that place...."

Most of the members were first surprised, then disappointed. They all thought they had ringside tickets to a good fight. And all Coach Murphy really wanted to do was come forward and remind the legislators of that night's Heart Fund basketball game against the Senate.

"George T. said he could've killed me," Murphy says.

It wasn't the last time the Georgia House would see his stubbornness or his humor. He had come to the House in

1961, an eventful year for the state and the General Assembly. Federal judges had ordered the University of Georgia to admit its first black students and there was trouble on the all-white campus. Governor Ernest Vandiver had promised "No, not one," when asked about school desegregation, so the state was wondering if the governor would lock the doors on Georgia schoolhouses now that the two black students were going to class in Athens. There was also talk that the House and Senate soon would be facing the end of the age-old County Unit System, a change that would forever alter the course of the legislature.

Murphy was elected in 1960. He attributes that election to his father and his brother James. "Their reputation got me elected, not mine," he says. But Tom Murphy did have a reputation. He was a pretty good lawyer and he had done all the things active people do in a small town. He had been president of the PTA. He had been on the school board and when his kids were involved in something, there was Tom. So people around Bremen and Haralson County already knew Uncle Bill Murphy's youngest boy.

Noise was being made all over Georgia and all over the historic capitol, but when Tom Murphy got there, he stayed uncharacteristically quiet, listening and learning. Only now and then did people see flashes of the Irish temper that often boiled inside him as he studied how things worked.

"He was very brash and very active," says Tommy Irvin, who was a member of the House when Murphy was sworn in on 9 January 1961. "From the very beginning, he didn't follow the leader, he wanted to be the leader."

"You didn't have to worry about where he was at on something," says Marcus Collins, who that same year came to the House to fill his father's unexpired term. "If you asked him, he told you and I think that's one of the things that has always helped him."

He felt his way along slowly, but that first year Murphy introduced a bill to abolish capital punishment. The bill failed, but people remembered the confident way he handled himself when he spoke in front of the House explaining the controversial proposal. They also noticed how the idealistic newcomer dealt with the complaints that followed from the people back home in his district who didn't agree with his stance. "From the very beginning, his delivery and his knowledge of his subject matter was impressive," remembers Irvin, whose early impressions of the rookie legislator would later help Murphy get his first taste of leadership in the House.

George L. Smith was the Speaker of the House in 1961, a position to which he had been appointed by Vandiver in 1959. But as speaker, George L. was only as good as the governor allowed him to be. Vandiver was the head coach. Without even leaving his office, he could call every play, just as governors had always done in Georgia. It was also that way for committee chairmen as Murphy would learn during his second term.

Carl Sanders may have asked others for a scouting report on the second-term legislator, but Murphy is much more realistic about why in 1965 the new governor chose him to chair the House Hygiene and Sanitation Committee, an advancement that he didn't expect so soon. "It was obvious," Murphy explains. "Every elected official in Haralson County had gone for Marvin Griffin but one—me."

Marvin Griffin eventually carried the West Georgia county by just seventy-eight votes. The chairmanship was Murphy's reward for political loyalty and with just two years of experience in the House, he was a committee chairman, knowing he wasn't ready and knowing even then that there would be problems.

Sanders expected him to do as he was told. No questions. No debate. Just do it. This didn't set well with Murphy. "That just wasn't my idea of leadership," he explains. When legislation sponsored by the governor came up on the floor, the governor's people were expected to lock arms and show their unqualified support. Not Mr. Murphy. "If some of the governor's legislation came up that I didn't agree with, I'd let it be known on the floor of the House or by my vote."

So Sanders gave him his pink slip. The four of them had been butting heads constantly over legislation so the governor told reporters he was firing three of his chairmen. Murphy shouldn't have been surprised. When Sanders became governor in 1963, citing loyalty as his primary reason, he had fired George L. Smith of Swainsboro as speaker and replaced him with George T. Smith, a Grady County attorney. "He had been telling everybody that George Smith would be his speaker. We just assumed it would be George L.," Murphy laughs.

Since Sanders already had that big of a notch on his gun, running three of his chairmen out of town was nothing. "He fixed me up good. But then they had to put me on the back row in the back corner, just as far away as they could move me," Murphy says, still upset at that new seat assignment. "Now that teed me off."

Murphy waited. He knew payback would come, and it did. Meanwhile, he continued to flex his muscles as a legislator. When the State Properties Commission started considering a lease for the old state-owned W&A Railroad, it caught Murphy's attention. Railroads were personal to him. His father had worked for the Central of Georgia forty-four years, staying on a few extra years because management personally asked him. Railroads had fed the Murphys when others were hungry. Then, years later, he had seen what happened when the Central of Georgia was swallowed up by the much-larger Southern Railways. Now Southern was competing with the L&N for a lease with the state on the A&N.

The State Properties Commission would represent the House in the lease negotiations and Murphy wanted to be part of that process. "I went to see Governor Sanders. I told him, 'Well, governor, if you set your mind to take me off of it, you can, but I want you to know I am going to be a candidate for the commission.' I was elected on the floor of the House and he didn't say anything one way or another," Murphy said.

That was only the beginning of a squabble between the railroads. Nobody gave the state much of a chance to beat them, but they finally did in 1967. All of the legislators from Georgia's 7th Congressional District were opposed to leasing the W&A to Southern because such a move would give that line a monopoly in that part of the state. "They had ruined us in northwest Georgia when they bought the Central of Georgia and practically shut it down. Thank goodness, they utilized it later," he said.

Murphy was the primary spokesman against the lease with Southern. On the day of the decisive vote, he went down to the well of the House with all of the legislators but one from the 7th District flanking him in a show of solidarity. High above them in the House gallery were lawyers for the two competing railroads—Phil Lanier of L&N and W. Graham Claytor for Southern. Watching what was going on below them, Claytor turned to Lanier with a comment: "Phil, I guess you know how they do it in Washington, but I'll be damned if I know how they do it in Georgia."

It was a stinging and unexpected defeat for the railroad. W. E. Dillard had been president of the Central of Georgia. Earlier in his career he was trainmaster at Cedartown, just up the rail line from Bremen. He and Uncle Bill Murphy were good friends. One morning, Dillard called the young legislator from his office in Savannah and told him how disappointed his Daddy would be in his stand against the W&A lease. "Of course, I was respectful to the old gentleman, and I didn't blame him for doing his job," Murphy said. "But there was no way they could change me."

The payback between Sanders and Murphy finally came during a special session of the legislature that the governor had convened to rewrite the state's election code, a tedious task at best. The governor had refused to allow them to adjourn until they had finished. The next day, Murphy and his cohorts used a parliamentary ploy that soon got the governor's attention. A fight was about to break out and Murphy didn't run from it. "I always have loved a good fight," he says. "It makes the world go round."

The ploy was that within the rules of the House, members were allowed to ask for clarification on any matter before them and they were going to use the red book of rules to their advantage. Murphy and friends made a motion the next morning asking for the election code to be read and explained—paragraph by paragraph by paragraph. Sanders and his people were paralyzed. Murphy had used a trick play and it worked. By mid-day, the House had covered just two pages—two out of a seventy-eight page bill.

Moody Daniel, the governor's runner, came to the floor of the House and found Murphy, telling him that Sanders wanted to see him as soon as possible, as soon as the House recessed for lunch. Murphy said he would be there and after the House took its break, he went down the marble steps to the governor's second-floor office.

"I'm sorry, but Governor Sanders is busy," Murphy was told.

"That's okay with me," he said. "I didn't want to see him anyway."

Sanders was playing games with him and Murphy was not about to have his heels cooled out there in the lobby. He stood up and started to leave, but suddenly the governor was no longer busy. He could see the legislator now. The door opened and Murphy walked inside. Sanders was waiting for him. "Tom," he said, "You've made your point."

"What do you mean, Governor? We just want to get the bill explained so everybody will understand what we're voting on."

Sanders repeated himself. "You've made your point."

For the two of them, it was politics more than personal. But down the road, when Murphy became speaker, Carl Sanders came to see him at his law office in Bremen. Murphy's office next to the railroad tracks is hardly a big city practice. The chairs in his lobby aren't usually taken by corporate clients. A hard-of-hearing old fellow in a ball cap may just need someone to draw up some papers and help him get a person evicted from a house trailer he has on his land. Some folks don't need legal advice at all. They just need to talk.

Into that setting came Sanders, by then a partner in a major Atlanta law firm. He congratulated Murphy on his rise to the speaker's office, then he told him that the Georgia Power Company might want to hire him to do some legal work for them. "I thanked him, then I told him no. For two reasons. I didn't want my young partners getting used to making all that money then having it taken away if I wasn't speaker anymore. 'And besides,' I said, 'I can make more money fighting Georgia Power than I can representing them.'"

Murphy also remembers his next election. He had a strong opponent and it wasn't an easy race. Sanders, still the governor, allowed his driver—in a state car—to visit his uncle who lived next door to Murphy and ask him to vote for his challenger.

"It didn't work," Murphy says. "The fellow said he was going to vote for Tom, that I was his friend."

The two politicians long ago made their peace. But when you ask Tom Murphy about Carl Sanders firing him from that chairmanship, he often refers you to Sanders' 1993 biography, *The Spokesman of the New South*. There's only one reference to Murphy in the book (page 290). Sanders's version of what happened then is identical to Murphy's. But author James F. Cook quotes Sanders as urging Murphy to "get on the team" and the biographer said he was "as stubborn as a Georgia mule." Only Murphy doesn't mention those descriptions. "He calls me 'a gangly young lawyer from Bremen,'" he recites from memory.

SANDERS WAS AMONG the state's most popular governors, but under Georgia law at the time, governors were relegated to a single four-year term. They could run again, but not for consecutive terms. As Sanders was preparing to leave office in 1966, one of the most memorable gubernatorial campaigns in modern Georgia history was picking up steam.

The field for that year's Democratic Party primary was as crowded as an Atlanta freeway at rush hour. The laundry list of candidates was a long one—including a pair of former Georgia governors.

There was Ellis Arnall of Newnan, Gene Talmadge's harshest rival, a legend from the 1940s, a New Deal Democrat who served as governor from 1943 to 1947. There was Ernest Vandiver from Lavonia , the governor who kept Georgia's schools open, a rumored nominee to John F. Kennedy's cabinet and Georgia's chief executive from 1959 to 1963.

There was even serious talk circulating the state that Herman Talmadge might want to come home from Washington, giving up his United States Senate seat for another run for governor. He had been governor from 1949 to 1955, passing the sales tax that had given the state's economy the boost it needed.

As the field was evolving, Vandiver shocked everyone by saying that the heart trouble with which he suffered while governor would keep him from running for the post again, that a spirited campaign might threaten his life. Insiders had bluntly advised Talmadge that he was more needed in the Senate than the Governor's Mansion so he never formally entered the race. But even with those high-profile names off the potential list of candidates, it was still a lenghy ballot.

There was Albany media magnate James Gray, a wealthy newspaper and broadcasting owner. There was former lieutenant governor Garland Byrd, a Butler lawyer who had flirted with the race before. There was Jimmy Carter, a peanut farmer from Plains who had served with distinction in the Georgia Senate. There was Hoke O'Kelley, a perennial candidate from Gwinnett County who wasn't a serious threat.

Then there was Lester Maddox. Everybody knew Lester. Everybody enjoyed the fried chicken he used to serve at The Pickrick, his working class Atlanta cafeteria. But few had ever voted for him. Mainly he was known for waving an axe handle to keep blacks out of his cafeteria and for the humorous but outrageous political ads he bought every Saturday in the Atlanta Journal. He had unsuccessfully run for local offices around Atlanta for years, twice for mayor, including an outspoken campaign for mayor against Ivan Allen just five years before. Later, he had run for lieutenant governor, being the runner-up to Peter Zack Geer. But nobody had ever taken him seriously as a candidate–much less for governor.

Finally, on the heels of their party's success in Georgia with Barry Goldwater's 1964 presidential campaign, the GOP had its first serious contender for the state's highest office since Reconstruction, Third District Congressman Howard "Bo" Callaway.

A one-time Democrat, just two years before he had become the first Republican to represent Georgia in Washington. Callaway was well-known and well-heeled. His parents Cason and Virginia had planted and founded Callaway Gardens, the popular resort in Pine Mountain. A graduate of West Point and a veteran of the Korean War, he had also followed his father on to the prestigious Georgia

Board of Regents—appointed by Herman Talmadge, the state's best-known Democrat.

While others were running traditional political campaigns—making speeches and buying ads—Maddox was driving around the state in a rundown station wagon, stopping to tack up obscure "Maddox Country" signs on any vacant tree. A few of those faded signs can still be found on Georgia back roads. Without the support of Democratic Party regulars and with the news media poking fun at him, Maddox kept working.

After the first round of the Democratic primary there were just two: Arnall and Maddox. Third was the previously-unknown Carter who soon would launch a four-year campaign that would earn him the governor's office in 1970, eventually leading to the presidency.

With closet Callaway supporters crossing over to help him, Maddox became the Democratic nominee for governor in 1966. Many Republicans had changed parties to vote for the outspoken segregationist, assuming that in the general election he would be an easy mark for their dignified, polished candidate. Once again, people underestimated Lester Garfield Maddox.

When at last it came down to Maddox and Callaway, traditional Democrats responded by mounting a write-in campaign for a third candidate. Their choice was Arnall, who although his strident campaign style didn't translate well to television, was still a formidable figure. Arnall didn't support the write-in effort. Nor did he decline their support. And for the third time that year, Georgia voters were headed to the polls.

The race was a contrast in style and presence: Callaway with his military demeanor and a campaign that featured computers and smiling young people versus Maddox with his bouncy "Everything's Pickrick" personality and a low-budget machine that usually needed oil. More than that, the differences were evident in the two men. "He shook hands with the restaurant managers, I shook hands with the cooks and the diswashers," Maddox declared.

But the morning after the November election, Georgians still did not have a governor and none of the candidates could claim a clear majority. Arnall had attracted 52,831 write-in votes, and those votes were the key to what was beginning to unfold. Callaway had 453,665 votes to Maddox' 450,626—a margin of only 3,039 individual votes.

Georgia had never faced such a dilemma before, so no one knew what would happen next. The state constitution said any election in which a single candidate did not receive a majority should be decided by a joint session of the General Assembly with that body considering the two highest vote-getters on the ballot. Because the General Assembly was so clearly dominated by Democrats, this outcome was not what Callaway and the Republican Party wanted to happen.

Two lawsuits soon challenged the legislature's right to elect the governor. One suit said that by doing this, the one-man, one-vote principle would be violated. Another called for a man-to-man runoff between Callaway and Maddox with no write-in votes allowed. There was even talk suggesting that Carl Sanders might step aside and swear in George T. Smith as governor. Smith, giving up his House seat, had been elected lieutenant governor on that same ballot in November. Smart money was on another runoff between the Republican and the Democrat.

To everyone's surprise—especially Maddox's—a ruling by the United States Supreme Court sent the election to the Georgia General Assembly, saying that's what the state should have done in the beginning.

Amid this conundrum, key members of the Georgia House had been privately talking among themselves. Even before the election or the court ruling, there had been serious discussions about the body seeking its independence from the governor. Under their plan, the House membership—not the governor—would select the speaker of the House and speaker pro-tem. The speaker would then choose the committee chairs and make the committee appointments.

At a secret caucus, the House had elected George L. Smith, who had been speaker before for four years, as their first independent leader. For first time in Georgia's history, the General Assembly was about to become a true third arm of government.

With Republicans making headway in the state, House members also formed their first Democratic Caucus. They would need a majority leader and the names of George Busbee and Tom Murphy came to the top. Busbee won that election by six votes and eight years later he would be elected Georgia's governor, the first to be allowed to seek two consecutive terms under an amended state constitution. As for Murphy, his first taste of leadership was also drawing closer. Sanders, meanwhile, continued to act as governor.

Be it Callaway or be it Maddox, the new governor would be working with handicaps his predecessors never had. Sanders, with representatives of the two candidates working with him, was drawing up the proposed state budget, taking away influence from the new chief executive. Moreover, neither of the two hopefuls knew much about the inner workings of state government—especially Maddox, who during his campaign had even promised legislative freedom. And now, with the General Assembly casting the deciding votes, Georgia's seventy-fifth governor would owe his position to each and every member.

Lieutenant Governor Peter Zack Geer called that historic special session to order. Seated before him that January were members of the previous House and Senate for the election of the new bodies had not been certified and the new members had not yet been duly sworn. The lieutenant governor always presides over joint sessions and it was ironic that Geer had the gavel because just four years before Lester Maddox had been one of his challengers.

After wrangling over a number of issues, the roll call of names began. To win, one of the candidates needed 130 votes. One by one, the names of legislators were read beginning with Billy Abney. Finally the clerk came to Representative Thomas B. Murphy of Bremen. He cast his vote, calling out the name of Lester Maddox. Maddox carried by a 182-66 margin. The oath of office only made it legal. Murphy's vote had made Maddox the Governor of Georgia.

Murphy had not been a Maddox man during the long campaign. He had eaten in his cafeteria, but the two of them had never met. Murphy had originally supported Jimmy Carter. But Haralson County went for the staccato-speaking Maddox and when the time came so did Murphy. Besides, Maddox was a Democrat and Murphys always voted for Democrats.

Earlier, in December, Maddox had begun pulling together his own team and one of them he chose was Tommy Irvin, a member of that outgoing legislature. The rangy Habersham County legislator would become the new governor's executive secretary. It was Irvin who eventually would recommend a former state senator named Zell Miller for the governor's staff and it was he who first mentioned Murphy's name to Maddox.

ON A SUNDAY afternoon in December 1966, Tom and Agnes Murphy were relaxing in their den in Bremen when he received a call from Lester Maddox. Figuring it was somebody playing a prank on him, Murphy said something silly. No, the voice said, it really was Lester Maddox.

Turning serious, Murphy assured Maddox that he was going to vote for him when the special session was held. The candidate said fine, but that wasn't why he called. He said he wanted Murphy to come to Atlanta to talk. "I'm here with Agnes," Murphy said.

"Bring her along," Maddox said. "Virginia would like to meet her."

Getting into their car, the Murphys went to Atlanta. Once they had sat down and talked for a little while, Maddox told them why he needed to meet with the Bremen legislator. He said he wanted Murphy to be his administration floor leader. The floor leader carries the flag for the governor in the House. He is the governor's eyes and ears. Remembering his experience as a committee chair, Murphy was typically candid. "Governor, you may not want me. I'm a pretty independent fellow."

"I know. That's what they tell me. That's why I want you."

"Well, I won't go along with you if I don't believe in it," Murphy warned Maddox.

"That's the same thing Tommy Irvin told me."

Thus began one of the most unusual relationships between a governor and a floor leader in memory. "That was one of the unique things about that administration. If the governor had something that Murphy didn't think would fly, we'd just iron it out down in that corner room near the governor's office. If Murphy didn't agree with the governor, he'd say so," says Irvin, now the state's veteran agriculture commissioner.

The relationship between the administration and the newly-independent House was also tenuous. Nobody knew where anyone else stood. There was a governor elected by the grace of the legislature. There was a speaker and lieutenant governor sailing on uncharted waters with George L. Smith wanting his finger on every button. There was the newly-vocal Republican party. There was a restless group of urban members who were increasingly unhappy at their role in a rural-dominated legislature. "It's a period of testing for us all," Maddox said at the time.

As might be expected, one of the first battles fought was over money. The House wanted a line-item budget but the governor didn't want to give up total control. A compromise was reached in which the governor had the ability to transfer funds. Everyone was having to give and everyone was having to take. As the governor's floor leader, Murphy soon became a key player in the budget process, beginning an influence that has continued for nearly four decades.

And still Murphy and the governor were having their daily debates—a situation Maddox appreciated. "I like mavericks more than politicians," he said. "I like people who think for themselves. I didn't want people who had to say 'yes' no matter what I told them."

Murphy and Maddox worked together for the first three years of Maddox' administration and Murphy is proud of the programs and changes that the governor made. "History will record that Lester Maddox was a good governor," he says. "Who among you will laugh at the efforts of of an honest, sincere Christian man whose honest desire is to keep the state ahead?"

Because of his position with the governor, Murphy was confronting George L. Smith more and more over legislation, and the powerful speaker usually prevailed. On a personal level, Murphy was growing uneasy with the way the House was being operated. The speaker ran things like he wanted them run. He told his committee chairmen what he wanted and he expected them to blindly go along with him. There was very little difference in that from the way things were when the governor had control.

Murphy was loyal, however. He was brought up that way. But he also wanted more of a voice. "He was smart on his feet. It didn't take a smart person to know he was going to be a leader," Marcus Collins remembers.

His opportunity to become a leader came soon. Maddox Hale, the veteran speaker pro-tem, died unexpectedly in 1970 and Murphy let it be known to his colleagues that he wanted a chance at the job. He had been in the House for nine years and "I felt it was time to move up in the organization."

That he would be in that position is wrapped in a layer of irony. Had he prevailed instead of George Busbee, Murphy would have been House Majority Leader and probably not interested in being speaker pro-tem and had Busbee been defeated, he might never have been governor. And down the road three more years, had Murphy not been speaker pro-tem, he would not have been as strong of a choice for an advancement that was to come.

"I've been blessed, real blessed," Murphy says.

The race for speaker pro-tem came down to Murphy and Elliott Levitas, a skillful representative from DeKalb County. Levitas, later a United States congressman, was the favorite of the urban coalition. Murphy, however, got the job with much of his support coming from rural legislators—a group he prefers to classify as "independent cusses like me." Four years later, they'd have another chance to voice that independence.

6

THE

UNEXPECTED

SPEAKER

GEORGE L. SMITH grew power the way South Georgia farmers grow corn. He planted it. He cultivated it. He fertilized it. Then, when the ears of corn were just right, he picked them and put back seed for another year.

That was his way of cultivating the power and influence he needed to reign as speaker of the Georgia House. It was a tedious crop. One year he would plant, cultivate, and fertilize—any good politician knows you have to fertilize— then when time came for the General Assembly to convene for another year, he already had the seeds he would need for another crop.

It was a Sunday in November. The 1974 Legislature would report for duty in less than two months and George L. had gone to his law office in Swainsboro to catch up on some legal work, some phone calls and to do some planning for next year's session.

For several years, he had been suffering from heart trouble, worsened by diabetes, and at the office that Sunday afternoon, he suffered a massive stroke. A day later, his doctors there at home moved him to Piedmont Hospital in Atlanta where, in a few days, he would mark his sixty-first birthday.

Twenty-seven days after the attack, after being unconscious nearly three weeks, George L. Smith died. He was buried in Emanuel County. But before going home a final time, with a flag draped over his coffin and somber state troopers standing guard, he became just the twelfth Georgian to lay in state under the capitol rotunda. It was a scene George L. would have relished.

Flags were at half-staff in honor of the man political folks called George L., differeniating between him and George T. Smith, the Grady County lawyer that Governor Carl Sanders had made speaker after he fired George L. just eleven years before.

Editorial writers around the state praised his years of service. "George L. Smith has brought new dignity and significance to the deliberations of the House that he loved," wrote the *Atlanta Constitution*.

George L. would have understood the events that followed his stroke. Naturally, he was news. He had been making news since Emanuel County voters first elected him to the Georgia House in 1945. He made headlines when Governor Ernest Vandiver appointed him Speaker of the House in 1959, made the front page when Sanders unceremoniously fired him in 1963, and once again four years later when newly-independent House members voted the gavel back to him.

More than all of that, he would have understood how the members of the Georgia House responded. These were his friends. Old friends. Good friends. He had been around the House nearly twenty-nine years, twelve of them as the body's presiding officer, so he would know very well their reactions.

Naturally, they would be shocked and genuinely concerned at news of his illness. And like most God-fearing Christians, they'd pray for his complete recovery—and mean it.

But once their saintly prayers had been delivered and they had gotten off their knees, the inevitable political questions would follow: Would he recover? Would he ever be able to come back? What about the upcoming session? Would someone be Speaker on an interim basis until either George L. returned or an election was held? What would this mean to their committee assignments? What about their political needs? And, finally, if he couldn't return, who should be his successor?

The public face was upbeat. People talked of the speaker getting well. Governor Jimmy Carter visited him in the hospital and came out hopeful. George L.'s brother, Doctor Wilder Smith, told reporters that when his brother recovered he wouldn't advise him to get out of politics. "It would kill him," he said. "This is his life." Out of range of notebooks and TV cameras, talk was not so optimistic.

There was a move to have a one-year caretaker in 1974, until either the popular George L. returned or a permanent selection was made. With the second most influential job in the state capitol at stake, that wasn't likely and soon legislative counsel Frank Edwards offered a ruling that an immediate election would be legally required if the speaker couldn't preside come January. After a brief rally, George L's health was declining fast and after he lapsed into a coma, names of his successors were being tossed around like a Frisbee at the beach.

There was Speaker Pro-Tem Tom Murphy of Bremen, the second in line, a legislator seen by one Atlanta reporter as "a brooding enigma" an atypical House member who could be "silent, withdrawn and unapproachable."

There was Elliott Levitas of DeKalb County, a former Rhodes Scholar, a background that George L. once joked qualified him for the Transportation Committee. Two years before, Levitas had unsuccessfully opposed Murphy for speaker pro-tem.

There was Denmark Groover, the old war-horse from Macon along with Robin Harris of Decatur, Al Burruss of Marietta and everybody's dark-horse, Roy Lambert of Madison.

But all conversations began with George Busbee. The veteran legislator from Albany was George L.'s protege. He knew the House and the members knew him. He knew how things worked, or had worked. He knew the state budget. He wasn't flashy, just steady. However, Busbee had already announced that he intended to run for governor in 1974, probably challenging Lester Maddox who had taken a "temporary job" as lieutenant governor so he would be ready to move back into the Governor's Mansion in 1975. Busbee had already spent nearly $100,000 on that race so no one knew if he'd give up that opportunity to be Speaker.

Some of Busbee's advisors were telling him he owed it to the House to return, including Al Holloway, his close friend and a veteran state senator from Albany. People were saying that without him the race for speaker would turn into "a gun fight"...that he was the only one who could fill his mentor's shoes...that he was heir apparent, the chosen one.

Had George L. Smith been able, he would have called those talkative colleagues into his office and, gently or not, told them to keep their mouths shut—or else. Busbee himself was uncomfortable with all the talk, saying it made him appear to be a political vulture.

While most of the public talk involved Busbee, Murphy's forces looked in other directions. While the media focused on the majority leader, they didn't see him as an officer of the House. As speaker pro-tem, they thought Murphy should be the obvious successor.

Ten days before George L.'s death, the House Democratic Caucus convened at the capitol. They had only three options:

(1) ask Busbee to withdraw from the gubernatorial race and take the Speaker's job; (2) ask Busbee to take the job for the 1974 session, leaving time for him to resume his run for the governor's office; (3) promote Murphy into the job–with Busbee's support.

Murphy was poker faced, telling reporters he thought it was in poor taste to talk about such things while Smith was ill. "I am going to do what I am supposed to do and that's all I'm going to do," he told reporters, walking away before other questions could be asked.

Options centered on the Albany Democrat and so did most of the news reports around the state. The *Atlanta Constitution*–on the day of George L's funeral–even reported that sources were saying he was leaning toward the House post and that his formal announcement would come after the services in Swainsboro. If Busbee gave up the governor's race, most people assumed he would be George L.'s successor.

Before the funeral on 12 December Representative Marcus Collins asked Murphy if they could talk. They spoke the same language. Collins was from Pelham, in Mitchell County, just one county removed from Busbee's home county of Doughtery. The burly farmer was a second generation member of the House, having filled his father's unexpired term in 1961–the same year Tom Murphy arrived. Both Collins and Busbee had served a tour in the Pacific during World War II. Both were from rural upbringings. They became fast friends.

"George," Collins said, "we've been doing some counting." According to Collins's numbers, reports of Busbee's coronation were very premature. While the political reporters had been busy speculating, Murphy and his supporters had quietly secured the South Georgia votes everybody had assumed would go to Busbee–and he was a South Georgia boy.

Busbee wasn't too surprised. He had been majority leader while Murphy was Maddox's floor leader. The two of them had tangled often so he knew how tenacious Murphy could be. Murphy's position only added to Busbee's dilemma. He was really at a crossroads now.

Run for speaker and lose and he could soon be back practicing law in Albany. Run for speaker and win a close race and the House would be divided, setting up forty painful days that would hardly provide a proper push for the governor's race. His pending campaign against the ever-popular Maddox would not be a sure thing.

Busbee had a choice. Murphy didn't. "If George had decided to run for it, it would have been the gut fight described in the papers," Murphy says. "I really don't know who would have won if he had stayed in it. It would have been close."

Murphy claims not to know, but Collins did. And so did Busbee. He had been around politics. He could count. The Bremen lawyer had been promised forty-one votes from the caucus. He was only thirty-five shy—and he hadn't even asked anybody for a vote yet. Busbee also realized there was no turning back for Murphy. "I hold the second-highest position in the House," Murphy said, "and for me not to run for speaker would have meant of the loss of respect from the House." Such a loss would pain anyone, that would mortally wound a proud man like Murphy.

After George L.'s funeral, Busbee announced he was going to stay in the governor's race. It was a wise decision on all counts. He knew what the results in the House would be. And a year later, forcing a primary runoff with the favored Maddox, the self-described work-horse defeated the show-horse. George Dekle Busbee would serve two acclaimed terms as governor of Georgia.

Murphy says that's what Busbee wanted all along. "He just had a real burning desire to be governor—something I've never had," Murphy says. "Besides, he never was the primary candidate for speaker. That was just media inflation."

Some thought it was not just the media who had been setting Busbee up for a fall, but rather Maddox or other would-be candidates for governor. John Grier, at the time a veteran House member from Atlanta, put that theory into words befitting the rural legislator he once had been. "I remember what Ed Rivers used to say and I believe it's still true," Grier observed. "He said the governor is a public coon dog. Everybody wants you to run their coons and rabbits for them."

By then, the media was focusing on Murphy, and, predictably, he wasn't comfortable with the attention. While George L. Smith had been the darling of the press room, Murphy never was. George L. loved to cajole with the press, particularly the late Celestine Sibley, a veteran *Atlanta Constitution* columnist who delighted in telling of his colorful exploits. Often he would call Sibley aside and predict the outcome of particular bills—and he was usually right. He was good copy. Murphy wasn't—and didn't care.

In print, capitol reporters remembered Murphy as a Maddox floor leader, labeling him as "the epitome of old-line reactionary county unit politics." They remembered his sage comments about Governor Jimmy Carter's highly-proclaimed inaugural address in 1971—a speech that got the future President of the United States on the cover of *Time*. "It was a good speech," Murphy said. "I just didn't agree with much of it." They remembered his ongoing arguments against the governor's proposed government reorganization, a plan that Carter saw as the hallmark of his administration. "I don't just blindly follow anyone, he explained, saying his views had nothing to do with his friendship with Maddox, the governor's primary adversary.

He was everything Smith was not. The only resemblance anyone could see was they were both small-town lawyers. They also remembered him baiting their friend George L.

from the floor of the House. "Your honor, if it pleases the court," he would often begin, railing against the speaker's plan to reduce the size of the House. He deferred only when he saw "an express train coming down the tracks and I'm fixing to get obliterated."

At the age of fifty, Murphy was described as a champion of lost causes and a maverick, a guy who didn't want to be a team player. Call him what they want, they were about to call him Mr. Speaker. Democrats were planning a meeting 19 December hardly two weeks before the 1974 session would begin. Murphy said publicly that he had 102 strong commitments, a statement that moved Denmark Groover to whimsically confirm that he was out of the speaker's race. "The statesman-like reason to give would be that I did this in the interest of unity," the colorful Groover said. "Fact is, my canvas of the situation is that Mr. Murphy has the votes." And he did.

Using a symbolic tactic he would use twice more in the future, Murphy asked the erudite Elliott Levitas—his opponent for speaker pro-tem two years before—to place his name into nomination at the party caucus. The vote was unanimous. Thomas Bailey Murphy was Speaker of the House.

He said the right things. He thanked his friends and supporters. He was humble. He was proud. He properly praised George L. Smith. Then, typically, he moved away from the sweet talk and got down to the business of the moment, reminding the 133 Democrats present that "the time has come to turn from the past to the future."

House Republicans had already agreed that once elected Murphy could immediately move into the speaker's second floor suite of offices. So after the caucus adjourned, there was work to be done. To the media, he talked about his temper and his future. "I know that what I do with it in this session will have a lot to do with who presides in 1974," he said. "I know some people say I have a temper—and that's true. I used to not try and control it. But now I think I can control it as well as any man."

But first, he made a statement to the House members who had elected him that over the years would get him into trouble with some and at the same time forever endear him to his fellow democrats. "I am tied," he said, "to no one except to the individual members of this caucus."

A statement House Republicans wouldn't soon forget.

7

ALONE

AT THE

TOP

TOM MURPHY WAS the new Speaker of the Georgia House and he was alone. There was no one to counsel him, no one who had been where he was. The only man who would understand the challenges he was facing was George L. Smith and he was dead. The ones who came before them could only help so much because their gavel had belonged to the governor. Tom Murphy was alone.

Jimmy Carter was the governor and Murphy had slowly grown apart from him, even though he had actively supported the Plains peanut farmer in his gubernatorial campaign. He wasn't alone there. Few members of the House were that close to Carter. When Representative Al Burruss, the governor's floor leader, was being interviewed by a reporter for a story on Carter allies, he quipped, "It's not going to be a long story is it?" That situation made the new speaker even more isolated.

Every morning his committee chairmen would show up at his office looking for their marching orders, just as they had done when George L. was in charge. That's the way George L. wanted it. As far as he was concerned, he didn't want a bulb changed in the House without him knowing it. So first thing every day, the chairmen filed in and asked Murphy what he wanted them to do. Fed up, Murphy finally put a stop to that. "Listen," he said. "If you people can't run your own committees, tell me. I'll get somebody who will. I am just plain tired of you coming here."

The individual members also learned there was a new sheriff in town, one who was giving them a voice. Ward Edwards, now the House doorkeeper, was a legislator from Butler in 1974. He remembers when he got that message. "We had our first policy meeting with the new chairman sitting at the head of the table. We walked in there with an issue of some kind and Murphy said, 'Let's discuss it.' We did, too. We went all around the table and he asked everybody what they thought. I really appreciated that, because right then I started seeing that I had some input into what was going on around here," Edwards says.

It was a learning experience for the House members, too. They had elected Tom Murphy, but they didn't know him all that well. They respected him as a legislator. They knew he was a leader. Over the past few years, when he was speaker pro-tem, George L. had given him experience presiding, but this was different. Now he was in charge and the House members quickly learned of his distaste for yes-men. "Most useless person in the world. Tell me if I'm making a mistake. One of us will change our mind." But, with a twinkle in his eye, he confesses that it is much easier to convince someone you're right if you are the Speaker. "I have to admit that," he laughs.

Knowing his years of influence around state government, Carter had given George L. Smith more breathing room than he did Murphy. Now he was quietly maneuvering to regain some of the controls the governor's office once had over the House. As governor—and later president of the United States—Carter preferred to put things in writing. So, on almost a daily basis, he was forwarding detailed messages to Murphy. "He'd send me handwritten memos just about every day and I would wad them up and throw them in the waste basket. I wish now I had saved them," Murphy says.

As for the news media, there had always been a level of mistrust between the capitol press and Murphy and it grew even more intense when he became Speaker. Quickly, he had agitated the *Atlanta Journal* when, after a single session, he canceled weekly conferences with the newspaper's editorial board. It was a meeting George L. Smith always kept on his calendar. "We didn't agree on anything," Murphy recalls. As his colleagues in the House began watching Murphy take the heat, they realized that in many cases he was being hammered for things others had done. This only endeared him more to the membership.

Lobbyists also were trying to understand this new leader. They knew how to operate under George L., but Murphy was a different animal. "If George L. didn't particularly like a bill or proposal that was introduced, there wouldn't be a hearing. The committee chairman might just carry the bill around in his coat pocket. We called that a 'coat pocket veto.' With Murphy, you always got a hearing. You might not like the results. But you got a hearing," remembers capitol lobbyist Bryce Holcomb.

In the Georgia House, as in the forty-nine other statehouses, there was a natural inborn competition with the body across the hall. This competition intensified within the first year Murphy was Speaker. Zell Miller, a former state senator, was elected lieutenant governor and in 1976 he began to make changes that seemed to be directed at the House. Miller was trying to reinvigorate his own group and soon both presiding officers were setting up the other side as the legislative enemy. In Miller, Murphy discovered a competitor who enjoyed a good sparring match as much as he. Thus began a sixteen-year political duel.

Maybe by instinct or maybe by just plain luck, these factors forced Murphy to look within, not just at himself but at the members of the House. It was a process at which he became a master. He had a group of friends who were loyal and experienced. He trusted them implicitly. Then, man by man, he began to get to know better the individual members — who their constituents were, what their home district was like and personal information such as who their daddy was and who their spouse was. He learned about their pet issues, their interests, their abilities, their weaknesses. He decided for himself who could lead, who could follow and who could do neither. He was compiling a mental data base that would serve him well for the next quarter of a century.

It was a kind of bunker mentality — us against the world. Almost a holy war. This attitude rallied the House members together as a tight-knit group that looked at Murphy as its leader. As for Murphy, he was creating the very distinctive character that became his political persona. Doctors advised him to keep the sun off his face because of skin problems so he had started buying big-brimmed LBJ Stetson's at Lipham's Department Store in Tallapoosa. He was never without one. Doctors also told him to lay off the cigars he had enjoyed smoking for many years so he put out the fire and started chewing on them, a habit he has never broken. He was the bully, putting those pesky Republicans in their place to the delight of his Democratic gallery. He said things others wished they could say. He was a man's man, in what at that moment was definitely an all-male fraternity. All of these elements solidified Murphy and his leadership — both of which would be severely challenged within two years.

Murphy was putting a face on a position that had historically been faceless. Few men had ever held the job for any significant length of time. William Cecil Neill, the author of the controversial County Unit System Legislation in 1917, was Speaker of the House for five years (1921-1926) and later presided over the Senate. His death shut down the capitol as most state officials went to Columbus for his funeral. Richard B. Russell was speaker for four years (1927-1931) and went on to become the state's youngest governor. But his mark on history, of course, was his legendary service in the United States Senate. Roy Harris served five years spread over two terms in the position (1937-1940 and 1943-1946). Fred Hand, other than Murphy, held the job for the most consecutive years, holding the gavel seven years (1947-1954). George L. Smith also had the honor of seven years, but it was over two stints (1959-1962 and 1967-1973).

Without knowing it, Murphy was building a foundation unequaled in the history of the House. "I never thought I'd stay in the job very long," he says. "I never even imagined I'd be Speaker when I first went there."

Murphy soon became active in several national legislative organizations, including the Council of State Governments and the Southern Speakers group. Such organizations bring together people facing similar challenges, giving them a chance to share war stories with people who have been there, too.

It was in these groups where he became close friends with Ned McWherter. Like Murphy a big old country boy from Palmersville, Tennessee, McWherter was elected to the Tennessee House in 1968. Within two terms, he was elected Speaker of the House, a job he held for fourteen years. He gave up his gavel to become governor of Tennessee in 1987, serving two four-year terms as the state's chief executive.

Their friendship has grown over the years and McWherter knows Murphy very well. He also knows the skills and traits that are needed to be the presiding officer of an unwieldy and diverse body of legislators. The things he talks about as prerequisites for the position parallel the early years of Tom Murphy. "First off, you have to know your membership.

When I was elected in Tennessee, the House was half Democrat and half Republican. I got elected by one vote. You get to know what kind of constituency it is. Is it urban? Is it inter-city? Is it rural? Is it suburban? These are traits Tom has naturally. He understands all these people. He comes from Bremen, but he knows the needs of Atlanta and the urban centers of Georgia."

McWherter knows the power in the position. It comes with the gavel. Knowing how to use that power is another matter. "As Speaker or as a leader, you don't use it unless it is absolutely necessary. And when you use it, you don't disclose it. You just make things happen. If you know the history of your state this gives you a unique understanding of issues. Murphy knows it well and respects it. He is able to get things done, and that is a characteristic of a good leader and a good speaker."

The Speaker is usually a conduit for everything that happens in state government. He is part of the vision. He is part of the action. And unlike the chief executive, he even has a vote. To McWherter, who has experience in both positions, this is gratifying. "You feel challenged every day. You're doing the best you can for your state and for the body that elects you. I've told Tom this and I told Zell Miller this—he's also a friend of mine—the speaker of the house or the leader of the senate can make more things happen in a state than all the governors put together. Governors propose. Speakers dispose. As speaker, you have one vote. As governor, you have none," he says.

Zell Miller, who followed a trail similar to McWherter's and became governor of Georgia, says the job of a presiding officer is uniquely different from the person elected statewide. "It is hard to understand, almost impossible to understand, unless you have been there or close to it. To be a presiding officer, it requires a different set of skills and a different kind of politics than it takes to be elected statewide or to govern the state."

Miller also talks about the need to understand the membership and their needs. "Whenever you run statewide you come to have a different, broader outlook on the state. As governor, you look at a Savannah or Chatham County and think about what its needs are. As Speaker, you would look at the legislators who represent that area and what would make them happy. Let's use Muscogee County as an example. It is much more important for the Speaker to keep Tom Buck and the other members of that delegation happy than it is to keep Jim Blanchard of Synovus or Bill Turner of the Bradley Company or the newspaper down there happy. As a statewide candidate, those legislators may not even support you, but you go over their heads to the people."

In 1999, Mark Taylor was in a position similar to Murphy's in 1973. As Georgia's newly-elected lieutenant governor, he took over the State Senate at a time when partisan politics was beginning to become an issue. He not only sought Murphy's advice, he also studied his style as a presiding officer. "To do as well as the Speaker, you either need the respect or the fear of the body. He has had both. His survival has been on the fact that his troops know there are ramifications if they don't follow his lead. The trick is to accomplish these things without abusing those powers," says Taylor, who believes a comparison of himself and Murphy is similar to comparing a South Georgia gnat and a Lockheed C5A.

At the same time he could be the House bully, Murphy wasn't afraid to show his softer side, opening up and sharing personal memories of his brother James and of hungry families riding the train through Bremen during the Depression years hoping somewhere there would be a job. He would even cry in front of them. "He has a soft heart," says Calvin Smyre, who was elected to the House during Murphy's first term as speaker. "Even those that are very, very politically opposed to him, people he vigorously fights, he can have a soft spot for them. He's always been a master of the political game, but there is also this soft side to him."

As much as anything in those early years, he endeared himself to the membership, especially the Democrats. George L. Smith had begun to evangelize among the Republicans, giving them office space and a few other amenities. Murphy reversed that trend. With the small number of Republicans, he could afford to do this since it played so well with his Democratic leadership. He wasn't afraid. He knew he had the votes to do anything he wanted to do. So he did.

To the members of the House, his office door was always open. His policy wasn't first come, first serve. For while a lobbyist or a news reporter might have been waiting longer, the House member who just walked in would see Murphy first. This was Murphy's way of showing respect, but at the same time it was a way to make those 179 people feel important — not that some of the egos he worked with needed stroking.

At the podium, he knew the rules of the House and he had an unparalleled awareness of the issues. He was confident with the gavel and he was confident as a leader. He knew his primary task was to facilitate the thousands of bills that are introduced every year, efficiently turning them into law or turning them away. That was primary in the job description of a speaker as described by Bill Bulger, whose retirement as president of the senate in Massachusetts in 1997 made Murphy the nation's senior presiding officer. "He or she is there to accomplish legislation, not to sell newspapers or enhance broadcast ratings," wrote Bulger in his 1996 autobiography, *"While the Music Lasts."* After retiring from politics, he became president of the University of Massachusetts. He described his idea of an effective presiding officer. "It is one who works to bring about the consensus necessary to accomplish legislation seasonably — which is the reason for a House and Senate."

Bulger said a presiding officer is often a mediator, and to do that he or she must be a sympathetic listener. "I view leadership as a catalytic function. One discusses issues with members. One asks questions in an effort, not merely to know, but to understand diverse positions. To an extent, it is not unlike the role of a mediator. The job requires a great deal of sympathetic listening—listening for points of agreement that can be developed into a base upon which to build, listening for areas of compromise, urging their exploration. A leader must welcome initiatives and encourage creativity to bridge any final gaps between dividing members."

Like Murphy, Bulger was a lawyer and like Murphy he fought for years with the Boston press. He said the media often told him he had an obligation to provide headlines and sound bytes—which like Murphy he usually did whether he planned to or not. Bulger was a combative, forceful leader. But the fiery Irishman also cautioned about abusing the power that goes with the position and often the person. "The end product—whether to support or oppose a bill, or whether to agree on a viable compromise—is not something that can be inflicted by leadership; it is a consensus resulting from the communal wisdom and goodwill of the membership."

McWherter knows about consensus. You don't spend eighteen years in the Tennessee House and eight more as governor without understanding that principle. He used consensus building in both offices and he says he has often asked his friend Murphy why he didn't go after the statewide post.

"Look what happened to you," Murphy told him. "You lose all your leadership abilities when you become governor."

McWherter laughs and says that isn't too far from the truth. "I remember what we speakers always told our governors—and I tried to tell myself that when I got elected governor. We always said 'Don't get carried away.

Remember who makes the laws.' I tried to take my own advice."

Though essentially retired from public life, McWherter, a Democrat, is now a member of the Postal Service Board of Governors. Recently, he was asked by Governor Don Sundquist to co-chair a bi-partisan committee with former Senator Howard Baker that will examine and identify new revenue sources for the state of Tennessee. He is also a colorful story-teller and one he enjoys telling shows leadership, vision and consensus building. It involves four speakers from four Southern states — including Tom Murphy of Georgia.

Billy Clayton was Speaker of the House in Texas and he invited two other speakers to go dove hunting with him just over the border in Mexico. McWherter and Murphy flew out of Atlanta, going into Austin to meet Clayton. The group boarded a small plane Clayton had secured and flew to McAllen, Texas. They were going to cross over the Rio Grande there and head for a hunting camp that Clayton knew about in Mexico.

"We got to this check point where the Mexican authorities were and we had a station wagon full of shotguns, two or three each. The official looked into the car and saw all those shotguns. But he was more worried about how many cases of shells we had. He said we could only carry nine shells each," McWherter recalls.

Nine shells each wasn't many. McWherter says he needed a case a day by himself. But these were innovative leaders. They had a plan. So Clayton turned the station wagon around and the Texas speaker, the Tennessee speaker, and the Georgia speaker retreated to a service station they had seen up the road on the Texas side of the border.

Hiring a young Mexican boy, they assembled the materials they needed: a plywood plank and an old intertube. Quickly a make-shift raft was put together which was sturdy enough to float the Mexican boy and several cases of shotgun shells across the Rio Grande into Mexico.

"We got back into the station wagon and went right through that same check point. No problem. When we got on the other side, our driver went down in the woods, found the Mexican boy and came back up with our shotgun shells. In a few days, we came back through there with a station wagon full of doves we had killed. I don't know how we got them across the border, but we did."

It was the kind of ingenuity a speaker needs every day.

8

MISBEHAVING

IN THE

HOUSE

ALTHOUGH ITS MEMBERS sometimes act like college frat boys away from home and Mama for the first time, the Georgia General Assembly keeps alive the rituals and traditions of the stodgy British Parliament. The pomp is there. So is the circumstance. Only you will probably get a mess of hush puppies with your order of fish and chips.

Why else would Ward Edwards, a Southern-fried doorkeeper from Butler, Georgia, bow to the left and bow to the right before announcing an invited guest to the Georgia House of Representatives? Really, Edwards is just following a life-and-death tradition that began centuries ago in Great Britain.

When the Queen would come to call on the House of Commons or the House of Lords, the doorkeeper would first bow to his friends, then bow to his enemies, then scamper down the aisle before someone stabbed him in the back. Sort of like when the Georgia House and Senate start fussing.

Tradition is why His Excellency the Governor of Georgia can't visit the House chambers without an invitation and even then has to knock three times and wait to be introduced. That's why when a House or Senate member rises — they must always stand — they can never refer to a colleague by name but instead must call that person "the gentleman from the 135th" or "the lady from the 43rd." And, as if they were a contestant on "Jeopardy," members must always begin their remarks with a question: "Isn't it true that this is a horrible bill?" Tom Murphy's reply has the bite of an Alex Trebek when he answers: "That's a matter each and every member will have to decide."

Well, it is true that the General Assembly of today is much calmer and better behaved than the one to which Tom Murphy first came in the winter of 1961. Then, it was a body with time on its hands, for while the voters back home elected them and sent them there, the membership actually worked for the governor on the floor below. That would change in six years when the House declared its independence, but until then the governor was without a doubt the man in charge.

The governor appointed the leaders. The governor handed out committee assignments and decided who the committee chairmen would be. The governor decided what bills would be heard and what bills would become law, even though he never openly cast a vote. For forty days and forty nights, the governor was boss. Legislators had little to do but show up and pull the lever when told to, so there was plenty of time for fun and frolic — even on the floor of the General Assembly.

The governor had other influences, according to the late Elmore Thrash. Thrash first came to the Georgia Legislature as a page in 1927 when Richard Russell was governor and later served as House Messenger for many years. When he first came to Atlanta, the General Assembly met for eighty days every two years. His grandfather and his father had been legislators, but he never chose that route. He recalled the scene in the governor's office during a session. "Used to be, everybody up here owed his or her job to the governor," Thrash said. "You didn't hire a janitor or secretary without asking him first. You go to his office now and there's a few folks down there, but back then it would be teeming with folks. All of them wanted a job—for themselves, for somebody they were related to, or for a friend back home. You had to stay on the governor's good side if you wanted a state job."

For many years, legislators stayed at the Henry Grady Hotel, which in those days sat on Peachtree Street where the Peachtree Plaza now rises far above the Atlanta traffic. Everybody stayed there and everybody played there. It was the scene of politics and parties.

"That Henry Grady was like a dormitory," said Thrash, who died in 1998. "There were hospitality rooms going all day long and most of the night. You could walk the streets of Atlanta at night and not be afraid, so we would all walk to the nightclubs, close them down, then come back to the hotel for a party. You didn't get to bed until 2:00 A.M. or later and you'd be back at the capitol first thing the next morning. It was fun then. It's not that way today."

Parties carried over to the floors of the House and Senate and into the ante-rooms of the capitol. In 1999, after celebrating the closing of the legislative session, some staff members of Governor Roy Barnes left the capitol in the wee hours after having too much to drink. One of them received a DUI and he was forced to resign his position. In the 1960s, that staff member might have been given a Merit Badge.

That party spirit used to carry over to the daily proceedings. With time on their hands, there was time for mirth and time to play out their political games. Such as an incident that occurred in 1958, Marvin Griffin's final year as governor. George Bagby, a representative from Paulding County, had been one of Griffin's faithful supporters, carrying out the governor's bidding whenever asked. But now Griffin was a lame duck leader with waning power and the short and feisty Bagby had set his eye on the speaker pro-tem's job, a position he would eventually earn. To get in line for the job, he knew he would need votes from the people he had been opposing so Bagby decided to defy the governor on a major issue. He chose a bill on rural roads, something sure to be noted by the anti-Griffin faction.

Griffin sure noticed. "They took George up to the countryside and showed him the green pastures," the colorful governor said when told of Bagby's public defiance.

The bill and Bagby hit the floor at the same time. He went up and down the aisle working against it, finally going to the well of the House to speak out. Wanting everyone to feel his courage, he told his colleagues that he was doing this knowing full well that the governor would take vengence against his brother John—a state patrolman. "I've written John," Bagby told the House. "I told him it'll be all right. If he has to come home, there's ham in the smokehouse, corn meal in the barrel, and we'll split a hoecake."

Griffin had never even heard of brother John, but after hearing of Bagby's speech he sent out orders that he wanted John Bagby unemployed and he wanted it done by sundown. And so it was. He sent his former supporter a note: "Dear George: Get the ham out of the smokehouse, take the corn meal out of the barrel and start dividing up the hoecake. John is headed in your direction."

There were no hard feelings about such things in those years. Politics was politics. If he didn't know it before, Griffin learned that in 1962 when he returned to the campaign trail in an unsuccessful attempt to be governor again. He was in Rockmart when he spied a face in the crowd—one he felt he was supposed to know. It was John Bagby, and he was applauding right along with the other Griffin supporters. When Griffin shook his hand, he asked Bagby how he could support him. After all, it was he, Marvin Griffin, who got him fired. "It wasn't your fault, Governor," he said. "It was my damn fool brother's big mouth."

The Atlanta newspapers were often the topic of fiery speeches in those years as members would rise to talk about things that were written about them in that day's editions. Griffin was certainly not immune from such articles and on one particular day his controversial brother Cheney—who during his administration got the governor in more than his share of trouble—came bounding into his second floor office. "We're in trouble, Marvin," Cheney said, with a rolled-up paper in his hand.

"What's the trouble?"

"It's them lyin' Atlanta newspapers again."

"You had me worried," the governor said. "For a minute, I thought they were telling the truth."

It was the Senate where the late Culver Kidd wore his Roman toga to give special effects to a speech so the Senate chambers aren't immune to outrageous antics. Many can be traced to Bobby Rowan, a former senator and public service commissioner. He tells this story on himself, a candidate for governor, involving Roscoe Dean, who served several terms in the senate and a term in prison for taking money when he shouldn't have. Rowan was, and is, a colorful storyteller and a talented speech-writer. Dean, it seemed, wanted to use those talents. This is the *Reader's Digest* version of the yarn. Rowan can turn it into a lengthy monologue.

Dean, a cartoon-like character from Jesup, wanted to come out against Governor Carl Sanders on a bill that called for a tobacco tax and he asked Rowan and some of his henchmen to write him a speech. Collaborating with his friends, Rowan started out drafting a serious text but as it is with anything the Enigma, Georgia native is involved with, it turned to foolishness.

A speech was written and Rowan had it done on a special typewriter that put the words in large type. It looked real professional. The text dealt with the tobacco tax as Dean had requested, but there were also words nobody could define and phrases that made no sense at all, a kind of South Georgia double-talk. The next morning, Rowan presented Dean the speech, which he glanced over quickly.

"Senator, this is good," Dean said. "But what about jokes? I've got to have jokes."

Rowan told him that you cannot write down jokes, that you just have to tell them. He shared a couple of appropriate ones with Dean and showed him the places in the speech where he could tell the jokes. They were marked by big block letters set off by parentheses.

Thanking Rowan over and over for what he had done, Dean took the speech with him and said he was going to rehearse it that night. And the following morning, soon after the Senate convened, Dean rose on a point of personal privilege, a parliamentary procedure that means the legislator is not necessarily going to speak on a bill, that he is going to share something personal with the body.

Rowan and his co-authors scampered to the rear of the chamber to listen. "When Roscoe got to the double-talk, we were elbowing each other in the ribs and laughing it up. You could see senators all over the room looking at each other and asking, 'What did he say?' Old Roscoe was pleased with himself. He was waving his arms and extending his hands at just the right time, just like he had practiced it in the mirror. He was on a roll. He was getting to the good part: 'And so gentlemen, today I remind you *READ THE JOKE!*'" That was the last time Roscoe Dean ever asked Bobby Rowan for a speech.

It wasn't the last time the Senate ever resorted to foolishness, however. Once during debate on an election bill, someone mentioned how dead folks sometimes vote, an age-old habit in some Georgia counties. They then proceeded to argue at length over how long a person had to be dead before they qualified to vote.

Years ago in the House, someone told a hushed chamber about how a biologist from the Department of Game & Fish had killed a hound-dog named Cleo, suspecting the animal had been killing deer. Member after member came forward to eulogize the slain dog. They were using their most eloquent words, almost resorting to tears as they talked about the late and lovely Cleo. Someone finally proposed a $300 award to the dog's owner then somebody else suggested a proper monument. The clock was ticking and there were other more-pressing matters on that day's calendar. Finally, after hearing all he could stand about the dearly-departed animal another member rose and said "Let's bury Cleo and get to work."

Their hijinks were often reported by the late Celestine Sibley, an *Atlanta Constitution* columnist who loved to write about the goings-on at the capitol. She was a favorite of George L. Smith and she was also adored by Tom Murphy after he became speaker.

Their relationship with her was unlike those with other members of the media, mainly because they knew she appreciated the legislative game and the people who played it. That was never more clear than in the summer of 1999 when Sibley became only the second woman in Georgia history to have a road named for her and when Governor Roy Barnes offered the beloved reporter's family the capitol as a site for her funeral—an offer they declined. Years ago, Sibley was sometimes part of the frivolity.

One of those times was a tale she often repeated in her column and one Sibley, already ill with cancer, told the House in 1999 after receiving an unprecedented invitation to speak to the body. The story involved a call girl known to many who frequented the Henry Grady Hotel. Wearing pink and blue and decked out in matching shoes and gloves, the woman showed up in the gallery of the House one afternoon. It was a slow day at the house and George L. Smith—in his first year as Speaker—had left the gavel to someone else and was off the floor.

Noticing Smith's absence, a prankster smuggled the fallen woman to a seat on the House floor, the seat of a kind, elderly member who was home sick that day. Members of the press corps also hung out at the Henry Grady so they recognized the flashy prostitute. One of them suggested a prank of his own to Sibley. "Let's shake them up, Celestine," he suggested. "You go over there and sit next to her. Pretend you're interviewing her."

Showing her floor pass to the doorkeeper, Sibley made her way to a seat next to the guest in pink and blue. She made a grand gesture of throwing back the cover to her notebook and the two women started talking. All the time, Sibley was furiously taking notes.

A hush fell over the House. The eyes of every member seemed transfixed on that one conversation. The woman was saying very little but Sibley still took notes and nodded her head. The men of the House could almost see the headlines in next morning's Atlanta Constitution. Each man feared his name might be there in big bold letters.

"Are you a constituent? Sibley asked the woman.

"A what?"

"A friend."

"I'm friends with lots of the gentlemen," the woman said, coyly.

Meanwhile, someone rushed to find George L. When the Speaker heard what was taking place, he rushed back to the podium and pounded his gavel like a sledgehammer on Peachtree Street. "Mr. Doorkeeper," he bellowed. "Clear the hall of the House! Mr. Sheriff, escort all persons not entitled to the privileges of the floor of the House."

Heads bowed as the call girl was escorted to the door. The members feared eye contact.

Elmore Thrash also starred in one of Sibley's numerous columns about the House. When Thrash died, Governor Zell Miller delivered a moving eulogy and his old friend Tom Murphy wept, for the Valdosta resident had become an institution. He was also a cut-up. Sibley had written about one of his exploits one morning and as often the case in the newspaper business a headline writer committed the mortal sin of having an error in the headline:

Thrash became Trash.

Sibley came into the press room that day and she was met by George Bagby and Jake Cullen, both longtime members of the House and both members of the Georgia Bar. Bagby did the talking.

"Miss Sibley, I hate to do this, but I have been retained by Mr. Elmore Thrash in a law suit against you. Mr. Jake Cullen of

Bartow County will assist me. You will be getting a registered letter from us stating these facts," Bagby said.

"I guess I'd better get myself a lawyer," she said.

"That would be wise," answered Bagby. "Of course, if you should be able to prove that Elmore *is* trash as well as Thrash, then Mr. Cullen and I might be willing to work out a settlement. Say, a couple of Cokes?"

In 1967, with the election of Lester Maddox, the House gained its independence from the governor. No longer was there a telephone on the speaker's podium so the governor could call and bark orders. The House controlled its own destiny with George L. Smith as the first speaker not personally selected by the governor. But still, there were members selling and delivering men's shoes from their seats on the House floor and others sitting there reading newspapers or catching a quick nap. When Georgia Public Television began turning its cameras on the chambers, legislators began to behave differently, but even then there were moments when boys were boys—such as an incident not too many years ago when a couple of members passed around a graphic sex toy on the floor of the House.

The language is still colorful. More Foxworthy than Leno. "I can't pick all the fleas off this dog—because we inherited part of this dog," a senator might say. Translated that means not to blame him for that particular bill because it came over from the House. "I don't have a dog in this fight," means "that's not my battle, but I do have something to say on the matter."

The House reflects the speaker. George L. Smith was a quiet man who while politicking acted as if his hair was on fire. Tom Murphy, though certainly Irish and predictably volatile, quickly tried to transform the sideshow atmosphere of the past into something approaching decorum. He even set his sights on the pressroom, requiring reporters to stand during the morning prayer and to recite the pledge to the flag.

Mixing stuffy British traditions with down-home traditions he brought with him from Bremen, Murphy will slam the gavel on the podium and threaten to verbally slam individual members when the noise level gets too loud to conduct business.

"All members will take a seat and cease all audible conversations," he says over and over, sounding like an auctioneer as he turns the phrase into a single run-together word. Like first graders told by their teacher to get back into their seats, House members meekly do as they're told. Then, in a matter of minutes, they're up roaming around the chamber again visiting and politicking. That is when they hear the threatening voice of God. "I really don't want to do this again because if I do, I'll embarrass somebody."

Which is still better than having to run from your enemies.

9

THE

TIMES

ARE

CHANGING

THIS MUCH WE know. It was the closing night of the General Assembly and with the legislative clock ticking, there was no time for a dinner break. Tom Murphy bought some sandwiches and they were spread out in his office. Mitchell Kaye, a legislator from Cobb County, ate one of them—a turkey sandwich, he insists. Tom Murphy got mad, real mad—mad enough to attack him, he confesses. The rest of the story ought to be clear because, if you believe the 180 members of the House of Representatives, each one of them was standing right there when it happened.

Meet the participants.

Mitchell Kaye is a Republican from Cobb County's 37th District. *Creative Loafing*, a weekly newspaper in Atlanta, once called him "Jumping Jack Flash," a description that had nothing to do with the Rolling Stones, more to do with how many times the legislator jumped up out of his chair in the House on a given legislative day. Tom Murphy is the Speaker of the House and a Democrat. Legend has it that instead of sandwiches Murphy prefers to dine on Republicans, sometimes eating two or three just for an appetizer.

By now, the story about the sandwich caper has achieved legendary status. The episode has festered. It wasn't sandwiches. No, it was hot dogs from the Varsity. It was a turkey sandwich, or was it ham and cheese? The Republican legislator ate one of them. Maybe more. They called each other names. The Democratic Speaker hit him with his fist. Or was it his gavel? Since there are so many versions and so many differences of opinion, let's hear from a few of the witnesses.

First, the Speaker of the House, Tom Murphy: "It was something silly. I pride myself on control and I lost my temper. I had bought my family some food and put it in my office. He went in there and was told he couldn't have a sandwich. Then he brought some other representatives back and told them 'Go in there and get them so they can't eat them.' When I heard that, I thought he was talking about my family. I rushed down there and I would have killed Mr. Kaye if I could have gotten to him. When they saw what was happening, Bill Lee and George Brown grabbed me to keep me off him. It took three of them to hold me. It was something silly and I'm ashamed of it."

Now Mitchell Kaye from the 37th District: "There were a bunch of sandwiches in the Speaker's office and it was late. There were Democrats and Republicans sitting around eating sandwiches and I asked where they got them and they said in the Speaker's conference room. I was hungry. It was me and four other representatives and we go in there for sandwiches. Steve Anthony, the Speaker's aide said they were lobbyists' sandwiches and were only for Democrats. They threw us out of the office. I went down to the Speaker. He was at the podium. I told him we had just gotten thrown out and he picked up his red phone and said 'Let these folks in.' I'm one of only three Jews in the General Assembly and I almost felt like Moses as the crowds split and we were allowed inside. I had a turkey sandwich with cold fries. I was given permission. I was clueless I had done anything wrong. Next thing you know, I'm talking with Bill Cumming, the chairman of the Retirement Committee in the ante-room, and here comes the Speaker and it's like there's fire coming out of his eyes. He lifts me off the floor by the back of my neck and arm. He was threatening to beat me up and they had to hold him. He kept saying, 'You took that sandwich.' They weren't protecting the Speaker from hitting me for my benefit. They were protecting him from hitting me because it would have ended his career."

From former Representative Bill Lee, a Democrat, and at the time the senior member of the House: "I stopped him. I got between them and I told Murphy he wasn't going to do this. He's strong now, don't you believe he isn't. There was a lot of tension for everybody down there. Some people try to create that kind of situation. Murphy doesn't, but he gets in a position sometimes where they test him pretty good and they try and make him mad. When I see that happening, I go up there and sit right by him and say, 'Be calm.' He doesn't appreciate me doing that until I do it."

From former Representative Matt Towery, a Republican: "I was on the phone with my wife and I saw Murphy storming by about ninety miles a hour with two or three people following him. Then, about two minutes later, he comes by again headed toward his office and a few more minutes later he comes flying out of his office again and this time five or six people are with him along with a bunch of reporters. It was like a comedy. I said 'Marylee, I've got to find out what's going on.' Somebody said the Speaker just punched Mitchell Kaye over a sandwich. You know how folks at the capitol exaggerate everything so I go back there to his office. I had been back there earlier and had a sandwich. If you were part of our (the Speaker's) little group, you could have one. If you weren't, you couldn't. And that was his right because he paid for them.. It wasn't like the House had paid for them. Apparently, Mitchell had caught wind of this and had opened the door and was telling people they could come get a sandwich because he had been denied access to a sandwich. Primarily because none of us wanted him back there eating."

MATT TOWERY WAS right. That scene does sound like a comedy. Only less than a week after that episode, Tom Murphy suffered a heart attack. Two years later, he suffered a light stroke. Granted, he has celebrated seventy-five birthdays and he had suffered from heart troubles before, but no one would doubt that the growing stress of the General Assembly contributes to his health problems. Warhorses such as Murphy have seen these pressures intensify every election season, leading to the contentious spirit that is so prevalent in contemporary politics. Much of this can be traced back to the ongoing change that has taken place in society and in Georgia politics.

Little of this spirit and attitude was around when Murphy took his first oath of office as a House member in 1961, mainly because the membership shared such a common background. They looked the same. They thought the same. Their backgrounds were much the same. Their color was the same. Their genders were the same. They mainly shared the same party membership. Surely not all of them agreed on every matter, but even if your feelings and opinions were different you kept your mouth shut and cast your votes. With so much unity, it was an easy world to live in and to manage.

The world now is very different and so is Georgia's House of Representatives. And this is the diverse 180-person world

Tom Murphy must organize and lead. It is a juggling act for Murphy to keep a liberal black Democrat such as Billy McKinney of Atlanta content at the same time he tries to mollify a conservative white Republican such as Vance Smith of Pine Mountain while at the same time remembering that the House is no longer a Men's Club, or that female legislators such as Jeanette Jamieson of Toccoa also have a point of view. Sandwiches and health problems aside, Murphy has dealt with these changes amazingly well.

Butch Parrish calls Murphy the glue that has kept state government together through all of these changes. "And sometimes he gets himself in trouble by taking the heat for some of us or promising things it is hard to deliver on. He walks a high-wire with the balance between Democrats and Republicans getting so close. And you know, the perception is all of us Democrats are wide-eyed liberals and the Republicans are the conservatives. Well, that's not the case. When somebody asks me if I'm a Democrat, I say 'Yeah, a Georgia Democrat.'"

Former legislator Matt Towery, a Republican and a confidante of the Speaker's, says Murphy has adjusted because he has had to adjust—in order to deal with the young whipper-snappers—and to keep his job. Numbers explain Towery's words.

When Murphy was elected Speaker in 1974, there were twenty-nine Republicans in the House. In 1999, there were seventy-eight, ten more than in 1996. Arithmetic tells you that ninety-one votes are required to turn a bill into law. Politics tells you that Murphy cannot control all 102 Democrats on a given measure so he often needs help from the Republican side of the aisle.

"What saves Murphy is this unspoken fifteen or sixteen Republicans who, when push comes to shove, cross over and vote with him. What you have is a cadre of Republicans and Democrats who work together, spend time together, go to dinner together, who view themselves as good friends. It is a working coalition that not enough has been written about," Towery says.

To their peers, these crossover Republicans are often not seen as "good Republicans." However, Georgia Republican Chairman Chuck Clay is not so harsh. "The Speaker just knows how to reward and punish," he says. Nor does Clay argue with the fact that a speaker must sometimes be a tyrant. He just thinks Murphy ought to include Republican House members in his circle of leadership. "He is excluding forty percent of his talent pool and this is short-sighted," Clay says "When there were only a handful of Republicans in the House, they could be the brunt of jokes. It didn't matter. It does matter when it is forty percent Republican. You'll never take the politics out of politics. It's a full-contact sport with no prisoners taken. But the voting public wants to see us work together."

Clay, a former state senator and candidate for lieutenant governor, is low-key, and throws more than a few compliments in Murphy's direction. His approach is far different than Rusty Paul, his predecessor as party chairman. To Paul, Murphy was the Poster Boy for everything wrong in Georgia. He said Murphy and the Democrats' long hold on power was unhealthy and pictured Murphy as evil incarnate.

"The Democrats have been in control of this state longer than the Communist Party was in charge of the Soviet Union, longer than Castro's been in Cuba, even longer than Queen Victoria, the longest-serving monarch in the history of the British Empire. That's about as close to absolute power as you can get. The old adage is 'Power corrupts and absolute power corrupts absolutely.' When I say corruption, I'm not talking about thievery, but having an inbred system closed to all but a few decision-makers, which is the practical definition of a dictatorship," Paul said in an interview with *Georgia Trend* magazine.

Towery ran for lieutenant governor in 1990, losing to Democrat Pierre Howard. After his experience in a statewide race, he believes efforts to make Murphy a symbol are not the way to go. To average Georgians the Speaker is not a household word — even after a quarter of a century with the state's loudest gavel and despite the fact that he is the self-proclaimed keeper of his party's banner, Towery says.

"He's partisan, don't get me wrong, but I think he really wishes now that we no longer had to be so partisan. You know he's exasperated by the fact that it appears Republicans are taking increasing control. But he has taken the view that he is the spokesman for the Democratic Party and its flag waver. But the problem is, there are Democrats who don't want him to do that because they, as incorrectly as Republicans, think he is a liability, not realizing that so many people don't know who he is — and those who do like him," Towery says.

Political insiders can identify him, but Towery maintains a poll taken in a shopping mall somewhere across Georgia would show that people don't know who the Speaker of the Georgia House is. So how do you run against him? "I tell Republicans that first we will have to spend a million dollars to explain who he is. I know because I tried."

Republicans have been trying to have a louder voice in the House for decades. In 1986, when Joe Frank Harris was governor and he was bickering with Murphy over problems in the Georgia State Patrol, the twenty-one GOP members in the House saw this as an opportunity to flex their muscles. Led by Minority Leader Johnny Isakson and John Linder — both future congressman — they talked with the governor and the speaker.

Eventually, they sided with Murphy.

"We went with him on that issue and in return he said he would put Republicans on every conference committee during the next session," remembers Linder, who in 1986 represented a district in DeKalb County. "We gave him our votes and he won." Only Murphy reneged, which Linder pointed out to him. "I told him we had delivered and now we wanted him to deliver. He said he couldn't and I wanted to know why. 'Because Marcus Collins won't let me,' he said. 'Well, who's the speaker?' I asked.

After defeating Murphy in what came down to a head-to-head duel over legislative salaries, Linder ended up being the one embarrassed. It was in 1974, just after legislators' pay was raised from $4,200 to $7,200 a year. Murphy wanted to index the salaries to the State Merit System so they would never have to be voted on again. Linder was fighting this and went to the well of the House several times to speak, as did Murphy.

"I beat him on the floor. He brought it back up for reconsideration and I beat him again. I was supposed to be on the McNeill-Lehrer Show that night talking about Jimmy Carter's Reorganization Plan. Robert McNeill was there to interview me himself. Like a fool I told my wife who called folks all over and said I was going to be on TV. When I showed up, Robert McNeill said, 'Oh, weren't you informed? The speaker said you weren't going to be able to be with us.' I just walked away."

But Linder, like so many others who have had hand-to-hand combat with Murphy in the political arena, says he never disliked him and even praised him for his fairness and his ability to get things done for the state.

"We just have two different approaches. He takes things personally. I don't. When he would be in the well singling me out, which is clearly against House rules, it didn't bother me. I always said I went down there to makes changes—not friends," Linder says. "But he was always very fair. He did his best to be fair to the entire state. And he had a heart as big as the world. He loved kids and he was a softie. But as the chair, he also tried to be fair only sometimes he got too personally involved and too angry."

Angry or not, Johnny Isakson says Murphy never lashes out first. "Lots of people think he does, but that's not true. He never throws the first political punch. But when he counter punches....Boy!". And to Isakson, such punches were not reserved for Republicans. "Murphy's Law doesn't stop with the party. If a Democrat throws down the gauntlet, he will fight you. But whether you were a Republican or a Democrat, if you shoot straight, he'll shoot straight."

As their numbers have increased, Republicans in the House have grown more impatient than in previous generation and Murphy has continued to play into their hands by refusing to appoint the GOP to leadership roles—even when forty percent of the body is non-Democratic. Kaye certainly is impatient, sometimes to the extent it rankles his own party. A member of the House since 1992, he has been a gnat constantly buzzing around the leadership's face.

"When I was running the first time, someone asked me what I hoped to accomplish if I was elected. I hand them all this stuff, you know, Mom and country, God and apple pie. They turned to me and reminded me I was going to be a freshman Republican in a Democratic dominated body. 'How are you going to be effective?' they asked me. Then they said that someone in that situation who is effective has to become the conscience of the body," says Kaye, one of the founding members of the Conservative Caucus.

Conservative is the label that divides some of the Republicans. Such as Matt Towery who criticizes their way of doing things. "Some of the newer legislators just want to play to the crowd, to do what they think is going to be popular," he says. "As a result, they don't really give a damn if you go back to Tobacco Road as long as they make their constituency happy and they come across as being 'conservative.' Murphy stands in the way of that attitude."

Kaye says he doesn't worry about popularity.

"As a freshman Republican, I was catching a lot of heat because of a sales tax issue. I joked that the arrows in the front of my body came from Democrats and the ones in my back came from Republicans. Lester Maddox was on the floor of the House and he put his arm around me and pointed to the voting board where everybody's names are. 'Mitchell,' he said, 'Just remember if everyone around here likes you, it's time to go home.' "

That came up a few years ago during a debate on the floor when Kaye was trying to rally partisan support on a bill that was before them. He rose and asked the chair for a ruling. "Is it not true to my sixty-six other Republican colleagues in the House, that if we do not all hang together, we will all hang separately?"

"I don't believe if I was you I'd say that, because some of them might want you hung separately," Murphy dryly answered him.

Later that same day in 1996, Kaye accused Democrats of toying with election laws and compared their tactics to someone rearranging deck chairs on the Titanic. Murphy jumped in with an observation of his own. "If the Titanic's going down," he said, "I'm glad you aren't on it with me."

Despite their frequent exchanges, Kaye seems to admire Tom Murphy at some level. The speaker apologized for the sandwich incident long ago and Kaye says he accepted. At times, the Cobb County Republican talks about Murphy's brilliance and how he has held on to his power for so many years. He believes the two of them have achieved a begrudging respect for one another.

"People have told me that he sees me as almost a Tom Murphy of years ago when he was a bull in a China shop where no one wanted to sit next to him on the floor. I would take that as a compliment," the outspoken Republican says.

Not that Kaye apologizes for his past tactics; he obviously enjoys sharing play-by-plays of his favorite moments. One tactic that Kaye and others used to infuriate Murphy the most was when they tried to play the Speaker's own game. Kaye tells of former Attorney General Mike Bowers advising some young Republican legislators that the primary way they would be successful was to learn the rules of the House—a Murphy specialty. A few years ago, Kaye set out to do that, even soliciting the help of Democrat and former House member Denmark Groover, considered a master of gamesmanship and procedure.

"I adapted the strategy that the best way to hurt those good old boys was to use the rules they wrote against them. And in doing so, they keep saying it's not that much fun anymore. And for us, we never had so much fun in our lives," he says.

In 1994, on the first day of the session, it was a routine table-setting day. Few were paying much attention. They had heard it all before, because these house-keeping measures have to be taken care of every year. Resolutions were being introduced to invite the Chief Justice of the Georgia Supreme Court for a speech and to formally arrange for the governor's State of the State address, a time that was pre-arranged and scheduled to be broadcast live on Georgia Public Television. Most of the legislators weren't tuned in to what was being said that day, but Kaye and eight others were ready for an ambush. They had even written out scripts, ready to make a calculated series of parliamentary moves.

"When the resolution was introduced to have the governor come at 11:00 A.M. on Tuesday, we tried to amend it to have him come at 1:00 A.M. We had a series of people asking questions, then we moved to reconsider. This put it on the board and had people hopping up and down all over the House. The whole thing was to show not only did we know the rules, we weren't going to take it anymore. We were organized and we were ready," Kaye says.

The young legislators, mostly Republicans saw it as a no-lose situation. "So by the fact that it was impossible for us to win, we couldn't lose. Just the fact that we forced the debate with zero change made it a complete success. So the game was much more important than the outcome," Kaye says.

Former Democratic Caucus leader Bill Lee says his old friend Murphy is his strongest at such moments. "He's at his best when he is handling surprises. He's tough. A storm-trooper. No, he's not as much gruff as he is a master at handling difficult situations and surprises." But when Republicans such as Kaye were raising Murphy's political blood-pressure, Lee used to amble up to the podium and tell Murphy a joke. Clerk of the House Robbie Rivers likes to slip the Speaker a small card with a prayer on it, something he can take out of his pocket and read when the action gets hot.

More than it used to, such things are helping. Murphy seldom explodes these days, at least not with the bombasity of the past. A few years ago, after hearing a ruling from Murphy he didn't like, an exasperated Garland Pinholster threw papers up in the air and slapped the top of his desk with his hand as he marched out the side door of the chambers. It brought back memories of when the vice-chairman of the Republican caucus was drawing technical fouls as the hot-blooded basketball coach at Oglethorpe University in Atlanta. There was a time when Murphy would have slammed his gavel and directed a wise-acre comment at the legislator from Ball Ground. This day, he just smiled.

When a partisan outburst is heard from the podium, Chuck Clay considers it part of the game. He understands that when warranted Murphy must be heavy-handed. Even the terms tyrant and dictator don't entirely bother Clay, an Atlanta attorney.

"You better have someone in that job who can, when necessary, be a little bit of a tyrant. Whoever comes behind him will have a big pair of shoes to fill with so many people looking for a more democratic institution. I don't question either his leadership or his accomplishments. I take my hat off to his history. But on the stump we will run against him because of his brand of politics. I will say this—though not on the campaign trail—this state has been well served with Tom Murphy as speaker. He doesn't deserve all the credit or all the blame. His Achilles heel is how he won't deal with reality, that this is not only a multi-racial state but a two-party state," the GOP chairman says.

It is a two-party state to Clay. Not Murphy.

"I've never knowingly voted for a Republican in my life," Murphy says proudly. "I still remember '29 and 30.' " That is why he likes to say he's only two things: a Baptist and a Democrat. Part of that rancor comes from his role as party flag waver. Part of it comes from the intense animosity he has for the religious right and its identification with the far-right of the Republican Party.

"I have a pet saying. We have way too much religion but not nearly enough Christianity," says Murphy, whose father was a Primitive Baptist preacher. "That's the reason I don't have too much respect for the Christian Coalition. I say ninety-nine percent of the membership are good honest, decent, God-fearing law-abiding American citizens. Problem is, those folks who run it and get all the money take half-truths, absolute fabrications and dispense them under the guise of Christianity and those good honest, decent, God-fearing law-abiding American citizens believe them. You take me. I don't campaign on Sunday. I refuse to. I won't even let my radio spots be run on Sunday. But those folks go into *church* and politick on Sunday. If that's Christianity, I don't want any part of it."

Murphy is saddened by some of the racial implications of Republican politics and he says it can sometimes be seen in the House. "I have no problem with the number of black legislators growing. I have no problem with the number of Republican legislators growing. As long as it is issued based. The sad part is it has become a black-white issue between some Republicans and Democrats. That causes strife, and it's sad. And Republicans agitate anyway they can."

Of course, he welcomes the help of Republican legislators — "Some of them wear that label because the only way they can get elected is to be a Republican." But he also thinks mean-spirited Republicans and ultra-liberal

Democrats leave a big chasm for others in both parties to bridge.

"There are thirty-five out there whose first conscious thought each morning is who can I hurt today. Then there are thirty-five out there whose first conscious thought is what can I give away today. The rest of us are in the middle getting beat to death," he says.

Murphy also had taken opportunities to deal with Georgia's most famous Republican, Newt Gingrich. In 1970, Gingrich became a professor of history at West Georgia College, just ten miles from Murphy's home of Bremen. He immediately became active in state Republican politics. In 1973, the year Murphy became Speaker of the House, Gingrich ran for Congress for the first time. Murphy, in fact, has told friends that his wife once voted for the Republican candidate. Gingrich eventually was elected, beginning his rise to Speaker of the United States House of Representatives. So at one time, Gingrich was Murphy's Congressman and Murphy was Speaker of the House in the Republican's adopted home state.

Murphy and Gingrich worked together to secure federal funds for the widening of US Highway 27 which comes right through Haralson County. But more often than not, they've enjoyed taking pot shots at one another from afar. Their most public conflicts have come over the reapportionment of Gingrich's congressional districts back in Georgia. Privately, it has been more personal.

Mel Steely, a professor of history at West Georgia and a former aide to Gingrich, remembers being with Murphy and Gingrich in a hamburger place in Bremen where the two men met to discuss building a major reservoir in the area. Steeley had his camera with him and it seemed natural to take a photograph of the area's most prominent Democrat and Republican together.

"Okay, if I take a picture?" Steely asked.

"No pictures," Murphy said, jumping out of his seat.

Later, Murphy explained his reluctance to have his picture taken with Gingrich. A few years before Gingrich was Speaker, he came to the Georgia House for a speech. As is often the case, after a guest finishes speaking, he or she poses for photographs with Murphy and with their local legislator if they're from Georgia. So Murphy ended up in a photograph with Gingrich and Bill Lee, who represented the Republican's district there in Atlanta. Harmless. Dozens are taken every year. Only this one ended up in a Gingrich newsletter, trying to send out the message that he works well with Democrats.

At first, Murphy did not see Gingrich as any kind of threat to his politics. But by 1984, the Republican Party in Georgia was better organized and making stronger noises so Murphy helped recruit someone to run against Gingrich. Former State Representative Gerald Johnson was the candidate and Gingrich gave him a resounding defeat.

Six years later, the Georgia House redrew Gingrich's district again, this time forcing him to run in a newly-constituted 6th District around Cobb County. Murphy told people he thought Gingrich's pride would force him to run in his old 4th District, but he didn't. It proved to be a mistake for Georgia Democrats. Gingrich swept to an easy victory in his new district and Republicans overnight dominated the Georgia Congressional Delegation.

These days, after Gingrich has given up his job as speaker and resigned from Congress, Murphy loves to jab at him when someone asks about him. "I feel sorry for Newt," he says. "The press said I was mean, a tyrant and a dictator. But at least they've never accused me of lying and stealing."

Gingrich is no longer the issue in Georgia politics that he was, but the movement he helped begin continues to advance. There were seventy-eight Republicans in the Georgia House in 1999 and the GOP forecasts more gains in the coming years. Yet, they are no closer to becoming part of the leadership than they were when Republican members could be counted on a single hand.

African American members, despite their smaller numbers, have become a factor. There were just thirty-three African Americans and a like number of female legislators in 1999. Each of the thirty-three black members is a Democrat so their influence on the leadership is evident. In 1992, when Murphy faced a challenge from within the ranks, only one black legislator voted for his opponent. Of the thirty standing committees in the House in 1999, twenty-four were chaired by white Democrats and six were chaired by African Americans. Three committees are chaired by women and one of them is black.

African Americans have been part of the General Assembly only since 1964 when Leroy Johnson of Atlanta was elected to the Senate after court-ordered Reapportionment and the legally-mandated death of the rural-based County Unit System. The House was not desegregated until 1966 when six African Americans were elected. One of them was Julian Bond, whose seating was contested after he marched in demonstrations against the Vietnam War. What riled House members were his inflammatory statements about Vietnam, including a charge that it was a racist war.

As a youth growing up in Atlanta, Bond had been evicted from the House gallery when he questioned its all-white seating rules. In 1963, Speaker George T. Smith had quietly changed those rules, but the arrival of the black legislators was another matter. Some old line members boasted openly they would never sit next to a black person. Smith answered that threat by assigning to seat No. 1 Grace Hamilton of Atlanta—a black woman who became the body's second female.

Bond, later a state senator, did draw most of the attention that January. House members refused to seat him and it would take a decision by the United States Supreme Court to change their minds. It was a group Murphy did not join.

Albert Thompson, later a Superior Court judge in Muscogee County, was among that group of six African Americans seated in 1966. He did not feel totally welcome, but he remembers no open animosity from his fellow members. He says most of the anger was directed at Bond, whom he described as "the lightning rod." For Thompson, it was a learning experience and one of his teachers was Tom Murphy.

Thompson concluded that if a person amended your bill, they were attacking it. When Murphy noticed Thompson vote against a bill that had passed through a committee he was on, he explained the philosophy behind an amendment, that an amendment might even strengthen a piece of legislation. "I had never thought of it that way," Thompson says. "That was one of many things he taught me."

Thompson says he admired Murphy even before he became speaker in 1974, eight years after the Columbus lawyer's arrival in the House. "He would give intelligent leadership from the floor. Sometimes, I thought he was the conscience of the House. I remember one bill that had racial overtones and people were skirting around that issue. Tom got up and said, it was racial. He just cut to the core. He was always very blunt and very frank, but I thought he was on the side of the angels."

In 1974, legislators had gathered at the University of Georgia in Athens for the annual pre-legislative forum. Murphy called Thompson aside and told him he was planning to appoint him chairman of the Special Judiciary Committee. Thompson became the first African American to chair a standing House committee.

"He was an extremely fair man who did what he thought was the right thing to do—not just the politically correct thing to do. This was both political and fair. No one in all the history of Georgia had ever taken a step like that before," said Thompson, now retired in Columbus.

Thompson's appointment was well received. The only open opposition expressed came from a fellow black legislator. "He was from Atlanta, and he thought the Speaker should have made someone from Atlanta the first black chairman," he says.

Six African Americans chaired committees in 1999, including another Columbus legislator, Calvin Smyre, who Murphy appointed to chair the all-important Rules Committee, the panel that tightly controls each day's agenda during the latter stages of the General Assembly. Smyre, a former administrative floor leader for Zell Miller, succeeded the retiring Bill Lee. When Smyre's name was proposed after Lee's retirement, the color of his skin was hardly mentioned.

"He was just the right person for the job," Murphy said.

Smyre, an influential Democrat at the national level, was already a key member of Murphy's leadership team. He has proven adept at working within the system, patiently gaining the seniority and experience to become one of the most influential members of the House. The Muscogee County legislator traces that back to one of his first meetings with Murphy after he was elected to the House—the same year Murphy became Speaker.

"It was my first sit-down with him and he asked me what my interests were. I told him that for the long haul, I wasn't that interested on most issues, that I was a finance person. I had gone to school to be a CPA or a math instructor and had wound up majoring in accounting. I just loved numbers. Many people's attitude about blacks was monolithic, assuming we all thought alike and all had the same interests. For me to be interested in the budget seemed to intrigue the Speaker," Smyre says.

Smyre soon moved into an influential role on the budget-writing team, working alongside his Muscogee County colleague, Tom Buck, the chairman of the Ways & Means Committee. Smyre gave up the chairmanship of the University System of Georgia committee when he became chair of the Rules Committee but continues to be a member of the important Appropriations Committee. He is one of several African Americans in leadership roles. In 1991, when Representative DuBose Porter was challenging Murphy, Smyre gave one of the Speaker's nominating speeches.

For him, it goes further.

"When Mrs. Murphy died in 1982, I went down to his house in Bremen to pay my respects. He is my friend. It was the right thing to do. I looked around and I was the only black person there," he says.

Jeanette Jamieson is one of thirty-three women in the House, but she says she would have to look at the legislative guide to be sure. "I just don't keep up with that kind of information," she explains. Years ago, it was much easier to compute that number. There were no women there when Murphy arrived in 1961. Five years later, Janet Merritt of Americus was the only woman in the House when Grace Hamilton of Atlanta became the second and the first African American woman. Jamieson believes her personal philosophy has helped her move into a leadership role as chair of the House Education Committee.

"If you come here with an attitude that you are a female member and that is the major part of your philosophy, then you will only be a female in the House—and that is very limited," she says, preferring to be thought of as a legislator who is a woman. In a male-dominated group that can be jocular and often crude, the Toccoa accountant reports no difficulties. "There may be other women in the House who could give a totally different attitude but I have accomplished everything I have wanted to accomplish. Never, to my knowledge, have I been denied action on my legislation or an opportunity because I was a woman. If it was a closed shop, I would not be where I am today."

Not that she has always been on Murphy's team. It was she who gave the nominating speech for Representative DuBose Porter when he unsuccessfully challenged Murphy for the speaker's position in 1991. It is something she and Murphy have never discussed. "And I applaud him for the way he handled that," she says.

"There needed to be change in the House at that time and I have never apologized to the speaker for that. There were concerns among the Democratic members that needed to be addressed. We needed to bring about a consolidated effort among Democrats. I have never repented. I think DuBose is an outstanding gentleman and an outstanding legislator," Jamieson says.

She is also a strong supporter of Tom Murphy.

"When people say he has lost a step, I just laugh. Give him credit. He has been willing to make changes, sometimes going against his own philosophy. He has had to deal with the concerns and needs of this state and he has done that. He has seen tremendous change during his tenure. He has made changes to meet the needs of Georgia and the House. He has to be strong to keep the other 179 diverse members in tow, but to see the real Tom Murphy, you have to see the issues that concern the man. That is when the real Tom Murphy rises to the surface."

Jamieson's mention of concerns among House Democrats and the need to consolidate those members is in line with Chuck Clay's observations about the General Assembly and Georgia politics being in a period of change. "Among younger Democrats, the question is how long he can serve. It is like when a high school football player being recruited by Penn State asks, 'Is Joe Paterno going to be there when I graduate?' Those Democrats are wondering where to cast their lot. I can see Terry Coleman and Larry Walker jockeying among themselves," he says, referring to the two House members usually mentioned as Murphy's eventual successor—if Democrats still have the majority.

Matt Towery believes Murphy is smarter than any of them. "Murphy may be the smartest man in American politics. He does such a wonderful job of dealing with the myriad of individuals he must deal with every day. The system works in Georgia because of Murphy. People who love to go down there and harp and complain about the way he operates, they're also darn thankful that there's that stability. You have this big overpowering, overwhelming bigger-than-life character holding a gavel and he's going to maintain order in a House that could easily dissolve into one like other states where you have fist fights breaking out on the floor. That will never happen under Tom Murphy."

While Clay also praises Murphy at many levels, he always returns to the speaker's lack of respect for the Republican membership's potential leadership in the House. As a member of the Senate, he saw the success of Democratic Lieutenant Governor Pierre Howard's effort to reach out to the Republican senators. He sees nothing like that on the horizon for the House.

But maybe Murphy is also tired of the bickering.

After a mud-slinging general election campaign against Republican Mitch Skandalakis, Mark Taylor took over as the Senate's presiding officer in 1999. His approach to running the Senate was far different from Howard's. Before Taylor took over, Sonny Perdue—a high-profile senator from Bonaire in Middle Georgia—surprised the state by switching to the Republican Party. That move shook up both parties and later spurred a lot of heated partisan exchanges on the floor of the Senate. Taylor was a combatant Democrat and a vocal lieutenant governor, making it clear to everyone which party was in charge. He used his office and he used his gavel to make that point.

Every Monday during the session, Governor Roy Barnes assembled the Democratic leadership for a strategy session in his office. It was growing late in the session and it had been a tough week. In the Senate, the lieutenant governor was again squabbling with the GOP. People were slow to get to their seats but Murphy and Taylor were already in theirs when the speaker turned to the rookie Democrat—a person in whom Murphy could see traits identical to his.

"Mark, I want to tell you something," Murphy said. "I'm going to tell you something somebody should have told me. You are making some of the same mistakes I made. You're too partisan. You're too hard."

Taylor listened, but Murphy wasn't through, telling the Albany Democrat that if he continued this he was going to make a martyr out of Sonny Perdue and the other members of the minority party.

"You can tell me to kiss your foot, but I'm telling you. You're making some of the same mistakes I made."

Does this mean Tom Murphy is about to get soft and cuddly and welcome House Republicans into his loving arms? There probably will be tarnish on the gold atop the capitol before that happens. But it does show how he thinks. He knows that the Republicans' conservative views of spending are closer to his than some of his Democratic colleagues. He knows that some of the Democratic members who want to be leaders are not as bright as some of the people on the other side of the aisle. He knows he needs that small group of Republicans who vote with him to keep his truck on the road.

But he's a Democrat, and he's not about to change that label. And as he looks ahead to a time when he will no longer hold the House gavel, he must be conscious of doing whatever he can to make it easier for the Democratic Speaker he hopes will follow him.

As Jeanette Jamieson says, "He has changed with change."

10

ALL

IN THE

FAMILY

They're Murphys. So you know they're seldom short on opinions. They're Tom's kids. In their own way, each is political and each one believes in God, apple pie, and the Democratic Party. And they can't talk about their father very long before their devotion to him becomes apparent.

Their personalities are different and so are their interests. They don't always agree. They don't always get along. But when the subject is Tom Murphy, the wagons are circled and the guns are cocked. They will fight you over their family and over their father.

Mike was born in 1947, while his father was in law school at the University of Georgia. Martha was born in 1949, the year her parents came back to Bremen for her father to practice law. Lynn, the shy one, was born in 1950. Mary was born in 1956, so she remembers little about their family's life before her father was in the Georgia House.

Michael Louis Murphy will be the first of the children to be on a ballot. He was appointed to an unexpired term on the Superior Court in the Tallapoosa District by Governor Zell Miller in 1998 and faces re-election in the fall of 2000. In 1999, wearing his somber robe, he swore in the newly-elected members of the Georgia House—including his proud father.

Martha Murphy Long operates an insurance company around the corner from her father's law office in Bremen. She is outspoken. She chairs the local Democratic Party Committee. Because of the traits she shares with him, some folks around Bremen laugh and call her "Tom Murphy Junior."

Lynn Murphy McAdams is the thoughtful, quiet member of the family, so unusually reserved that her very vocal siblings like to tease about being adopted.

Mary Murphy Oxendine is the youngest of the family and is the school teacher her father sometimes quotes and consults when an educational issue is coming before the House. She moved back home to Bremen in 1998, teaching Georgia History to students in nearby Paulding County.

But on most Sundays—forty or more out of fifty-two, their father guesses—his children and his grandchildren gather around Tom Murphy's dining room table for Sunday Dinner. Most of the time Martha, Lynn and Mary prepare a lot of the food, but their father is also a good cook. As for the vegetables that fill the table, most come out of the Murphy garden out back.

When they come together, there is food and there is noise.

On this particular evening, the Murphys gathered in the board room of Murphy & Murphy, Attorneys at Law. A tape player was running and they talked about two of their favorite subjects: their father and politics.

They also talked about growing up in a small town and about life in a political family. They described the influence their Uncle James had on the entire family. They shared their own hurt-to-the-bone feelings about the news media and its treatment of their father and how those reporters' stories contributed to the death of their mother

GROWING UP AND LIVING IN BREMEN

They bemoan the fact that their children can't experience life in Bremen the way it was for them — and the way it was for their father. In a town as small as Bremen, everybody was your surrogate parent. Everybody was ready to correct you if you misbehaved. Everybody knew your parents and their phone number. But it was especially tough when your father was in the headlines and on the six o'clock news.

MIKE: "Our childhood was a lot like our Dad's. He's told me when he was working at the theater in Bremen that Grandpa Murphy wanted to see the movie the 'Union Pacific.' Dad took an easy chair and put it in the aisle so Grandpa Murphy could be near the back to go out and smoke. He wanted him to watch that movie."

LYNN: "And remember, he took us up to Rome to see *Gone With the Wind.* That was big because, he didn't really like to go to movies. He said he had seen enough of them when he worked in the theater as a boy."

MIKE: "He just wanted to do things for his kids and now his grandkids."

LYNN: "To this day, he still goes to see the local high school football and basketball games. Our kids aren't playing anymore. He just supports all kids."

MIKE: "Bremen High School has never had a better fan than my Dad. He runs their auction every year. He gives them a gavel to raffle off for the booster club."

MARTHA: "We were in a community where we would have people in town call Mama and Dad and say 'Saw Martha driving today. She sure was going fast coming over that hill. You need to talk to her.' Everyone looked out for you. And we knew we were responsible for our actions, that we had a good family who loved us. The worst thing in my mind that I could have done was disappoint my Dad or hurt my family."

MARTHA: "I remember when we were children living on Sharp Street. We had some city employees that were called our garbage men. I can remember us taking them lemonade or something to drink. Not many people did that for them. About a month ago, I saw one of those guys at a nursing home...I didn't even know his name...and I went up to him and told him how glad I was to see him. And I was. Because I remembered him [from my childhood]. I didn't think of him as a garbage man. I just remember how good those fellows were to us. They spoke to us. It never entered my mind not to offer them something to drink because they looked so hot and tired."

MIKE: "Dad was an attorney. We didn't have that much money all the way through high school, but I can't remember us wanting for a thing. First bicycle I ever had was a girl's bicycle that my Dad had put together. I put a broom handle across there so it'd be a boy's bike. I got all the clothes from my cousins up at Rockmart. But we were always proud of who we were. I don't remember being conscious of a dollar sign. That was the beauty of living in Bremen. Money was never an issue. There were people here with money, but they didn't lord it over anybody. They were generous to our school system and to our community. And they always spoke to us kids. Everybody loved them and had respect for them. They taught us by the way they lived that when you have a lot, you give a lot."

MARTHA: "If people would give Dad credit, he was one of the first ones to support 'Women's Lib.' I was about fourteen and I was the bat girl on the American Legion team when we went up to Chattanooga. They freaked up there. A girl was in the dugout being the bat girl."

MIKE: "We grew up in a town with blue-collar people and the blue-collar people were always the underdogs. Dad wore a suit, and he represented them as a lawyer."

MARTHA: "And when people couldn't pay him, he took chickens, anything they had to give him."

LYNN: "We all played basketball and Dad would come home from the legislature to every game he could. It was more enjoyable for him when our kids were playing because they won. We only won one game a year."

MARTHA: "It wasn't our fault. We were guards and in those days we weren't allowed to shoot. But if we had been able to play a full-court game we'd have kicked some tails. Lynn and I could shoot the ball, but we had some forwards who couldn't shoot a lick. It was frustrating for me because we didn't get to shoot the ball."

A LEGISLATOR'S FAMILY

After Christmas, they knew what was coming. Their father would pack his bags and move to Atlanta in early January and they would have to share him with the Georgia House of Representatives until sometime in March. He came home to cheer them in their ball games. Miss Agnes was basically in charge. Of course, they also know that having a father who is Speaker of the House also brings opportunities.

LYNN: "I remember my Dad getting in the car on Sunday afternoon to come back to Atlanta. We'd all be lined up. I'd cry, of course I cry easily. Mike as the older brother, would pull us all in and say it would be all right. But from the time we were born, it seems, from January through March, he would leave us and Mama would take care of us. She'd go up there when she could, but we wanted her home with us if we couldn't have Daddy."

MARTHA: "I don't remember crying."

LYNN: "I did. And I still do. I cried when I heard over the news that he was going to run for re-election because I wanted him to be home."

MARTHA: "We had discussed that. He knew we wanted him home but we said we'd support whatever he did. It's his life."

LYNN: "But I believe he would have already retired if mother lived."

MARTHA: "It is just in his blood. It's what makes him happy."

LYNN: "He and Mama had talked about all the traveling they would do but things just don't work out like you plan them sometimes."

MIKE: "It was like we had to overachieve..."

MARTHA: "To stay even?"

MIKE: "No, to gain acceptance."

MARTHA: "Do you remember getting on the Greyhound bus in Bremen, Lynn, just you and I, and riding the bus to Atlanta and the old Georgian Hotel? We were young, about twelve. We got off that bus. Daddy told us how to come out the door and we walked from the bus station to the hotel by ourselves. He met us. He had to go to a meeting so he gave us some money and we walked to the movie theater. Can you imagine little kids getting off the bus like that? I think we were more frightened about the bus trip than being turned loose over there."

LYNN: "We always went over there and paged every year."

MARY: "I've never had anyone say anything negative to me when I was campaigning for him. It happened to the others, but not me. I would go with him to the plants when I was so little I'd sleep in the car while he met people."

TRAVELING WITH THE MURPHYS

Long before talk of "Family Values" the Murphys were a close-knit group. They visited their grandparents on Sundays. They went to Atlanta for the General Assembly. They went to political conventions. But with four high-spirited children crowded into a car, traveling was an adventure.

LYNN: "We played poker for matchsticks. I was the ring-leader and they thought Martha was."

MARTHA: "I just looked like I should have been the one."

LYNN: "And then there was the National Legislative Council in Portland, Maine and Dad took his entire family again plus Martha's boy-friend and my sister Mary's three-foot tall doll."

MIKE: "That was the year Uncle James died. He died when we got back."

MARTHA: "In a blue Ford Galaxie."

LYNN: "It was awful."

MIKE: "The point of all of this is to say that we have always been family oriented."

LYNN: "We didn't take a lot of vacations then. Daddy always worked. So when we did something, we did it as a family."

MIKE: "On one trip, we stayed in a motel at the foot of Lookout Mountain. Dad said that was the last time he stayed anywhere without asking how much it cost first."

MARTHA: "He couldn't *beeelieeve* how much that cost."

MIKE: "He always included us, though. Like that time he took us to eat at the Ship Ahoy restaurant in Atlanta. I was just a kid, and when I looked at the bill I said, 'Did we eat all of that?' 'Son,' he said, 'you pay for the atmosphere.' I told him that surely to God they've got it paid for by now."

MARTHA: "One of the best times was when we took that train tour of Georgia. Dad took all of us. He always did when he could and so there he was, with his four kids. Not many folks brought their kids."

MIKE: "It was on the Nancy Hanks. We went all the way to Savannah. Remember, I took you girls to see the *King and I?*"

LYNN: "We went to Jekyll. It was the first time I had been to the beach and I brought back all those sea shells. Nobody told us we were supposed to boil them and when we opened our purses when we got home there were these sea creatures."

RELIGION

Tom Murphy's father was a Primitive Baptist preacher and he reared his children in that church. Today, they are all members of the Methodist Church, but they each recognize the influence that their father's faith had on him and on the way they were reared.

MARTHA: "We were blessed. They were the best parents any kids could have. They instilled values in us. I don't know anyway to put it other that we were always for the underdog, trying to help people who needed help."

MIKE: "I remember that I was there, Martha was there, and Carol came. We went down to the Holly Springs Primitive Baptist Church for a meeting one Sunday. It was the last Sunday of the month and the association meets down there. I hadn't been with him in a while. Last time I went it was to Little Vine, out near the golf course. It was real cool, the wind was just blowing. It was so fresh looking. All those windows were down and the doors flung open and there was about five people there. We sit there and both speakers were elders that I've known forever. The first speaker was talking about Solomon, about his wisdom. He was speaking from the heart. The other fellow got up and he talked about faith and works, that if a person believed, he had a responsibility to try and help people. I'd say that's been my Dad all his life. I said to Dad that's funny, that in my Sunday School class when we get through with the lesson I stand up and summarize and just say whatever is on my mind. He said, that's what a Primitive Baptist is. It never dawned on me before and it's taken me all these years to understand and appreciate that. It makes me think, why couldn't I have known this when my mother was alive."

MARTHA: "I was talking to a chaplain at the hospital, talking about my faith. He said 'You sound like a good old Southern Baptist." I stopped him, 'Excuse me...Primitive Baptist,' and my Dad would be so proud to hear me say that.'"

MIKE: "He's taught us to be judgmental, because we're all trying to do the right thing and live the right way. He taught me that. Some people think he doesn't even go to church, but he goes to some church every Sunday morning. He's not a member of any big church. He's a member of a little Primitive Baptist Association. The members have all died out. There's not many young folks in it either."

MARTHA: "And they have a meeting at a church somewhere every Sunday."

MIKE: "He thinks everybody should do that as an individual. It's everybody's responsibility to make a better life for somebody else, the best you can. I find myself being a lot more like him in ways that even my sisters aren't. We're both extreme realists. Though bad news may affect us like it does everybody, you just have to deal with it. You take it in. You do the best you can with it. But you've got to keep moving ahead, stay focused and try to make the best of whatever situation you have. It sounds like I'm insulting my sisters and I don't mean to be."

MARTHA: "Do you think we stew about it too long?"

MIKE: "No, we all stew about it. But on the other hand I know when our mother passed away in 1982, Dad and I had this office. I loved Mama, and I remember the night before she died she called me. It was a Sunday morning after Herschel Walker had played his last game at the University of Georgia. Our family went to that game, except Mama. She didn't feel good. We all came back to Bremen and I didn't go out to the house. I stayed home and listened to the LSU football game on some AM station....Anyway, the phone rang and it was Mama. She asked me what I was doing. I'm so sleepy, I told her. I just laid here listening to football and fell asleep. I can hardly keep my eyes open. She says, 'Well, that sounds like a good idea. I just wanted you to know I loved you.' 'I love you, too Mama,' I said. And that's the last conversation we ever had. I don't why she called me. It can still make us all cry. But Dad and I could come back up here to this office and plow into our work. My sisters, it bothers them even today. I loved my Mama more than you can know, but I keep thinking that if we live the kind of life the Lord wants us to live, we'll all be together again someday."

MIKE: "We've been a fortunate family. We've had it instilled in us to help folks. Forever and ever. I can look anybody in the eye and tell them I'm probably a better person today than if Dad hadn't been in politics. All of the things that come from people looking at you, waiting for you to stumble, to see you fall. I dare say that some of them would want you to fall. There was always somebody looking, to see if we lived up to standards. But it's made me better than I probably had the capacity to be. I've been so conscious all my life not to let anybody down. We always cared. Nobody can say we didn't try."

MIKE: "Every generation wants to push the one ahead of it out of the way. I probably feel this way because of who I am, but in my Sunday School Class at the Methodist Church, there are people Dad's age and older. And there is so much cumulative wisdom there. If young folks would just sit down and listen to what they have to offer, we'd be so much better off. My notion is that as long as they want to make a contribution, let them. The time will come when there's nobody there and we have to do it but while there are people with wisdom and experience, listen to them."

MARTHA: "History is a great teacher. People like Dad, they've been there. They've done these things before. That disappoints me about my generation. There's a lack of respect for our parents and older folks. I see it every day and I can't understand it. Our family has such love and respect for these people and I think it goes back to our family's relationship with our grandparents, our great uncles, our great aunts. It never enters my mind not to respect and love these people and what they've done. I see people wanting to push them out of the way and it infuriates me. Not just my generation but the one coming up behind us. They're worse."

UNCLE JAMES AND CARING FOR THE UNDERDOG

They hardly remember their Uncle James without his crutches or his wheelchair. He died in 1966. But they know how much Uncle James meant to their father, and as adults they now know how much his presence and his disability affects the way they live their own lives.

MIKE: "Dad will cry about Uncle James right now if you talk about him."

MARTHA: "He was a wonderful uncle. I never thought about him having a disability. We would go to his house and Grandma Murphy's. He couldn't get out in his garden and dig but he had a fellow to do it for him. He was into organic gardening back then. He'd take so much pride and joy in that garden. He was a wonderful teacher for us."

MIKE: "I can remember being at Emory Hospital with my Dad and him when they were first working with a drug called Cortisone. They were experimenting with it."

LYNN: "And we'd go to Cave Springs, thinking that those people might help him."

MIKE: "We've been around handicapped people all our life. When we'd go to Cave Springs I'd go over to the deaf school there and see the fellows I played basketball against. They'd be in there playing ping-pong and it was quiet as a mouse. I'd start playing with them. It was one of those times where you wanted them to win, but you still played hard. They'd stop and watch you because you could hear and talk. Our entire life has been spent around people who were dealt a bad hand. It's taught us so much."

MIKE: "I would never tolerate anybody picking on another person. Because of my Uncle James's situation, I wouldn't tolerate anybody picking on somebody else."

POLITICS RUNS IN THE FAMILY

Up until now, none of their generation has seen his or her name on a ballot. That will change in the fall of 2000 when Mike Murphy runs for a full term as a Superior Court judge. This doesn't surprise them, for politics has been part of their lives for as long as they can remember.

MIKE: "As a young boy, I used to go to court all the time. One of our judges now, Bill Foster and his little brother John, we were all children of lawyers. We'd all go to court and we'd all play. We were all over Buchanan. I can remember seeing my Dad pull my Uncle James' wheelchair into that old courthouse. We're not talking about a lightweight portable wheelchair. We're talking about those old-fashioned ones. He'd pull it up thirty or forty steps and it was narrow. He would go get him in the morning, take him home at lunch, go back and get him. You can't imagine the devotion he had for his big brother. I think of the amazing things that have happened in my life. When my Uncle James passed away in 1966, my Dad had to practice law by himself. He had four kids at home. He wasn't making any kind of big money but he had unbelievable discipline and spent untold hours making sure his family was looked after...and he was also in the legislature. I don't see how he did it. He has incredible capacity. I'll never be a tenth of the man my Daddy is. I think about what he's done, what's he been through, how he's held up and it's almost incredible. That's that entire generation, which went through World War II. Makes me wonder if we'll live up to that."

MIKE: "He told me two or three years ago, 'Son, to be honest with you, I can't tell you that if I was a young man your age again that I'd be interested in running for public office the way it is today.' That does not speak well for the future of our state."

MARTHA: "I don't know why I do it or how I got into politics myself. I wanted to be a committee member so I'd be involved and know what was going on. I didn't show up for a meeting one day and they made me chairman (of the Democratic Party). I stay involved because my Dad is such a good man and has been such a wonderful public servant. This is my way of helping to perpetuate what he's done. Truth of the matter is, I want other people to give. I try and recruit so there will be others coming up. Seeing the challenge from the other party I want to do my best for the Democratic Party because I do believe in what they stand for. No, it's not just my Dad. It's important to me that we have compassion. The Democratic Party has that feeling. We're taking some hard licks because we are compassionate."

MIKE: "People don't like the criticism that comes from the media today. Ask Dad. I sometimes think the criticism comes disproportionate to the office you seek. The lower down the office, the more criticism. City council, school board, it's awful. There's just not a good feeling about public office holders today."

MIKE: "To my mind, the Murphys have always been politically active. They've always been part of the Great American experience. They've tried to participate and they've always been strongly opinionated. The first picture I can remember was Franklin Delano Roosevelt. It was in my Uncle James and my Grandmother Murphy's house from the time I was a little kid. It was probably a picture out of a Sunday newspaper that somebody had framed and put up on the wall. They've always been Democrats. My Grandpa Murphy was mayor of Bremen when Dad was a kid in the thirties. Uncle James was mayor and Dad was on the school board."

LYNN: "What about those signs he had on his bicycle when he was a kid? He told me about them one time, the three Rs: Roosevelt, Rivers, and Russell."

MIKE: "Every one of our kids have grown up with him being speaker essentially. My daughter is twenty-three and Holly is twenty-four and Chad is twenty-seven and our other nephew is thirty-one and one is eleven and they've all grown up with him in that position. There is no way they can remotely appreciate what it was like when we were kids. Like in 1965 when I graduated from high school, Dad had just finished his fourth year, or take that back, his fifth year in the Legislature. He was just learning. So there's no way they'd have any feeling for what it was like before."

MIKE: "As a citizen of Bremen, Haralson County, Georgia, if I ever had a chance to go over there to the Legislature I wouldn't be interested in a lot of ya-ya over the threshold issues. You're there to make a difference, and I think that's how my Dad feels. He wants to make a difference, a positive difference. Sometimes it's a far cry from what it ought to be. It's a frustrating place and I know it frustrates Dad. It's not an absence of ability. Sometimes it's an absence of maturity."

MARTHA: "I don't think some of them understand what job they're running for. They certainly don't have the commitment Dad has and others like him. Those fellows know what it means to be a legislator, that they're supposed to be a public servant."

MIKE: "Dad is loyal to the core. He will not turn his back on people He has been loyal to his party. He has looked after members of the Democratic Party. I think about presidents who have ignored the affairs at home and focused on foreign policy. Home for the Speaker, starts in the Democratic Caucus and they always know he'll be loyal to them."

MARTHA: "But a lot of younger members don't understand that. They don't know what seniority means. They don't understand the system and how it works."

LYNN: "And when he went there he just sat and listened for a long time."

MIKE: "He said he went there and looked for the person everybody respected for their work ethic. That was Mr. J. Roy McCracken from Augusta. He had been there for years and everybody respected him. He knew right then I was going to pattern myself after him. If Mr. McCracken told you something, he meant what he said and knew what he was talking about. When he spoke, everybody listened, the best way I can figure it out."

MARTHA: "I don't even like to think about my Dad not being there. It's important to all of us. Say what you always tell him, Mike."

MIKE: "We all worry about our Dad's health, to the last one of us, the kids, grandkids, daughter-in-law, son-in-law. We all worry about him. But every one of us has pretty much resolved ourselves to the proposition that as long Dad is happy, whatever he wants to do is fine with us. My attitude is that my Dad is a big boy; my Dad loves his family more than he loves his own life and as long as my Dad has peace of mind and a reason for living I want him to do it. One thing we don't agree about is my Dad dating. But in a lot of ways, he has committed his life to this state and in a lot of ways, the state is his mistress, his wife. He has devoted himself to this state, this county, this district. He's like a great-grandfather who has taken everyone under his wing. He's gonna look after them the best he can. We want him to have peace of mind. But I know if something was to happen to him today, as much I'd hate it, as much as we'd all hate it, I know my Dad is doing what he thinks he needs to do. My Dad sees he is in a unique position where he can make a difference. He feels obligation. And he will do it until he can't do it no more."

MARTHA: "More and more, he seems to be totally at peace...But if people only knew him like we know him."

MARTHA: "This is the one place he can come and he doesn't bring all those fusses he's having home with him. We hesitate to bring them up if it's been absolutely horrible....My Dad has never tried to be better than anybody else. I can't stand that kind of arrogance in other politicians."

MARTHA: "Sometimes I just cringe when I hear what they say about each other back and forth across the hall."

MIKE: "My Dad always laughs and says all good ideas start in the House...I look at the House and Senate as two small towns that are close rivals in football. They don't want to just beat the other one, they want to beat the living tar out of them. They want the other one to feel it to the bone and remember it until the next year."

LYNN: "That's what a democracy is all about. You have to have that debate so you can come out with something that is good."

MIKE: "We've been fortunate to be the Murphys that we are...even though great expectations were put on each one of us."

LYNN: "Me being the shy one, lots of people didn't even know I was one of Daddy's children."

MIKE: "You're adopted aren't you?"

LYNN: "They always tease me like that, because I'm quiet. I've stayed in the background because of the hurtful things that are done. If one of Daddy's opponents said 'hey' to me I'd be as friendly as I could be because every person has a right to run for any office they want to. I won't hold it against them...I don't want them to win...but they don't need to tell stories. They need to be running for something, not against my Daddy."

MARTHA: "I can remember going to Ladies Night at the Rotary Club a long time ago. Rotary isn't about politics, but we got to the room that night, there at every person's seat was a card for my Daddy's opponent. That hurt my Mama especially. But it also hurt me. Those are the things you can't dwell on. You know folks are sorry. They just didn't realize what they had done to a child. I can remember that campaign. I was with Dad at the polls. We were at all different places, giving out cards."

LYNN: "We used to stand in the entrances to plants early in the morning, six or seven in the morning."

MARTHA: "I remember one day when we left the polls. It was one of his early races. He said, 'Martha, I think we may lose this one.' I was shocked. I looked at him and 'Daddy, I've talked to these people all day and they say you're going to win.' I think it helped him at that moment. He needed to hear that. It was a tough campaign for all of us."

MARY: "We don't care what he does. If he wants to keep running forever, that's his business. We want him to be happy."

HIS PERSONAL IMAGE

Tom Murphy's big Stetson and his big cigar don't portray the usual image you expect of a politician in 1999, but they know that it goes beyond that. They recognize that their father's choice of clothes isn't always the best. It is a family joke, but it is one for which they plead innocence.

MARTHA: "He has more new clothes in his house, things we have given him that are still in the gift boxes...and he still wears the same old ones."

MIKE: "But he's never been what you'd call a fashion plate."

MARTHA: "I do buy him socks that come up high enough that his legs don't show when he crosses his legs."

MIKE: "He won't wear nothing but Arrow Shirts, their factory used to be just across the street from us. Dad is just not into clothes or a flashy look. His favorite TV show is *Matlock* or *Walker Texas Ranger*. He just is not concerned about those things."

MARTHA: "He's got Tommy Hilfiger shirts 'cause we gave them to him. If he knew what we paid for them, he'd be surprised."

MIKE: "Can you imagine Tom Murphy in a Hilfiger shirt? I don't think so."

MARTHA: "If you buy him a shirt without a pocket, forget it. He has got to have a pocket to put his cigars in. He just won't change."

MIKE: "He is not the guy you'd want waiting on you in a men's department."

MARTHA: "He misses mother's help with his dress. She'd see to it he was put together when he left the house."

MIKE: "And those LBJ hats he wears...he's worn those hats for thirty years."

TEACHING HIS CHILDREN TO WORK

He worked as a child and he expected his children to work. They earned money, but they also learned. Their father is proud that they are hard workers. His only bad memory is seeing Mike way down in an eighteen-foot deep ditch. At that, he drew the line.

MARTHA: "I can remember the summer he told me in the tenth grade that he had me a job at the Arrow plant. I had been working at the soda fountain fixing sandwiches and drinks. It was the first year I was going to be able to drive. He had me a job sewing. I worked in that plant that first year. I learned so much about life and people. I was a good seamstress and I started making production. That affected how much those other women had to sew. I didn't know anything about that. All I knew was that I was there to sew. They started giving me the inferior work to slow me down. But these other ladies came to me. They said, 'Martha, these women are giving you this bad work to do and we aren't gonna let them.' Then I understood why. This was their living. This was how they were feeding their children and I was just there for the summer. It was such a life lesson for me."

LYNN: "When I sewed, I sewed in my sleep, I sewed at the red light. All I thought about was sewing. We didn't know anything but do things 100 percent."

MIKE: "All those jobs were our Dad's way of letting us know what education was about."

ABOUT MURPHY THE MAN

They know his traits. They know his habits. They know what he's like when the front door shuts behind him. So they can compare the man they see at home with the man they see when he is front of the House and its 179 members.

MARY: "When people start talking about my Dad, I say 'You need to be careful he's my dad.' Then I ask them if they have ever met him. I don't know how can people can make judgements based on second hand information. But I've never confronted anyone."

MIKE: "When we're out there on Sunday and there's twenty bijillion people at the house, literally eighteen or twenty, he can be watching a ball game and just shut it all out. I've never seen anybody focus the way he can. He can shut it off and focus."

MARTHA: "But if he hears something he wants to respond to, he can do that, too."

LYNN: "Even with a lot of kids running around."

MARTHA: "Even with the kids and the ball game, he knows what's being said in that room. He can snap right of the game and tell you what he thinks, just like he can do up in the House with all that going on."

MIKE: "I like what Roy Barnes says, that the opportunities in this state didn't just happen. It is this way because of the people who made it happen. I like to think of my Dad as being in the vanguard of the people who set that standard and made this state, to the extent you can in politics, into the state it is today. Industry. Business people were there. Educators. They were all there together.

LYNN: "I remember Grandpa Murphy coming by every day with little containers of ice cream for us. Now Daddy keeps his freezer full of ice cream sandwiches. He doesn't bring them to us, but they're always there."

MIKE: "Dad is like the Shell Answer Man. People come in to that law office and ask him questions about every thing under the sun except the law. A lot of them just need an ear, somebody to listen to them. There's no telling how much free advice he gives out, how much good he has done for people in this town."

CAROL: "The night Mike and I got married, he came out in the parking lot as we were getting ready to get into the car. He said, 'Sugar, be good to each other.' Then he gave us both a big hug. He's always treated me....and this whole family has treated me....like a sister and he's always treated me like a daughter."

LYNN: "People used to think I was stuck up simply because I was shy. I have people come up to me who have known me for years and they say 'I didn't know you were Tom Murphy's daughter.' I tell them I'm proud of my Daddy, but I don't meet people and say Tom Murphy's my Daddy. I want people to judge me for who I am. If they like me, then they can understand that he brought me up and raised me to work hard and do the best I can and try and help people."

MIKE: "We were all in his room at the hospital and they were about to do that neck surgery. The doctor came in and said there were more ways than not that you were going to do. There we were, all in that room. He said we can let that go and you have about an 98 percent blockage. We can let it go and your chances of a stroke are going to grow daily. We don't have to do it right now. Daddy said, 'Let's do it tomorrow.' No hesitation. Let's do it. He never puts anything off. He tends to it. Only thing he said to us was to love each other. That's all he said."

LYNN: "Here at home or up there in Atlanta, he's just a good man."

THE MURPHYS AND THE NEWS MEDIA

They try not to watch and they try not to read, but they can't escape news coverage of their father and his activities. They know they're prejudiced. They know some of their feelings are because they love their father. But they can't help harsh, bitter feelings about the way these things have affected their family.

MARY: "Neal Boortz said if I'd come down there to the radio station he'd let me take a swing at him and he wouldn't file charges. People said they'd take me if I wanted to go. I told them that I was raised better than that. But I was tempted."

MARTHA: "He's doing all this because he wants to make this world a better place. That's what upsets me when I see and hear all the bad things that are said and written about him. That's politics. But he is a good man trying to do right. It drives me crazy."

MIKE: "A lot of his public image is paper-created. He's always told the story that when he became speaker the news media was used to sitting down and having their discussion with the Speaker. All of that changed. He wasn't interested in their agenda. He had his own notions. He is a natural leader. He's refined it. He can be as gruff or as kind as you will let him be. He will give you the shirt off his back but if you tell him you're going to take it, then that's another whole proposition. That's his Celtic background, the Scotch-Irish background so many people in the South have in common."

MARTHA: "People who don't know him, who only know what they've read or heard on the news, they think he's a mean, domineering, vindictive person. My daughter was at North Georgia College in her freshman year. She was in her room one night and the Atlanta news was on TV. It was during the session. A lot of the girls were from Hall County, Gwinnett County, Republican areas. They love him, but they don't brag about him or try and lord it over people. The news came on and there was her granddaddy. One of the girls just screamed and said *'I hate that man. he is just awful. we can't stand him.'* Holly looked at her and said, 'Have you ever met him?' Then she told her that was her grandfather. Later on, she brought the girls down here to meet him. And those things hurt our kids. They heard the Atlanta stations making fun of him. They read the stories.

MARY: "Sometimes people will say, 'I can't believe you didn't tell me who your dad was.' I don't why they say that. Everybody has a father. He's not all that to me stuff people say about him. He's just daddy."

MARTHA: "I was standing by some people at a meeting and this man said he knew Tom Murphy and told the woman he could take her over and introduce her to him. She said she didn't want to meet him. *'I can't stand him,'* she said. Can you imagine. She had never met him and she couldn't stand him. As devastating as that was, I thought that poor woman. What type of person is she? That's the way we get through it. Those kind of people need to be in church somewhere."

MARY: "When I met my husband, the fact that Tom Murphy was my father took him by surprise. It like to have taken the wind of him. All John knew was what the Journal-Constitution and the television stations said about him. He thought that Daddy was this horrible person that TV said he was."

MARTHA: "I watch that *Georgia Gang*. I watch Bill Shipp and read his newsletter. He never misses an opportunity to criticize my Dad. He even makes things up. It infuriates me. It doesn't hurt me anymore I won't let it. I say prayers for him now."

MIKE: "I'm gonna disagree with my sister about Bill Shipp. He's an interesting fellow. I know about his background, about his life and about his personal tragedies. I was watching one of those shows and I recall him saying at the end of the 1998 session that his winner of the week was Tom Murphy. He said he had a remarkably smooth session. I don't remember exactly what his quote was. But it came out of Bill Shipp's own mouth. I think he admires Dad, that he has a grudging admiration for him and I think Dad knows him as well as you can know another human being. I never have understood their relationship. They both got the Big Heart Award together one year. It is just an absolute shame. It's like Bill Shipp wants to do better by him but can't. I don't think Bill Shipp dislikes Dad way down deep. I really don't."

MIKE: "It's like when people run campaigns. Why aren't they for something instead of against Tom Murphy? They come up short because he is not the animal they try and make him out to be. People who've been to Dad know that 'Hey, this man will help me. All I gotta do is go see him.' He's nothing like he is portrayed to be. But you have to take that step and go see him."

MARY: "When he became speaker I was a senior in high school. We heard about his attack on the floor through the newspaper....When he was taken to the hospital reporters were there waiting for us. They should know that none of us are going to talk to them. It's mostly TV. it's their job, I know. But I tell my kids at school, if you go into that profession, have a heart."

MARTHA: "It doesn't matter if I read a story or not, there are people who will always ask me if I've read it. If I haven't, they tell me about it, not to be hurtful.

LYNN: "Lots of times people tell you about stories in the paper because they're mad and they're taking up for you."

MARTHA: "The last really bad thing was when Pierre Howard was talking about the DUI legislation and had the parents of a child killed by a drunk driver along with the members of Mothers Against Drunk Driving march across to Dad's office, as if Dad was responsible for the deaths of those people since he had stood in the way of DUI laws. For the news media, that was their story for a week or two. It made Dad look real bad. But if they had asked questions, they'd have found out that Dad had not seen that bill, that nobody had shown it to him. And the news media didn't' go into all of that. They stood up there and called him a murderer. The way I handled it that time was to stop (Atlanta TV reporter) Sally Sears in the hall at the capitol. I asked her if they ever thought of the consequences of what they do or the hurt they cause people's families. She did admit they had made a mistake. She apologized. But she said you know, your Dad doesn't help himself very much. He doesn't try to get along. I told her I was proud of him and glad to know that there was at least one real public servant in the Georgia House, not just somebody up there acting out something. She was saying he didn't fit the mold, that he didn't talk to them. She said he maybe ought to get some help from somebody in Public Relations. Another time was when Monica Kauffman tried to say that Dad wouldn't let a handicapped child on the floor of the House. That was most hurtful. I called her up after the news. She said I'll go back and look at our story and get back to you on how I feel about it. And she did, and she said 'You're right. It's not fair.' And they changed the story on the eleven o'clock news. When I've had it, I just call them. If they think Dad has a crazy daughter that he can't do anything about it, so what. I just let them know it. But really, how should you deal with it? Well, you pray a lot."

MIKE: "We've try to get Dad to take a little credit for what he's done. He says, 'Son, people know who does the things that are done.'"

MARTHA: "Or it doesn't matter who gets the credit. That comes from his religion."

MIKE: "I tell him it don't work that way. You have to start beating your own drum. He has always had the faith that the people who count know."

LYNN: "And the people at home, for the most part, do know."

MIKE: "If my Dad had been half the crook they've made him out to be, he'd have been out of office twenty years ago. He is not like other people who have been in the news media of late. He's not like those others who stand up and talk about family values. He's lived it. That talk is as alien to him as it can be."

LYNN: "Georgia politics has been colorful like this in the past, from Day One, so it is not that much out of the ordinary. People coming into the state don't realize this by what they read."

MIKE: "All of us are just letting off frustration. Sure, we've all benefited by his years of service. It's exposed us to opportunities that we wouldn't have otherwise. I don't really hate the newspapers. I don't even subscribe to the Atlanta papers anymore I get so frustrated. I try and give people the benefit of the doubt, to think where they're coming from. It's just been hard to over the years."

MARTHA: "We had just gone through the Joe Frank Harris campaign and my Dad was made out to be a criminal on TV."

MIKE: "My sisters and I and probably my wife and the whole family believe that if you had to issue an indictment today against anybody attributable to the death of my Mama that it would be the Atlanta news media. She was fifty-three years old when she died. I can't tell you the number of times that I went out there to the house and she was crying over something she had read in the newspaper, some cartoon she had seen, some editorial she had read, something she had seen on TV. She'd sit there in that house by herself and cry. She'd read and she'd cry some more. She might watch a soap opera in the afternoon, then pick it back up and cry some more. It absolutely destroyed my mother's health, as sure I'm sitting here. Here's the thing. My Dad understood it for what it was but my Mama never understood it. It killed my Mama. I will always have that in the back of the mind that the news media didn't like him because he didn't fit their agenda."

11

Murphy

and the

Media

HE WAS COMING, and nobody knew what to expect. Most of the news people who would be at the meeting weren't working at either the *Constitution* or *Journal* the last time Tom Murphy had come calling on the Atlanta newspapers. A few of them were in grade school then. Now he was on his way and they didn't even have to invite him.

While the news people wondered why he was coming, Tom Murphy's closest henchmen wondered why he was going. "You think the boss is doing the right thing?" Bill Lee asked after Murphy's car pulled out of his parking place on the Capitol Avenue side of the statehouse. Milo Dakin assured the white-haired Lee that Murphy was, but at that moment the former reporter and press secretary wasn't that sure himself.

Dakin had covered state politics for the *Atlanta Constitution* in the early 1970s and he had worked for Murphy. Now he was a political consultant in Alabama.

More than that, he had become a friend to Murphy. He knew both sides and he knew the history and that's what scared him. It was like an ex-husband meeting with his ex-wife for the first time after a nasty divorce. How could anyone be sure what the other one would say?

Betsy Weltner, an Atlanta public relations consultant, had arranged the session. Both sides agreed on a date just a few weeks before the 1998 General Assembly. After setting up the meeting, she told Murphy that the newspaper people were excited about him coming.

"You've got nothing to lose, Tom," she advised. "Best thing they'll do is write something nice."

When Weltner—the daughter of the late Charles Weltner, a Georgia congressman and State Supreme Court justice—called the *Journal-Constitution*, there was surprise on the other end of the line. Governors, even presidents, routinely sit down with the newspaper's two editorial boards on a regular basis. In today's world, such conferences are part of doing business, be it politics or news. But for more than twenty years, *Atlanta Journal-Constitution* editors had not bothered even to invite Murphy for a visit. Why should they? He never came. Sometimes, he just ignored their invitations. Years before, he had resolved never again to set foot in the building and he had stubbornly kept his promise.

Now he was here, alone, leaving behind the Greek chorus of House members who usually shadow him. He even bought a new suit for the occasion. Once he got to the papers' offices on Marietta Street, he was taken to the ninth floor, to a room that is more like a comfortable living room than a stuffy corporate boardroom.

Both editorial page staffs were there. The *Constitution*, led by Cynthia Tucker, is the more liberal group as reflected by the tone and stance of its editorial staffs. The *Journal*, with Jim Wooten in control, is generally more conservative. The two editorial pages are the last vestiges of the days when the morning *Constitution* and the afternoon *Journal* were entirely separate—even bitterly competitive. Now, though they still publish twice a day with different nameplates, the only real difference in content are the daily editorial pages.

The first question was a simple one. Or then again, maybe not. "Mr. Speaker, why are you here today?"

He didn't hedge. "Because Betsy Weltner said I ought to." Typical Murphy. No veneer. No double-speak.

The rest of the freewheeling meeting went the same way. Wooten remembers it well. As a former legislative reporter, Wooten feels at home in the capitol pressrooms. He and the Journal editorial staff routinely take pieces of legislation and follow them through the entire process so they see Murphy in action on a regular basis.

The *Constitution*, on the other hand, relies more on reportorial coverage, depending on its reporters to serve as its eyes and ears. Tucker and her staff seldom visit the state capitol, so their view of Murphy and the General Assembly was more second-hand. "I knew he was straight-forward, that he will generally tell you what he believes and not in a way that is necessarily antagonistic," Wooten recalls. "But I think there were a lot of people on the *Constitution* editorial staff who had just read the press clippings and had developed an image based on his gruffness. They had this idea that he was this really gruff old codger—and he can certainly be that—but he can also be really charming as he was that day."

The younger, more liberal people in the room discovered a Murphy they didn't know. Instead of a red clay conservative, they got a glimpse of the Murphy who was shaped by his father and the times he grew up in, the kid who delivered *Atlanta Journal*s with the Roosevelt, Russell and Rivers signs on the back of his bicycle.

"The *Constitution* people were really smitten by him because he sounds like—and I think he is—an FDR, New Deal Democrat. To me, that's generally consistent with the beliefs of the *Constitution* editorial board. I think many of them were very surprised at how much they identified with his philosophy. They thought he was a troglodite and they found out he didn't have horns," Wooten said.

As much as anything, Wooten remembers how at home Murphy appeared to be. He laid back and answered questions and told stories. Dealing with the news media is not his favorite chore, and he was on their turf. As Wooten notes, the Speaker was relaxed and comfortable. "He was charming. He was personable. And at the same time there was no doubt that he was in control of the meeting."

Back at his office, Murphy's cohorts were anxious to know how the meeting had gone. One look at his face and Dakin knew the answer. "He came back happy, just like he had been talking to fifth graders in Haralson County."

Months later, however, Murphy began to have doubts about whether he should have gone and what he had accomplished by the visit. He called Dakin, who is now a lobbyist and political consultant in Montgomery, Alabama. "Son, they haven't written a thing about me going over there."

"Good," Dakin said. "It worked."

Murphy will tell you that little has worked in his forty years of dealing with the statewide media. As a House member, he was portrayed by the press as a living, breathing epitome of the old-line reactionaries who had controlled the body during the four decades when the County Unit System set the tone. He came to the forefront when Lester Maddox, who has spent a lifetime lambasting the Atlanta media, tabbed him for a leadership role. To the more cosmopolitan reporters, he was seen as a rural legislator with rural ideas.

Murphy did little to shed this backwoods image. He simply didn't care what was said or written about himself and, accordingly, gave reporters very little time to get to know him intimately. He was never a back-slapping type of fellow and reporters thought he was snubbing them when sometimes he was just being himself. He was used to dealing with a friendly small-town press and for many years didn't bother to acquaint himself with the capitol press corps.

Besides, he thought, he didn't need those reporters. They needed him more than he needed their stories. He didn't aspire to a higher office. He had the job he wanted. Since he did, all he had to do was control 179 House members and please enough of them to keep his job.

Long ago, Murphy decided that he was there to take the heat, to be the whipping boy for his members. Let the cartoonists have fun with him. To Murphy, that's part of his job description. "If you can't take that, you don't need to be speaker," he says.

Some of his stand-offish attitude with reporters may be traced back to 1973 and an incident when Murphy was speaker pro-tem, a short time before Speaker of the House George L. Smith's fatal heart attack and death.

It was an incident Dakin remembers well for it eventually led to him to him leaving the newspaper business for the final time. In late 1973, he was one of the newer reporters at the *Constitution*. A native of Louisiana, he was new to Georgia politics but not new to politics. He was a stranger to Murphy, but they were about to meet—all because of a toilet.

The speaker pro-tem's office is on the third floor of the capitol building down the marble corridor from the Speaker's much-larger suite of offices and, at that time, just a few doors away from the crowded old press room. As speaker pro-tem, Murphy didn't have a private bathroom. He thought it needed one, so using state money one was created, taking away space from a busy public men's room next door. The *Constitution* city desk thought there was a story there. Dakin didn't. When he didn't—and wouldn't—write the story, another reporter did. Only Dakin's byline was put on the article. That decision still infuriates him. "The whole thing was a tempest in a teapot," Dakin says. "I had never dealt with anything so foolish and it drug on for about a week. Like Lester Maddox used to say, it made news but not sense. I finally went to Murphy and told him what was going on."

An editorial soon followed in the *Constitution*:

> "There is something about a little power that is just likely to go to a man's head, and after all what better sign of position and status than your own private bathroom.
>
> "Rep. Tom Murphy has a fair-sized office on the third floor of the State Capitol in tribute to his position as one of the official leaders of the Georgia House. The main men's room on that floor is, as it happens, literally right next to his office. Convenient, no. Not convenient enough. Rep. Murphy has seen fit, at considerable expense to the taxpayers, to blast holes through the walls of his office so that part of the now public restroom facility can be incorporated into his private office.
>
> "We feel certain that the Boy Scout groups and visiting tourists who already often found such facilities a bit crowded in the State Capitol will remember Rep. Murphy in the future. After all, a man in his position probably deserves a private bathroom. We suspect maybe some of the voters in his district may remember too — at election time."

Murphy's reply to the stories and the editorial was brief and sarcastic. It came while plumbers were at work on the new bathroom and while the public facility was temporarily closed. "As long as the press is going to use that restroom, I'm glad it's sealed off," he said. "They might infect someone with their brains."

That episode was still in the news when word came that George L. Smith had suffered a heart attack and was gravely ill in an Atlanta hospital. The press that saw Murphy as a rube had for years depicted George L. as progressive. He had led the first independent House. He was comfortable in the company of reporters and their stories reflected his easy manner. And in the days that preceded George L. Smith's death, the media around the state—particularly in Atlanta—gave Murphy little chance of becoming speaker. The press focused most of its attention on George Busbee, even though the Albany legislator already had announced he intended to be a candidate for governor.

Editorialists were describing Busbee's "style of careful negotiating and bargaining" as being compatible with George L. Smith's. When Murphy was mentioned, writers said he wasn't a team player and didn't work well with other House members. All of this agitated Murphy. House members twice had elected him speaker pro-tem, the second in line for the top spot. Busbee was majority leader and, more importantly to Murphy, he knew he had the votes he needed to become the next Speaker of the House.

When he officially became Speaker during the 1974 session, Murphy tried to play the game as George L. Smith had played it, even agreeing to have regular meetings with the *Atlanta Journal* editorial board. It was a decision Murphy soon rescinded.

"George L. met with them every week and they kind of shaped his thinking," Murphy said in a 1997 interview. "I met with them that first week. After we didn't agree on ninety percent of what was discussed, I didn't do it again and they've hated me ever since. They couldn't shape my thinking."

In February of 1974, at the halfway point of Murphy's first session as speaker, the old *Atlanta Journal-Constitution Sunday Magazine* featured Murphy in a four-page layout. Included was a photograph of Murphy with Al Burruss of Marietta, his successor as speaker pro-tem. The caption under the picture said Burruss might run against Murphy for the top spot—a race that would not really begin until the following year. The main headline for the piece by veteran *Journal* political writer Margaret Shannon was "The Unexpected Speaker."

The first paragraph of Shannon's article talked about the late George L. as much as Murphy.

> "Thomas B. Murphy of Bremen, the new speaker of the Georgia House of Representatives, is a small-town lawyer, as was his predecessor, the late George L. Smith II of Swainsboro. It's about the only point of resemblance. The speakership was Smith's ambition and obsession most of his political life. Murphy never expected to be speaker. Murphy, who will be 50 next month, is rough-hewn, rumpled in dress, country in speech. Smith, who had just turned 61 at the time of his death, was suave, a considerable sophisticate as the years went by. Murphy has a reputation as a firebrand, moody and mercurial in temperament. Smith was low-key all the way."

Larry Walker is one of just eight current House members who has served under both men. He came to the House in 1973, eleven months before Smith's death. He tells of a conversation he had with Murphy about how the two men compared. "I served a year with Speaker Smith and I've served about twenty-five years with you. I don't mean this to be demeaning to George L. Smith, but I find you superior to him in almost every category but one," he told Murphy whose ears perked up at that suggestion.

"What's that?" he said.

"Public relations," Walker said. "Public relations."

Not that Walker was advising Murphy to cow-tow to the news media, just court them. "I don't think you ought to go out of your way to thumb your nose at them, but I do think you ought to do what you think is right. And then let the hide go with the hair."

During the first few terms Murphy was speaker, he was a frequent target for reporters and editorial writers. Initially, he was seen as only a caretaker for the position. With strong backing from editorial writers around the state, Cobb County legislator Al Burrus made his unsuccessful attempt to topple Murphy. Then, with former House members George Busbee and Joe Frank Harris serving four terms as governor, Murphy was labeled a king maker. The press saw both of those men as proteges of the Speaker. On the night Harris was elected, Murphy stayed out of the spotlight as supporters celebrated at an Atlanta hotel. He used a secluded service elevator to go upstairs and congratulate the new governor. More and more, Murphy hid behind his cigar, taking on almost a bunker mentality to the press.

Former House press officer Jet Toney says Murphy has never sought to use the press and really didn't even want to talk with reporters. "For many years, in the 1970s and 1980s, I think he was almost antagonistic about the media wanting to know how he felt about things. As the years have progressed, he still doesn't use spin doctors—he doesn't even have a news secretary—but he is more accessible. He's calmer, more thoughtful which I think is a byproduct of age and confidence with his position."

While most political figures today are mirrors of their advisors, Toney says Murphy has never allowed the House press officer or others to couch his phrases or tone down his views. "The first thing you have to get clear right off the bat is that the Speaker has never had anyone who performed the traditional role of a news secretary. He's never allowed that person to overly influence or even influence to a minor degree his comments," says Toney, now an Atlanta political consultant. "Today's politicians seem to rely on pollsters and spin artists to formulate their policies. Not Tom Murphy."

Years ago on a State Chamber of Commerce speaking tour around Georgia, Toney remembers making drafts of speeches for Murphy to deliver. They were a waste of paper, however. "He would kindly take them and read them, then put them on the carseat, and go about his business," Toney says. "He would talk about what he wanted to talk about."

What Toney observed in the past may have been Murphy holding a grudge after those early brushes with reporters. More of it comes from his innate shyness and his sometimes-abrupt natural manner. All of this has helped produce his cigar-chomping image. Toney doesn't think Murphy ever considers that image—positively or negatively. He remembers being with Murphy at a television station in Savannah where they had gone to tape a public affairs show with the Speaker of the House in South Carolina. It was around 1980 and they were in town for the Southern Legislative Conference. "I was always so worried about image. Everything had to be just right. The Speaker could have cared less," Toney says, laughing at the ridiculous memory. "It was a windy day in Savannah and just before they went on to tape the show, I whipped out a comb and recommended that he take those few strands of hair he had and maybe comb them over. They were wispy and hanging around his head. The Speaker looked me straight in the face and said, 'There's not really enough up there to matter and people aren't going to watch the show to see how I look.'"

Murphy has never understood reporters who've wanted to invade his privacy—which he values. He answers only the questions they ask—sometimes brusquely—and seldom volunteers anything. "Of course, they're interested in selling newspapers," he says, "I understand that. I have often wondered why I had to be the subject, though."

There have been times, however, that he has retaliated to what reporters have said or written—sometimes about his personal image. David Nordan, former political editor of the *Atlanta Journal*, wrote a newspaper profile of Murphy that was, as a whole, flattering. Only somewhere in the article, Nordan injected a descriptive phrase about Murphy's pants being too short.

An unsuspecting House member wandered into the Speaker's office and commented about what a good story that was in the *Journal*. The Speaker snorted, almost biting through his cigar. "He said my pants were too short," was all Murphy said.

DuBose Porter, who once challenged Murphy for the Speaker's gavel, was also the target of Murphy's Irish ire—but it had nothing to do with their past political differences. Porter owns the newspaper in Dublin and the newspaper published a photograph of Murphy and Mary, his youngest daughter, at a horse race in Birmingham. Friends know that Murphy loves to go to the track and that he tries every year to go to the Kentucky Derby. And yes, he will place a wager on a favorite pony. It is not something he tries to hide or spotlight. But this was different. Porter's paper had included his baby girl in this photo.

Though he may not openly cultivate an image, the persona he wears is well known—the LBJ Stetson, the ever-present cigar, the exaggerated features. To most folks, these things have become Tom Murphy. He has been characterized more than any other political figure outside of those who are elected statewide. His pronounced physical features lend themselves to the political cartoonists and so does the gavel he wields so provocatively and the oversized cigar on which he chews continually.

Jim Wooten think Murphy's gruffness was once an effective tool—keeping some people at a comfortable distance. "It worked well with lobbyists and legislators who might be seeking favors from him so there was a purpose for his gruff demeanor," the *Atlanta Journal* editorial page editor says. "There's also such a turnover among newspaper and television reporters that cover the General Assembly that they don't stay around long enough to get to know him and explain him in other ways. That has perpetuated his image to the extent that any nuance or subtlety is lost in the process."

Reporters do come and go quickly, but Dick Pettys has dealt with Murphy longer than any other active reporter in the state. He was around when George L. Smith was the speaker. The Associated Press reporter remembers going back and forth between Murphy and Zell Miller when the speaker and the lieutenant governor were in a grudge match that seemed to last as long as the 100 Year War. Murphy sometimes would want to attack the messenger, when all the reporter was doing was repeating what Miller had said. Murphy would then send the reporter back across the capitol with a stinging reply for the lieutenant governor. Pettys was often that media messenger. Later, he was also the primary reporter on a House slush fund and wrote a number of articles about members who had carried a sex toy on to the floor of the House. Pettys became an outcast.

Finally, one of the Speaker's closest friends sought out Pettys and advised him to go talk to Murphy. "Just tell him you're sorry," he suggested. Pettys didn't do that, because all he had done was his job. He didn't think he had done anything to warrant an apology. But their strained relationship was making it harder and harder for Pettys to be a reporter. "There was a period there where it just was very difficult for me to talk to him. He wouldn't return calls and was snubbing me," Pettys says. "We got past that and have a more cordial relationship now. And there's no doubt when he's mad at you. You absolutely know it. He doesn't flat out rip your head off, he just won't talk to you."

Perceptive insiders warn newcomers to be careful if Murphy refers to you by your last name, that a dart is about to be thrown in your direction. But Tom Baxter, the *Journal-Constitution*'s chief political correspondent, says a person should watch Murphy's body language for clues. "He can look past you in an expressive way," Baxter says. "I know that seems to be a contradiction, but he can do it. He can move right past you and shake another person's hand instead of yours. That really makes you notice when he recognizes you."

Over the years, Baxter has learned how fruitless a one-on-one interview with Murphy can be, how uncomfortable he can be and how he needs others to deflect his ideas. "That's why I don't try and interview him very often. Instead, I just watch him. It's in his body language, the way he stares, the way he stands. To me, that's the way he communicates best."

The press corps that Murphy worked with as a House member and in his early days as speaker was vastly different than the one that covers state politics today. When he became speaker in 1974, the reporting staffs of the *Atlanta Constitution* and *Journal* were totally separate, meaning that during a session there were two sets of reporters assigned to the General Assembly. That didn't count the newspaper's editorial department, its columnists or its photographers.

Along with them were year-round correspondents from the *Columbus Ledger-Enquirer*, the *Macon Telegraph & News*, the *Marietta Journal*, and the *Florida Times-Union* as well as a bureau person representing the *Athens Banner-Herald*, the *Augusta Chronicle*, and the *Savannah Morning News*. There were also wire service reporters from the Associated Press and United Press International. On the broadcast side, there were the three Atlanta network affiliates: WSB-TV, WAGA-TV and WXIA-TV. They were joined on occasion by reporters from television stations in other Georgia cities. Radio reporters also joined the contingent at times. By the 1990s, those numbers had declined dramatically.

Philosophies also changed. In the generation that preceded Watergate, news people sometimes saw themselves as an extended arm of the Legislature. They sat in on private meetings and didn't report the discussions. They shared ribald jokes with the members. They shared shots of liquor with the politicians — many times before the gavel had ended that day's workload. It was a cozy situation.

It was also an era when the capitol beat was one of the most coveted at a newspaper. Most of the time, Southern political reporters were next to sports editors in the freedom they received and next to them in the salaries they were paid. State government reporters named their hours, set most of their assignments and got to be friendly with most of the state's most influential figures. When it was time to decide which stories would go on a given day's front-page, political stories usually were at the top of the list, giving the reporters the prestige of Page One and plenty of space to tell their stories.

Eugene Patterson, editor emeritus of the *St. Petersburg Times*, was editor of the *Constitution* from 1956 to 1968, a period of time when political coverage was at its peak. He remembers the state capitol reporters having more prestige than the ones in the newspaper's Washington bureau "because that's where the big stories were and where the best people were."

Sometimes, prestige and influence offered reporters the opportunity to put a spin on news affecting their favorite political figure. That was certainly the case in 1936, two decades before Patterson arrived in Atlanta. Governor Gene Talmadge had set his sights on the United States Senate seat of Richard Russell. The two were native Georgians and both were staunch Democrats. In other ways, they were opposites — personally and politically. Talmadge had been talking about running for President against Franklin D. Roosevelt, but when that effort began to fizzle, he jumped into the Senate race at the last minute.

Clark Howell was the owner of the Constitution and was also a former Speaker of the House in Georgia. Fearing a Talmadge victory, Howell assigned Ralph McGill to cover that race. McGill was at that time the paper's sports editor, but he longed to be a political reporter. This was his chance. McGill's marching orders were to bolster the Russell campaign.

And bolster he did.

Russell, as McGill wrote, "has kept the faith and never betrayed his state, his party, or his friends." Talmadge, his reports said, was "a traitor and a deserter and one who would wreck his own party and his own state to satisfy his own insolent ambition." McGill's work was so flagrant that the *Macon Telegraph* wrote a blistering editorial condemning his articles. Its headline was "Crooked Newspaper Work." When the Talmadge campaign in turn included the Macon editorial in its campaign advertisements, McGill used the *Constitution* editorial pages to attack the *Telegraph*.

Talmadge, who was a three-term governor, suffered the worst defeat of his long and colorful career. Russell carried 143 of the state's 159 counties. Talmadge was only somewhat more successful two years later in an unsuccessful race for Walter F. George's seat in the United States Senate. But the damage had been done in 1936.

It was an era of personal politics and personal journalism. Candidates for years took to the stump all over Georgia to attack the "lyin' Atlanta newspaper"—turning that phrase into a political cliche. After World War II, race and civil rights began to emerge as a political and social issue. In 1944, a Columbus barber and minister, Primus King, filed suit in federal court after not being allowed to vote in the all-white primary. A federal judge in Macon ruled in favor of the Muscogee County suit, thus abolishing Georgia's all-white primary. In a one-party state, that meant black voters had for years been effectively disenfranchised. For the first time, black voters would be a factor in the 1946 governor's race. It would be a race the state would never forget.

An aging Gene Talmadge was making what would be his final comeback. His opponents in the Democratic Primary were former Governor E. D. Rivers and attorney James Carmichael, who managed the Bell Bomber Plant in Marietta. McGill, by then, was the editor of the *Constitution*, on his way to a prestigious career. Carmichael was the Constitution's anointed candidate in the first statewide election where black voters were given a voice. In an election day editorial, McGill called for Talmadge's defeat, saying his victory would "throw the state into discord, tension and fear."

Though Carmichael had more popular votes, rural support carried the election for Talmadge. It was the only time in history that the winning candidate failed to receive a plurality in the state's gubernatorial election. The power of the County Unit System was never greater, overcoming the new coalition of urban and black voters.

As was the case on most election nights in those pre-television years, most of Georgia's political leaders gathered in the newsroom of the *Constitution* to wait for election returns to trickle in from around the state. Ellis Arnall, the sitting governor, was among the crowd in McGill's office on Forsyth Street when Gene Talmadge suddenly threw open the editor's door, an unlit victory cigar stuck in the corner of his mouth.

Talmadge was weary but boastful. "Ralph, I give you a good whuppin' this time, didn't I?" he said.

It was their final duel. Talmadge was dead before the year was out, before he could be inaugurated. His untimely death set the stage for Georgia's infamous three-governor fiasco. Three men said the office was theirs: Herman Talmadge, M.E. Thompson and Ellis Arnall.

Talmadge, Gene's only son, claimed the seat since he had received more write-in votes than any other candidate — 675 to be exact. An *Atlanta Journal* reporter later discovered the fact that many of those votes were cast alphabetically by voters who were dead.

Georgia's new state constitution had only recently created the office of lieutenant governor and Thompson, a former teacher and school superintendent, had been elected to the post on the same ballot with Gene Talmadge. Thompson, therefore, claimed he should be governor since in the line of succession he would take over in the event of the chief executive's death.

Arnall, meanwhile, refused to give up the keys to the governor's office saying he would stay there until the courts made their ruling. When Talmadge's people changed the locks on the office overnight, Arnall set up shop near the capitol rotunda.

The Georgia Supreme Court eventually ruled in Thompson's favor and he became governor—only after Talmadge had held the office sixty-three controversial days. Thompson was governor for only two years, until another election could be held. Herman Talmadge was elected in 1948 and for a full four-year term in 1950. Six years later, he succeeded Walter F. George in the United States Senate, a role his father had desired twenty years before. He served twenty-four years, distinguishing himself as a member of the Watergate panel. But in 1980, Mack Mattingly, an unknown Republican from the Georgia Coast, would defeat the Georgia legend.

Talmadge was already crippled and bloodied before his race with Mattingly began. There were allegations of under-the-table campaign contributions that came out in court during his bitter divorce. Then there was his alcoholism, for which he eventually sought treatment. His political fate was sealed during the Democratic Primary when Zell Miller, then the state's lieutenant governor, was a pit-bull who wouldn't quit biting. In Miller's corner, egging him on at times, was the *Atlanta Constitution*, again on the attack against a Talmadge.

"The ill-kept secret of this Georgia political season is that Senator Herman Talmadge is the sawdust candidate, the hollow man, and even his staunchest supporters are beginning to suspect this is his 'last hurrah," *Constitution* editor Hal Gulliver wrote early in the campaign.

Miller forced a runoff but one more time the Talmadge forces marshaled and he easily emerged from the Democratic Primary. By then Miller was also wounded, and it would be a decade later before had recovered enough for a race for governor, a job he held from 1990 to 1998.

The 1980 Senate was a bitter political season on both the campaign trail and in print. The Constitution seemed to smell blood, Talmadge's blood, and the paper was relentless in its attacks on the state's senior senator. Gulliver was correct. It was Talmadge's last hurrah, but in retrospect some of the reporters who covered that race are apologetic about their role in that race.

"I think we all went too far on that one," says Rick Allen, the *Constitution*'s political editor in 1980. "I can remember, and I've apologized to Senator Talmadge, that I did one thing that was particularly bad. I violated an off-the-record confidence of his and I shouldn't have done that. I was wrong. But the newspaper itself went all out to get rid of him, and I don't think we should have done that. It was wrong. I was writing a column. I had always tried to be non-partisan in the column and I stopped doing that. I started taking out after him and I was still directing coverage of the campaign. So I think Herman's gripe about the paper is a fair one. I mean, he wasn't an innocent flower in all of this, but we went too far."

Former *Constitution* metro editor Bill Shipp says the paper was willing to be used by Miller and his campaign because they shared a common goal. "His goal was our goal," Shipp says. "We wanted to get rid of Talmadge. We wanted to get rid of everything that Talmadge had stood for and we saw Zell as an instrument to do that." This time, the newspaper gave a Talmadge "a good whuppin'."

There were ethical questions, as Allen and Shipp have noted, in the way the *Constitution* handled the 1980 campaign. At the same time, it showed the newspaper's almost obsessive interest in state politics. Within a decade, that interest had begun to wane. The *Constitution*'s change of attitude paralleled that of newspapers around the country where political news came to be viewed as boring and dry.

News that had traditionally been headlined on the front page was being relegated to the back pages. Resources were being invested in other departments in the newsroom, notably business and technological news. In the late 1990s, while the number of statehouse lobbyists was spiraling, the number of statehouse reporters was dropping.

The *American Journalism Review*, as part of an ongoing examination of the American newspaper, explored coverage of state government in its August 1998 issue. Zeroing in on Georgia, the headline on one of the articles said, "In Atlanta, even the governor wonders where the news went." AJR quoted one lobbyist as yearning for days "when journalists would get fire in their bellies and a commitment to issues." Zell Miller, who was the governor when the article was written, said Georgia reporters don't have context anymore. "There's no historical perspective whatsoever," Miller said.

Jack Nelson, who as a Constitution reporter in 1960 won a Pulitzer Prize for his stories revealing inhumane problems at the state mental hospital in Milledgeville, is now the Los Angeles Times chief political correspondent in Washington. Looking at his former paper today, he said, "it doesn't feel very good. I spent thirteen years of my life down there and I was always very proud of the papers."

However, in recent years the size of the state's overall capitol press corps has also declined. In 1998, the Atlanta newspapers had just four reporters on duty during the General Assembly, compared to a dozen or more in the past. Morris Newspapers had one reporter covering for its four papers in Georgia and Florida. Macon had a one-person bureau while Columbus sent a reporter from its local staff to be there for the session. Most newspapers in the state rely on the remaining wire service and the Associated Press maintains a three-person bureau, led by Dick Pettys, the dean of capitol reporters. Lobbyists in Georgia, according to the AJR, outnumbered capitol reporters 150-to-one.

Though most editors at the *Journal-Constitution* defended its apparent downgrading of Georgia legislative news to the AJR, its metro editor, Mike King, said he feared its reporters are missing state political stories. "The Georgia Legislature is an old-fashioned structure of government," King said. "It has a powerful speaker who can use it to his advantage."

The magazine, regarding the declining news coverage, also interviewed Murphy. His response: "It doesn't bother me at all."

In fact, however, he abhors the new reporters' lack of understanding of the legislative process and there is certainly a generational gap between Murphy and the younger reporters. When he's in a whimsical mood and is looking back at the past, he even talks warmly of some of the reporters with whom he worked over the years, sharing stories about them as easily as he does about former House members. However, he also relishes reminding people that he once had to force reporters in the press area to stand during the House's morning prayer.

The late Celestine Sibley was one of his favorite news people. Murphy was enraptured when the veteran *Atlanta Constitution* reporter and columnist spoke to the House a few years ago. She was sharing stories about her friends—and Murphy's—who were no longer around the General Assembly. When she became ill again in early 1999, she received calls from old House members as well as news colleagues. Just a few days before her death in the summer of 1999, Governor Roy Barnes and Murphy named a road near her North Fulton County home in her honor, and, in an unusual show of affection, Murphy has named the pressroom at the rear of the House chambers for her.

He also notices the generally good press he has been receiving. "They've been pretty nice to me these past few years," he says.

As Murphy shows flashes of nostalgia and mellowing, Wooten thinks he needs to force himself to become more open and articulate with the press. "He will tell you something deliberately inarticulate for effect. That has worked for him in the past, but it has gotten to the point that he needs to be softened and broadened. This is a very different state than it was fifteen or twenty years ago. There are a lot of people who have moved into the state and they are developing perceptions about the state, its politics and its political leaders. When these people read or hear these gruff statements they get the idea that we are a little backward or provincial."

Because Murphy personifies the House to so many people, his image extends to the entire body. So when these newcomers—many of them Republicans moving into the beltway around Atlanta—hear Murphy say "I ain't wearing no seatbelt!" they roll their eyes and assume this is the way everybody in the Georgia House talks even though Murphy often spouts such statements for effect. The historical shortcomings of political reporting in the state also breed this stereotype since so many reporters haven't been taken—or haven't been given—the opportunity to get beyond the Stetson and get to know the man who wears it.

As Georgia changes and the state's news media changes, Tom Murphy is also changing. It was no coincidence that he invited himself to that meeting at the Atlanta newspapers. It was no coincidence that he was on the cover of *Georgia Trend* Magazine in early 1999. Nor is it a coincidence that he has been openly cooperative with the writing of this book. Though he denies it, at the age of seventy-five, he is growing much more conscious about the way he will be remembered. "I just want to be remembered as a man who didn't steal and told the truth."

The 1981 House that Tom Murphy faced here was not as challenging or diverse as the ones he deals with in today's Georgia

As Speaker, George L. Smith wanted
his finger on every action of the House

In 1976, Al Burruss (right) offered the greatest challenge Tom Murphy faced for his gavel

During the sixteen years Zell Miller (right) was lieutenant governor, he and Murphy were not always laughing

Murphy and Zell Miller brought a continuity of leadership to Georgia that other states seldom enjoy

Tom Murphy served as chairman of the Southern State Speakers Conference. Here he is joined by (left to right) Joe McCorquodale of Alabama, Benjamin Cardin of Maryland, Ned McWherter of Tennessee, John Miller of Arkansas, William Kenton of Kentucky and C.B. 'Buddie^' Newman of Louisiana

Facing questions from the capitol press corps is not one
of Murphy's favorite chores.

When Murphy speaks, the House listens.

Tom Murphy has presided over the House longer than anyone in Georgia history.

When he talks to the House, Murphy doesn't hide his emotions.

Murphy talks on the phone, swings the gavel and listens to debate at the same time.

His cigar in hand, Murphy listens to former lieutenant governor Pierre Howard.

Nearly sixty years of state leadership was on the podium as Zell Miller and Pierre Howard applaud a waving Tom Murphy.

Tom Murphy is never far from a microphone.

Bill Lee gave up his seat in 1998, making Murphy the senior member of the House.

Many years, Murphy is part of the pre-legislative tour of the state. Here he visits with Columbus Chamber of Commerce president Mason Lampton.

The office of Speaker was turned over to Tom Murphy in 1974.

Senator Sam Nunn listens as Tom Murphy speaks on a Business Council of Georgia tour of the state.

Under George L. Smith, Murphy was
Speaker Pro Tem.

Representative Calvin Smyre of Columbus confers with
the Speakers as the 1980 General Assembly begins.

An intense Murphy fends off the challenge of
Al Burruss in 1976.

Murphy could have been describing either a big bill or a
big fish that got away.

They're never lit, but a cigar is usually in Murphy's mouth.

Traffic jams over occur around the House podium. As Murphy presides, Speaker Pro Tem Jack Connell of Augusta and Representative Tom Buck of Columbus wait for a word with him.

Governor Jimmy Carter

Governor George Busbee

Governor Joe Frank Harris

Governor Zell Miller

Governor Roy Barnes

Tom Murphy

12

THE STYLE

AND

THE SUBSTANCE

MOVING ACROSS THE state capitol from his third floor office to the elevator, Tom Murphy is a spectacle. It's winter, and he has traded his summer Stetson for a floppy winter felt. An unlit stogie is in his mouth and a stylish camel overcoat drapes over his shoulders like a regal cape. He walks with authority, his driver rushing ahead to save the elevator. A group of lieutenants walk with him as one. As he strides across the hallway, the crowd parts and people respectfully pay homage to Mr. Speaker, but he only nods, not stopping long enough for a conversation. The elevator waits and the entourage disappears inside. The door closes and he's on his way to a waiting car.

It's hard to know if this is a scene carefully choreographed or whether this is just a busy man leaving his office for the day. Either way, it's another piece in the mosaic of Tom Murphy. The lamp-sized cigar...the Texas Stetson...the sledgehammer gavel...they all make him easy to spot and sometimes difficult to approach. Packaged with his dominating nose and prominent ears, he appears larger than he really is—which comes in handy when you're trying to keep 179 unruly politicians in the same corral.

The covey of trusted henchmen who often encircle him are there to laugh when they should laugh, speak when they're spoken to and insulate when they should protect, much like the entourage that shadows a heavyweight boxing champion. His gruff reputation precedes him, so he doesn't have to be mean if people think he's mean. These trappings symbolize his power and influence around a building that was built on these things rather than brick and mortar.

For the people who do daily business with Tom Murphy as Speaker, there are other signals and signs. Overt gestures that to the insiders speak just as loudly as his voice when it booms across the House chambers. It may be a little nod or a quick wink that they think is just for them. It may be what he calls them. First name, okay. Nickname, he's in a good mood. "Son," he's happy with you. But if he puts mister in front of your last name, head for the nearest bomb shelter and throw your body on top of your favorite legislation to protect it.

Small but effective, such things are part of the bag of tricks that have kept Murphy in power longer than anyone in state politics. He is Speaker of the House—with twenty-five years of service and dean of presiding officers among the other forty-nine state legislatures. He has held that important position through the election and inauguration of five governors, longer than anyone in state history. He is both master and gatekeeper of the state budget. He is behind only the lieutenant governor in the line of succession should the governor be unable to govern. But his power goes beyond that prescribed by law.

Politicians are said to have three kinds of power: one that they own and two they only borrow. The power that they hold a deed on is the knowledge and experience they acquire through their years of service. This is nontransferable. The others are those powers that go with the office they hold and those powers that the person is perceived to hold — real or imagined. The power of the office is outlined by statute or regulations. The power they earn gives them respect. The ones that are perceived are sometimes the most useful.

In the case of Murphy, it is difficult to separate the inborn from the borrowed for so much of the sovereignty that goes with the office of speaker in Georgia has been created for him and by him. Before Murphy, there was George L. Smith and before him there was a list of well-meaning men who were little more than puppets whose strings were attached to the governor. George L. Smith had only seven years of independence and he had the special popularity that went along with being the first elected leader. Murphy took the power and influence that George L. had created and in twenty-five years has refined it and expanded it so that it is hard to separate the man from the position.

Some of his power and influence is nebulous. These things he wears like that cape he threw over his shoulder on his way to the elevator that night. Some may not be real, but perception overrides reality. The image and legend that has grown up around Tom Murphy is sometimes as much a part of his ability to lead as the gavel he wields.

Murphy has led Georgia through perhaps her greatest political and economic changes. Governors have come and gone. He is the constant. He was in charge of the House when Republicans were a true minority party, when blacks were not an issue and when women were ornaments. He was a legislator when the governor held the biggest stick and he has sat on the front row as the Speaker's leadership role has evolved. He has seen the House grow more cosmopolitan and urban, a sharp contrast to the aging rural twang that could be heard when he arrived in 1961. And still, he finds ways to lead.

It is not unusual now to see contemporary members of the House — some of them young and Republican — dressed like they are on their way to an important business meeting.

Some have a cigar that seems to be larger than their youngest child stuffed in the corner of their mouth, emulating one of the symbols of a man who is old enough to be their grand-father, and one they often politically attack.

Murphy's position is evidenced in many aspects of his political life. A special seat is always saved for the Speaker. Nobody sits in it. Nobody. Murphy neither demands it or commands it. That is just part of the ritual. He has his seat at the Monday morning breakfast held for committee chairmen. He has a reserved spot at Marcus Collins's daily breakfast. At the after-session parties, people know what part of the room Murphy likes so seats are saved for him and his buddies.

And at least once a year at one of these gatherings, the band will stop its normal set and somebody will invite "the best singer in the room" up to the bandstand to do a few numbers. *"So let's give a big Atlanta welcome to Tom Murphy."*

Usually, he gives his ageless version of "Your Cheating Heart," the way Ole Hank would have done it. And you get the feeling that many of the folks in the room think that heart would tell on you if you didn't stand up and give the best singer in the room a rousing round of applause when he's finished.

Veteran Associated Press reporter Dick Pettys talks about such things as the Murphy culture, most of it built around a strong feeling of old-fashioned paternalism toward House members. "First and foremost, he is a lawyer, a trial lawyer, which means he's an actor and good actors put on different faces for different needs. He has chosen to use this paternalistic yet strict father figure. One who has a temper and who will use it," Pettys says. "People don't want to risk incurring his wrath for fear of unknown punishments which is, of course, a great tool of power if you don't know what might happen to you if you do something that displeases the Speaker. You don't know, but you're fairly sure that there will be punishment."

Such a culture has to have a firm foundation and Larry Walker says it's substance. Walker is part of Murphy's inner circle and one he often calls "Son." Walker understands it as a term of endearment but knows other members might be offended. He says Murphy handles different people in different ways, including the manner in which he disciplines them. "Sometimes it's overt. That's the sign of a smart man. He's never really jumped on me and said harsh things to me, but he's let me know through the years that he hasn't liked things I've done. I've seen him be much more overt and much more direct with other people. But people should know that while sometimes his style isn't what you and I would think it ought to be, there is always substance. With most of us, it's style over substance. Murphy is substance over style," Walker says.

Terry Coleman calls it knowledge. "There are lots of people who could be the Speaker and not wield the influence nor command the respect that Tom Murphy does. He does it from something that I have learned from him, that knowledge is power. If you know what's going on, if you understand the bills and you understand the budget and you know the players, then you have power. It's the knowledge," says the Eastman legislator, the chairman of the all-important House Appropriations Committee.

Zell Miller understands power from all directions. He was a state senator. He presided over the Senate for sixteen years as lieutenant governor. Then he was governor for eight years. He understands that the financial side of government is a key to power whatever position in government you may hold. It's always the budget, Miller says. "You have a tremendous advantage over other legislators or other people in state government if you understand and have a good knowledge of the budget. It just gives you an advantage. So many legislators stay around the capitol for years and never understand that or never find that out. But the budget is practically everything. That is where Tom Murphy's strength lies. That understanding gives him power and he knows how to use it. He knows how to use that gavel. He knows how to use the power that the office has given, that the office gives anyone who serves in it. He has taken it and taken it to the 'nth' degree."

With Murphy, there is substance and there is knowledge. He is known to ignore basic rules of grammar and to freely mix his metaphors, but these things should not overshadow his brilliance and his mental dexterity. No one knows the rules of the House or parliamentary procedures better than he and the mental gymnastics he performs every day on the floor of the House too often are taken for granted.

Watch him at the podium. The floor buzzes with conversation and people. Upstairs, school groups are noisily finding their seats. Members are wandering from seat to seat shopping for votes or, more likely, talking about last night's sports scores. Pages are delivering messages. But there's also state business to conduct. One legislator stands at his side and talks about a piece of legislation. Across the room, Murphy is recognizing the next speaker. Meanwhile, he is posing for grip-and-grin photographs with an endless stream of visitors. And if the members are misbehaving, he swings his gavel. Yet, if a serious question arises about the bill that is being debated, Murphy never misses a beat. Somehow, he juggles all these things and still makes a cogent ruling.

House-banking chairman Butch Parrish thinks Murphy likes to be seen as a simple country lawyer. "Bless his heart, he doesn't try to help himself with that image. Yes, he's an old country lawyer—one who is dumb like a fox," says Parrish, a representative from Swainsboro. "He'll come across as someone who doesn't know what they're doing, but you better not ever believe he doesn't. How in the world can he stand there on that podium and carry on two conversations and bang that gavel and listen to the person in the well talking and recognize somebody to ask a question—all at the same time? I mean, his mind is going about 100 miles per hour."

"His country lawyer demeanor is disarming," says Tommy Chambless of Albany, who like so many other former House members is now a capitol lobbyist. "He has a steel-trap mind. I mean he doesn't miss a thing. He knows how to deal with people individually in such a way as to gain their confidence, to make folks think he cares about them and their future. The unspoken thing is that one day you can help me and I can help you. It is a personal kind of charm he has."

Not that Murphy won't play the anger card—when it's least expected. "There is an animal quality about him—and I don't mean that crudely," says Tom Baxter of the *Atlanta Journal-Constitution*. "He can just lie in wait, then pounce on people. It is a highly calculated thing. People don't see it coming."

Former House member Matt Towery, a Republican, wonders why anyone would show surprise about a person in Murphy's position flashing his tough side, not when he's the aging gun-fighter in a room of young guns. "Can he be tough? Sure. But so can everybody else. I mean, they act like Tom Murphy invented being tough. It's a roomful of tough people down there."

Parrish saw Murphy pull the trigger once in a meeting of the House budget subcommittee that was going nowhere. Nothing was getting done and the clock was ticking. Murphy came into the meeting, listened for a few minutes, then ordered anyone not a member of the subcommittee to leave the room. "Everybody!" Murphy bellowed.

"Boy, he just got on our case and read us the riot act. He chewed us up one side and down the other. I guess we needed it, because when he got through lecturing us we got down to serious business and got things done. I told somebody later that I felt like I was taken out to the woodshed by my father. After he got through, we all kind of hung our heads and said, 'Yes sir, Mr. Speaker.' That's the kind of respect we hold for him," Parrish says.

That respect or dominance makes it difficult for members and others to openly disagree with him, though at times Murphy wishes they would, recognizing that The *Speaker* usually gets his way. They are intimidated by the man and the aura he has created. Many nod their head like a lap dog when he says, "Don't you think we ought to do this?" Parrish says the more confident members will say, "Mr. Speaker, let's think about that," and Murphy will sometimes change his thinking if it is a position he believes should prevail. "He is not a closed mind," Parrish said.

But when Murphy takes a stance, the word is known. There are no written memos, no e-mails flashing on the screen. Members just know. "You knew when things were important to him," recalls Chambliss. "He won't come to you and say, 'You SOB, if you don't vote right on this one, you're through.' Nothing like that. But you knew it was important without him having to come tell you it was. On those bills, you knew where you had better be. But that was rare, very rare."

As a House member, Roy Barnes once confronted the Speaker on a bill on which Murphy's stance was highly personal. It involved former Attorney General Mike Bowers, one of Murphy's most bitter adversaries. Bowers and Murphy never got along, and those feelings grew when Bowers switched to the Republican Party. Representative Jim Martin of Atlanta had proposed a bill that would allow state department heads to hire outside lawyers, bypassing the attorney general. It was Martin's bill, but the Speaker had adopted it as his own, knowing it would agitate Bowers.

Coffee is served every morning in the Speaker's office and legislators who get to the capitol early wander in and out—especially if one of their pet bills is due to come up for a vote soon. Barnes came in that day and poured himself some coffee. People in the room, including Murphy, were discussing the Martin bill, which was headed to the House floor later that day.

"Mr. Speaker, I'm not going to be for that bill. It's bad policy," Barnes said.

"Bad policy?" the Speaker grumbled.

"Yes, the attorney general *is* the attorney general. He should choose the lawyers for the state of Georgia."

Murphy reared up at his friend, sounding wounded. "I can't believe you're going to choose Mike Bowers over me."

"This isn't about you and it isn't about Mike Bowers," Barnes explained.

That afternoon, Murphy spoke on behalf of the bill and still it just barely passed the House. Later, the Senate killed it. But it did not affect the relationship between Murphy and Barnes, a future governor. "You have to deal with him straight," Barnes says. "You deal with him up front. He may fuss at you; you may have some sharp exchange the next time you see him. But he understands."

When old-line Democrats dominated the House, Murphy did not have to be so understanding. He could cut a person off at the knees and never blink, knowing he had the votes then and would have them tomorrow. Johnny Isakson, now a congressman from Cobb County, came into the House at this time, one of just nineteen Republicans in 1977. "His power was complete," he says. "He had just defeated Al Burruss who had challenged him for the speakership and he may have been at that moment his most authoritative in the way he ran the House. He could bring out the best in you or the worst in you because he challenged you. Republicans were irrelevant. You could vote, and if you could find a reporter who would talk to you had a voice."

As the Democratic Party became more diverse and the number of urban Republicans began to increase, Murphy had to open his arms much wider. He was no longer assured of votes. He had to ask for them and cultivate them.

"In the early years, it was brute strength," Barnes says. "In the later years, as the House has become more fractious, more Republican, more African-American, more women, he has maintained his power because he is the only stable touchstone in the House. Even those who disagree with him know that he brings stability and order."

Adeptly, Murphy has been able to make each of these varied factions think they are participating in the leadership of the House. He has involved them and engaged them so that they were not easily enticed by opposing groups that might want to challenge him.

He has adapted—which *Atlanta Journal* editorial page editor Jim Wooten says goes against his outward persona. "To look at him, you would think he is incapable of change and quite the contrary is true. The way that he has been able to do this is as black legislators come along, or as women come along or as Republicans are elected, he reads these people, deciding which ones are intelligent, which are constructive, which can be brought along into leadership roles."

The key word has become consensus as he balances the interests of an increasingly varied membership. Murphy has skillfully come to this understanding, bringing together his traditional forces with the new factions that arrive in greater numbers every year. It is a balancing act few people would have imagined him performing as they watched him years ago acting like the statehouse bully.

But even then, Murphy understood a member opposing him if it involved their district politics. He knows the first rule of political survival: get elected. What he doesn't abide—and the examples are many—are people who tell him they will support a measure then vote the other way. "The worst thing you can lose up here is your credibility," Tom Buck says. "To be successful, you have to have it. You ever lie to somebody and you're dead. If you do, the word gets out don't believe that son-of-a-bitch. It's that way with Murphy. If you lie to him, you're dead."

Some of that goes back to Murphy's rearing in the Primitive Baptist Church where honesty is considered a major virtue. He says he plays by the same rules and in 1990, when he was running for governor the first time, Barnes learned how brutally honest Murphy can sometimes be.

Barnes was a law school classmate of Mike Murphy at the University of Georgia so he had known the family for many years, long before he came to the General Assembly, first to the Senate and later the House. As a senator, he often handled Murphy's bills for him when they were sent to the Senate. So when he decided to run for governor in 1990, he sought the Speaker's support. "Mr. Speaker, you need to help me with this governor's race."

"Can't do that, Son, 'cause I'm going to be for Bubba."

Lauren "Bubba" McDonald was a House member from Commerce and a Murphy favorite. He had been a key player in the budget process and Murphy was impressed with him much as he had been previously with Joe Frank Harris when he was in the House. He came out early for McDonald in the governor's race and he stayed with him, even when his protege's luster began to fade. Barnes concluded that McDonald's voters were his voters and rightfully feared that his support could keep him out of a runoff. Barnes went back to Murphy several times to no avail. "I've got one of my own running," he told Barnes.

Barnes was edged out of the runoff that pitted Zell Miller against Andrew Young. Miller of course went on to serve two terms as governor. Pundits assumed that Lieutenant Governor Pierre Howard would be the heir to that seat. So after first getting into the governor's race in 1998, Barnes changed his mind and said he would run for lieutenant governor instead, leaving Howard and the other Democrats to fight it out for the nomination. This time, Murphy had promised him his support so Barnes went back to him and told him of his change of heart. "We're fixing to split everything up and we could lose this whole deal," Barnes said.

"You can beat Pierre," was Murphy's take on the race. "But I understand and I really admire you. I know you don't want to be lieutenant governor and I'll stick with you whatever you do."

Murphy was right. Barnes did not have a deep interest in the second spot. When Howard shocked everyone and withdrew from the race, Barnes rethought his decision and got back in the gubernatorial campaign. Again Murphy stood by him and Roy Barnes was elected governor of Georgia in 1998. The loyalty he showed Barnes is the loyalty Murphy demands as Speaker. That is never more evident than when he appoints someone to a position that he sees as important.

Tom Buck has been in the House since 1967, one of the body's senior members. He chairs the powerful Ways & Means Committee and has long been one of the Speaker's inner circle. The Muscogee County legislator remembers when Murphy first put him on the budget conference committee, an influential group that is composed of House and Senate members who wrangle over what will be funded and what will not. Buck remembers the promotion and the dressing down that followed. "He called me up to the podium one morning and said, 'Son'...sometimes he calls me Tommy, sometimes he calls me Tom, and sometimes he calls me Bucko. When he calls me Bucko, I know he's in a good mood, that everything is fine. But if he calls me Thomas, I know he is a little more serious. Anyway, he called me up there to the front and said he was going to put me on the conference committee for the supplemental budget."

That was big for Buck and it would be big for the folks back home in Columbus. "I told him I was honored, flattered, that I appreciated it. I promised him I'd do a good job...then he really pumped me up. 'This is the most important thing that will ever happen to you as a member of this General Assembly,' he said. 'It's not easy. It's going to take a lot of time. You'll have to come early. You'll stay late. You'll be here on weekends and Sundays. We need you to do this because we all have to stick together."

His first ways and means meeting would be nothing more than an organizational session. Representative Terry Coleman, who chaired the committee, said it wasn't real important and wouldn't last long, which was fine to Buck because he was sponsoring a reception for higher education early that evening at an Atlanta hotel.

Buck's guests for the reception were on the capitol A-List: the governor, legislators, presidents of state colleges and universities, former governors, and presidents of a number of major Georgia businesses. Buck needed to be there early, in case he was needed to take care of last-minute arrangements. "I went up to the conference committee meeting and I kept looking at my watch. Terry Coleman saw me doing that and remembered I needed to leave early. He assured me it would be all right to go. Well, I hadn't been gone two minutes until Tom Murphy drops in. He was leaving the capitol and he sticks his head in on that meeting. First thing he says to Coleman is 'Where's Buck?' Terry reminds him about my reception. The reception went fine and I was on a high because I had been put on that conference committee. Murphy was there. He didn't say much to me, but I didn't read anything into that."

The next morning the Speaker's secretary called Buck early—before 7:30—and said Murphy wanted to see him. When he got there, Buck knew something was different. Then Murphy called him "Thomas." Right then, he became little Tommy Buck, a school boy who had been sent to the principal's office.

Murphy did most of the talking. He reminded Buck of the confidence he had shown in him, of how other legislators would be honored to take that assignment and of how important that assignment was to him and to the House leadership. All Buck could do was hang his head. "When he got through, I said, 'Mr. Speaker, I'm sorry I disappointed you. I regret I made a mistake and I assure you that it will never happen again. I'll do the best job for you that I am capable of doing.' He listened and all he said was 'All right, Son. I'm counting on you.' "

"I'm sorry I disappointed you."

"I'm counting on you."

Hardly phrases you might expect to be thrown around between a couple of powerful grown-up political figures. They sound more like words you would hear being thrown about in a family, between father and son. And in many ways, that is how the House is managed. Murphy is the father figure and the members are his children, just as Pettys described when he talked about that unusual paternalistic culture.

Murphy is the father you don't want to disappoint and you long for those times he is counting on you because you want to please him. Sometimes he's loving, waving you over to sit by him while he remembers when you were just a tyke. You want to make him proud. You surely don't want to disappoint him. And there are times you don't want to bother Dad because you know when he's crotchety. Sometimes he may think you need a good whipping, believing in the old Murphy adage, "Spare the rod and spoil the legislator."

Like other presiding officers, Murphy operates on the premise that legislators only understand two things: what you can do for them and what you can do to them. Murphy can influence them in a variety of ways, from committee assignments to a whimsical wink. What he can do to punish them is ignore them when they stand and want to speak, or he can bury a favorite bill. He could fire them from a key position, as a governor long ago did to Murphy himself. That is something he hasn't done, however.

Zell Miller did that, and he heard about it from Murphy.

Miller was lieutenant governor and as presiding officer in the Senate often clashed with Murphy the Speaker. Joe Frank Harris was governor at the time and he tabbed Senator Nathan Dean as his floor leader. That can be a difficult position since it often divides your allegiance, which is what happened with Dean, who Miller had made chairman of the powerful Rules Committee. On a piece of legislation vital to the lieutenant governor, Dean sided with Harris. The impetuous Miller fired him—by mail. "Even I've never done that!" Murphy told friends.

On the opposite end of the emotional spectrum is Murphy's propensity to tears. People who have been around the House of Representatives for more than a few years, estimate that he will go to the well of the House and cry at least once during every session just as he makes an annual appearance there to rebuke someone. Bets have been taken in the pressroom wagering when he would start to sob. However, more studious observers note that his tears usually come when the members are dealing with the most human issues, usually with old people, children, or handicapped persons.

Atlanta Journal-Constitution political correspondent Tom Baxter was moved himself by one of those incidents a few years ago. It involved a highly publicized charge by a fellow Democrat that Murphy had not allowed a handicapped child to bring his seeing-eye-dog into the House chambers. Murphy retaliated with both anger and tears.

"I don't question his sincerity about any of these situations, but the most sincere moment I've seen was when there were questions about being uncaring to the handicapped. He told about carrying his brother on his back. As he talked, you saw how that had shaped him. It showed how intensely loyal and caring he had been for his brother and it showed a lot about him. It was the most moving moment I can remember in there," Baxter says.

Murphy's tool box also includes the use of silence. Johnny Isakson says the speaker can say a lot by saying nothing. "He's from the old school that believes you don't learn anything with your mouth open," the former minority leader says. "When you're dealing with him politically, he says more by saying nothing than any man I've ever known. You're talking. He's sitting there chomping on that cigar not saying a word. You're still talking and you're hanging yourself with every word."

Like legislators and reporters, state officials and lobbyists also must understand the rules of the game. If they don't, they soon learn. Mac Holladay was new to Georgia, but he knew his way around government having worked previously in five other states. He came to the capitol in 1993 as the head of Governor Zell Miller's Development Council.

One of his earliest assignments in Georgia government was to secure legislative support for a state-incentive program for new businesses. Everyone had come aboard — everyone but the Speaker. Holladay soon learned that Murphy had never been inclined toward offering incentives, believing Georgia didn't need them. Holladay had barely met the Speaker, but he knew his major challenge would be convincing Murphy so he asked people who had been around longer than he had for advice.

First, he went to Ed Holcomb, the chief lobbyist for Georgia Power. He showed him seven things the Development Council needed to accomplish. Holcomb said he would be lucky to get two of them. His main advice was to boil down the request to a single sheet of paper. No more. The briefer the better. Then he might go see Robbie Rivers, the Clerk of the Georgia House. Rivers' mother is a former mayor of Bremen and he has known Murphy all his life. He might have some sage advice.

On Christmas Eve 1993, Holladay met with Rivers and the final strategy was mapped out. It involved Jim Blanchard, the chairman of Synovus Financial Corporation in

Columbus and Arthur Gignilliatt, the president of Savannah Electric Power—both members of the Georgia Development Council.

Key to the plan was that Blanchard's company had bought the bank in Bremen and that he was a friend of the Speaker. Gignilliatt had been a fifteen-year House member and had been one of Murphy's committee chairs. They knew Tom Murphy even if Holladay didn't. They brought credibility. Holladay brought a single sheet of paper. He would be the straight man. Early in 1994, just days before the General Assembly began, they went to the capitol for their appointment with Murphy. "I was just there," Holladay says. "I had my sheet of paper with the seven important items on it—in bullet form."

The speaker's office is more museum than office. His inner sanctum is the third of three offices. Pictures and artifacts cover the walls, the floor and the shelves. The frames on the wall are permanent. The pictures are rotated. It is a manly office. There is even one of those portraits of a bunch of dogs seated around a poker table. There are dogs of all breed and personality playing cards and over each of the canines someone has scribbled in the appropriate name of one of Murphy's inner circle.

The three men came into his office and Murphy rose and welcomed them. As soon as they sat down, Holladay briefly outlined why they were there and handed Murphy his sheet of paper. His work was done. Blanchard and Gignilliatt did all the talking.

Murphy listened, rolling his unlit cigar around in his mouth. He said little. He rocked back and forth in his chair and occasionally moaned or grunted. He did have one question, about exemption for major users of electricity. Holladay answered, and the other two men continued with their pitch.

Time was limited to thirty minutes. Forty minutes max. And they also had a plan for the finale. Tom Buck, the chairman of the Ways & Means Committee, was going to lunch with the Speaker and he was scheduled to arrive just as they finished. He would be their closer and he arrived on time and on cue. "Mr. Speaker, I hope you think this is a good idea," Buck said.

Terry Coleman, Larry Walker and some legislators came in about that time so the Speaker never really answered Buck. Murphy told Blanchard Gignilliatt and Holladay good-bye and left with his colleagues. Holladay was dumbfounded. He didn't know what to do. The others were calm and merely suggested they go downstairs to the governor's office and pay their respects to Zell Miller. "Jimmy, how did your meeting go?" Miller asked the Columbus banker.

"Best meeting I've had with the Speaker in ten years," he said, slapping his knee.

Holladay was stunned. Had they been in the same meeting he was? Miller could see he was puzzled. He looked at his department head and laughingly reminded him who the least important man in that room had been, then he explained the significance of what had just happened.

"You don't know what Jimmy's talking about, do you?"

"No doubt about that."

"It's kind of a game. If the Speaker doesn't say no, he means yes. So it sounds to me like you got everything you wanted," said Miller, who had been working around Tom Murphy since 1961.

Holladay was not entirely convinced until the following week at the annual Legislative Breakfast, which always offers a preview of the upcoming session. All the players are there. The governor speaks. The lieutenant governor speaks. So does the speaker. That morning, Miller mentioned the incentive package. So did Pierre Howard. And so did Murphy, who said it looked okay to him. "Right then," Holladay recalls, "I knew we had it passed. For me, it was a real learning experience about how things get done in Georgia."

For decades, the road to getting something done in Georgia has had an exit ramp to Tom Murphy's inner office. For those who haven't traveled that road before, it is an interesting stop. His office is interesting. He is interesting. So are his colorful trademarks.

Otis White, the founding editor of *Georgia Trend* magazine and a onetime *Columbus Ledger* reporter, is now a colleague of Holladay and the president of Market Street Services. He believes trademarks are useful to political figures. "Good politicians have always known how to use a few trademarks. It's like in a world of dark suits, a dash of red stands out. These people seem to know how to put a little spice in there so they can be singled out from the other politicians."

Trademarks help define Tom Murphy. Sometimes they get thoroughly mixed up with the reality. To the casual observer, he is the overstated character they have seen depicted in political cartoons. To the newcomer who only recently moved to Georgia, he is that cigar-chomping throwback who fits their stereotype of an Old South political boss. To the people who work around him in the House, he is larger than life. To his opponents, he is a vindictive dictator whose prime has passed, who should hang his Stetson at home instead of the capitol. To folks back home, he's still Tom.

To White, there is a touch of FDR to be found in Tom Murphy. "If you had taken Franklin Roosevelt and raised him in rural West Georgia, he would be a little like Murphy. Roosevelt had a flair for theatrics about him, you know. The cigarette holder, the jaunty wave of his hand, the pince-nez glasses balanced on his nose. There was almost a theatrical air to him and I think Murphy has a little bit of that, too." Murphy's theatrical style is apparently why the legend overshadows the reality.

13

BREAKFAST

WITH

MARCUS

HE HAD BEEN everybody's hero the day before and Larry Walker was still full of himself when he showed up at Marcus Collins hotel room early the next morning wearing Georgia Bulldog sweats and with a Superman ball cap cocked jauntily on his head. As soon as he walked in the room, folks started congratulating him for outfoxing the Republicans. Listening to their compliments, he got that 'deer in the headlights' look. He was going to be an easy prey for the experienced hunters who were just about finished with their first cup of coffee. Before setting their sights, they let him get his cup off the wall, the one with his name on it.

"Y'all sure did ambush those Republicans yesterday," somebody said.

"Bet Bob Irwin never saw that train coming," another guy added.

"What a move," a third fellow said. "Never saw that one before."

Walker filled his cup with hot coffee and his friends filled his head with praise. He sat down on the couch, all the time offering a play-by-play of the parliamentary ambush House Democrats had set for Irwin and his Republican counterparts during yesterday's session.

"We amended his amendment and it totally gutted his amendment," Walker said, sincerely proud of the slick maneuver that they had pulled off. It wasn't just the bill. To the old-time insiders, it was also an appreciation of the process.

His buddies listened and praised, waiting for the right moment to lock and load. It came. Time to fire. You go first, Newt. While most of the guys in the room had been bragging on old Larry, Newt Hudson, he seemed puzzled. He had a question for the Majority Leader.

"I was just wondering, Larry, where'd you get that idea?"

Elmore Thrash, right on cue, jumped in.

"He must have called Denmark," Thrash said.

Thrash, the longtime House Messenger, had invoked the name of Denmark Groover, who had gotten beat by a Republican and was back home in Macon practicing law after years and years in the Legislature. Groover knew the rules of the House like a Baptist knows the Bible. Surely, they hinted, Walker couldn't have figured out that ploy out himself. It didn't take long for Walker to realize that he was the one ambushed this time, and all of his buddies were laughing.

"You SOBs," Walker mumbled.

Every morning the atmosphere is the same as Tom Murphy's Inner Circle gathers for a piece of cheese toast and a hot cup of abuse. It is, in many ways, an early morning throwback to the days at the Henry Grady when that hotel was a political boarding house while the General Assembly was in session. There is no roll call, no votes are cast and Roberts does not rule.

Breakfast with Marcus, as Walker learned that morning, is not a place for the thin of skin. Abuse is always on the menu. Back and forth, forth and back, the regulars taunt one another. Nothing is sacred. Nothing is off-limits. Sometimes it is political, and sometimes it is profane. If authorities raided this gathering for political correctness, they would need a bus to haul in the violators. Neither is it a room where you should confess Republican leanings. To the early-risers who frequent Marcus Collins's room, a Republican is as welcome as Colonel Sanders at a hen house.

In the House pecking order, Collins's hotel room has always been only a door away from Murphy's. Their friendship dates back to 1961 and insiders have known for years that you get to the Speaker through Collins. He was the gate-keeper to the speaker's office and a good sounding board for legislators wanting to curry Murphy's favor on a favorite piece of legislation. And one of the best times to deliver your message was over breakfast. Sure, the wealthy South Georgia farmer cooks up some mean cheese toast and his coffee pot is always full. But between the taunts and the fun, there's political business being conducted. Murphy and Collins have not been too far apart since they arrived at the capitol as House freshmen. Both are fixtures under the dome. The two men came out of the same generation, and shared wartime memories and rural upbringings along with a fascination with the state budget. In recent years, Collins has served as a special assistant to Murphy during the legislative session.

That role will change, however. In August of 1999, Governor Roy Barnes tabbed the Mitchell county farmer to head the Georgia Tobacco Community Development Board, a panel that will distribute money to farmers from the state's $4.8 billion settlement with the tobacco industry. It was a controversial and expensive decision. After leaving the legislature, Collins was the state's Commissioner of Revenue, only to resign in 1996 after an audit revealed the department had lost track of about $1.5 billion in sales tax revenues. Barnes's appointment of Collins was seen as ageless good old boy politics. The move drew fire from all directions, leading an *Atlanta Constitution* editorial writer to say that Collins's appointment suggested "a conflict of interest about the size of Stone Mountain." A part-time job, the new position carried with it an $80,000-per-year salary.

IN THE PAST, it was Collins who the Inner Circle expected to deliver any bad news Murphy needed to hear. Sometimes, the news he delivered was not that bad. During a crucial House debate late in the 1998 session, Collins hurried into the chambers from the speaker's office and went straight to the podium where Murphy was presiding. Sidling up next to him, Collins drew close and whispered something in Murphy's ear. An observer would assume Collins was bringing a vital, important message. Afterward, Collins shared what he had said: "I gave him the Georgia basketball score."

But at Breakfast time, more was learned than just the basketball score. Lobbyists pushing a client's bill, show up just to show their face. Legislators who don't come every morning usually do when they have a bill pending, just to hear how it plays with the speaker's allies. Even governors need breakfast, and there are mornings when Roy Barnes drops by, leaving the pretense of office behind for awhile.

Most mornings, sitting in his favorite seat, there is Tom Murphy. He is not the cream in the coffee, but he does keep it stirred up, throwing in pithy comments from his seat by the end table. Before he arrives and after he leaves, he is the center of attention for these are his disciples. Most are close to his age. Most are rural. Most are part of the House leadership and, of course, they are all democrats. Yet, Murphy does not openly dominate the room, content to sit on the couch and listen, except for those moments when he agitates or throws a punch or a dart of his own. Usually, he arrives late, making a little bit of an entrance. He stays until he is ready to go and when he is ready to go it is a signal that maybe it is time for the others to knot up their ties and head for the capitol.

COFFEE IS READY every morning by 6:00 A.M. You need an invitation but not a key for Collins leaves the door ajar. Just come on in...unless your bulletproof vest is in the cleaners. After much high-level discussion, they even allowed a political reporter to join them, as long as his notebook was checked at the door. Collins greeted me, offering a piece of cheese toast, made with sharp cheese, of course. "This is the last time you'll be waited on, too," Collins said.

Introductions were made all around. Most of the fellows were House members, although some senators are welcome. All were Democrats, mostly from South Georgia. In and out of the room are lobbyists and state officials. On one end of the couch sat Thrash, who until his death in 1998 was House Messenger for years and years. He always sat next to the phone for he was the Speaker's morning wakeup call. If Murphy didn't want to come to the room for breakfast, somebody took his breakfast to him. "Elmore, how long you been coming up here?" Collins asked Thrash.

"Since Dr. Hardman was governor," he said.

Check your Georgia history and you'll see that Lamartine Hardman was governor of the state from 1927 to 1931. He was a physician when he wasn't picking peaches and as a state senator he authored Georgia's Prohibition Law. Thrash served as a legislative page when he first came to the capitol. A young Herman Talmadge was one of his fellow pages. At breakfast, Thrash—a frail little man with white hair—was sometimes the brunt of jokes and other times on the attack.

Thrash lived in Valdosta and on this morning Billy Langdale, his friend from Lowndes County was there for coffee. The day before Langdale had been re-elected to the influential Georgia Department of Transportation Board. From around the room came congratulations, then a jab.

"Billy, you know Elmore tried to run against you?" somebody said, pausing for just the right effect. "He got nominated, but he couldn't get a second."

Tom Buck, a veteran House member from Columbus, came in and fumbled around for his cup on the wall. He stayed in a different hotel so he wasn't there every morning. "But I come by here once or twice a week," he said. "You have to—just to see what they're saying about you."

"You can afford to miss a few days," Rep. Johnny Floyd of Rome explained. "This room is like a soap opera. You come back and pick right up like you had been here all the time. It never lets up."

Making a theatrical entrance, Bobby Rowan arrived. He came bearing fruit, cut up neatly in a Tupperware container. The others are just co-stars. Rowan is the feature act, the headliner. He is a former state senator from Enigma, a one-time candidate for lieutenant governor and a member of the Georgia Public Service Commissioner. But he missed his calling. The Lord intended for him to tell tales.

Rowan is writing a book about his experiences in politics and noting my presence Walker asked him if writers don't make up a lot of what they write. Rowan quickly pleaded innocent, but deflected the question toward me.

"No," I said. "I promised my Daddy a long time ago that if I ever started making up things that I'd quit newspapering and run for office."

"I think you just did that, so are you gonna run against Tom Buck?"

Now it was Tommy Irvin's turn to squirm. The Agriculture Commissioner is the dean of constitutional officers in the state so Rowan started targeting his remarks at the one-time House member from Fannin County. He zeroed in on how many times you can see Irvin's name if you travel around the state. Newt Hudson joined him.

"There it is, when you pull in a filling station," said Hudson, who represents three counties around his hometown of Rochelle. "Fellow told me that's why we can't rid of him. We couldn't get his name off stuff. It's everywhere."

"Oxendine's worse," Rowan said, referring to Insurance Commissioner John Oxendine, a Republican. "His name's on those gas pumps in even bigger letters than Tommy's."

Rowan then turned to Walker who was back lounging on the couch. Rowan said the Perry legislator ought to jump on Langdale and Frank Pinkston, another member of the DOT board who was there that morning. He said he had been driving down Interstate 75 and when he came up on Perry that the roads and exits were not properly marked.

"Larry, you gotta get Langdale to do something about this. If a fellow is looking for 'The Larry Walker Parkway,' you play hell finding it. A man of your stature deserves more respect than that," Rowan said. "It needs to be better marked, so folks will know you're from around there."

"Maybe they don't want folks to know that," Pinkston said.

"Tell about the road you got paved," Walker fired at Rowan.

"You mean the road that ran by my house?" he asked.

"That's the one."

"Well, when I got elected the first time, a fellow told me that a public official always gets the road in front of their house paved. Cause if you don't, people in your district will assume you can't get anything done up in Atlanta," Rowan said.

He continued, "For reasons that shall go unreported, the subject eventually turned to mule cuttin'. Should you not be from the country, that refers to the castration of mules. There was advice from every corner of the room. On which side you should approach the animal. On what kind of tools should be used. On very personal experiences in defrocking an animal. On the difference in cuttin' a mule and cutting a bull.

The talk went on for days, continuing from one breakfast to another.

"Several days later, I showed up again and mule cuttin' was still the topic of the day. Looking up, Thrash saw me come in."

"Got you a cup up there," he said.

"Nice," I? Who is this...?

"Third from the left, on the bottom," he said. "The one that says 'son-of-a-bitch' on it."

Actually, it said "Free-Loader."

Langdale said not to worry about names.

"Use one of those dead men's cups," he said.

No one is immune, which is part of the tradition. It is a tradition that is not likely to be continued when this generation passes from the scene. Walker is the youngest of the regulars. Most of them remember the World War, Korea and black and white TV. They also remember the County Unit System, the days when the General Assembly was dominated by folks who were as country as they are, when the House and Senate was filled with people who knew about 'cuttin' mules. As for the daily breakfast, black legislators only occasionally show up, and the same was true with women. Republicans don't bother. They'd be afraid to eat if they did.

It is a group that has prospered personally and politically under the New Georgia that has emerged in recent years, but they still like to fraternize with their buddies. Call them Good 'Ole' Boys or call them dinosaurs who were born in a Vanishing Georgia, but it is a fraternity that is going quickly away. With them will go history. With them will go a macho style at home on a hunting trip, a fishing boat or around a Thursday night poker game. With them also will go some things that are best gone.

But around Georgia politics, theirs is the generation that boosted the state to levels these 'ole' boys would never have imagined when they were the ones who dominated. They are the lonely survivors of that generation. One by one, they are watching their friends go away. Some are retiring. Some are being retired on election day. And, to their sadness, too many are showing up in the obituary section.

This is a colorful group and it is one that respects its leaders and its elders. Even the breakfast seating is part of the tradition. Marcus Collins has his private chair. Elmore Thrash had his. Newt Hudson has his corner of the room as do the others who regularly dine. No one saves a seat. They don't have to. They just know.

Such as the morning Hinson Mosely came in late.

"Just sit over there," someone said, not thinking.

Mosely, a lanky legislator from Jesup, got his coffee and sat down at the opposite end of the couch from Thrash. Walker moved over to give him more room. Mosely was telling them about a little barbecue that he was going to have for his closest friends. It was nearly 7:30, so nobody was really watching the door.

In walked Tom Murphy. While they were greeting the Speaker, nobody said a word to Mosely. They didn't have to. Mosely just picked up his coffee cup from the table and moved. He was sitting in the Speaker's seat.

As he looked around at the lineup of people that were there that morning, Murphy looked at me and shared a sharp observation. "Richard," he said, "you have had the privilege this morning of being in the presence of three of the state's biggest bull-shooters: Billy Langdale, Frank Pinkston, and Bobby Rowan."

A statement no one would dispute.

14

FEUDIN',

FUSSIN',

AND

FIGHTIN'

MILO DAKIN WAS sitting in the press office when Marcus Collins finally found him. The House was in session, and even over the annoying static you could hear the proceedings on the radio squawk box that broadcast the live action from upstairs.

Old Marcus had an idea. It had been bouncing around in his head and he wanted to bounce it off Dakin, the former newspaper reporter that Tom Murphy had hired to handle the news media. Even if you just ask him the time of day, Collins can make it sound as if he's sharing the secret of life with you, but he is also a man of few words. "It's time for Tom to patch it up with Al," he said.

Tom Murphy and Al Burruss had been at odds since Burruss threw a spear at the king and missed. More than a year before, Burruss had gone after the Speaker's job and failed. Since then, he and his followers had been political outcasts, shivering outside the door. The veteran House member thought it was time to open that door. "He ought to let Al preside," Collins continued. "You go tell him."

Milo Dakin is an impulsive Cajun, but this wasn't impulse, this was logic. "It makes so much sense I'm going to go do it right now," he said.

Collins and Dakin went straight to the House Chambers. The Mitchell County legislator casually strolled to the rear of the room and waited as Dakin made his way to the podium. A debate was going on, but Murphy motioned him to come closer and listened to what Dakin had to say. It took only a moment. Then Dakin stepped back to the floor.

In a single motion, Murphy turned the wooden gavel around in his hand and grabbed it by the head. Looking to his right where Al Burruss was sitting, he pointed the handle at the Marietta legislator. Burruss didn't move. He thought it was meant for somebody else. Realizing what was happening, he came forward and took the gavel. Murphy went straight to his own seat on the floor. Not a word was spoken, but a message was sent. Peace had been declared.

A simple gesture, but a major step. Murphy had offered his hand and Burruss had accepted it. A major wound was healed and Tom Murphy's position was rock solid. Essentially, it would never again be seriously challenged. But the defeat of Burruss in 1976 was not nearly as important as welcoming the prodigal back home, for now most of Murphy's enemies were again his friends.

Only a few weeks after Murphy became speaker in 1974, there were newspaper reports that Al Burruss might challenge him when the next vote was taken. Outsiders found it difficult to take the new leader seriously. They preferred to think of him as only a caretaker. By 1976, it was more serious than that. A powerful coalition, including Governor Jimmy Carter and a number of key lobbyists, wanted Murphy out. They thought their influence coupled with the large freshman class of black members who had been elected that year could easily elect Burruss, the slightly-built speaker pro-tem.

In the weeks leading up to the 1976 session, both men were busy.

"I was driving my car all over Georgia, just like he flew all over the state," Murphy says, years later still drawing a distinction about their mode of travel. For the members, that was a new experience. When George L. Smith became the first elected Speaker of the House, it was a quiet caucus vote with no opposition. When Murphy was elected the first time, it was also low-key since so much of the politicking was done while George L. was hospitalized in a coma. Now members were being openly courted by two of their own.

Harsh words were spoken in the process. Not by Burruss but by some of his supporters. Perhaps the harshest attack came from Representative Tom Blanton of Carrollton, who gave one of Burruss's nominating speeches. His words were so biting to Murphy that for a long time he kept a copy of Blanton's speech under glass on his desktop as a reminder of what was said.

The night before the vote, Murphy and a group of his strongest allies met in his hotel suite. Nearly a dozen were there—Collins, Joe Frank Harris, Crawford Ware, Tom Buck, Henry Reaves, Bill Lee and a few more. They went down the membership roster, person by person. Unless everyone agreed on a name, they didn't add him or her to their column. They came up with 118 positive commitments. "Twenty people lied," Murphy says. "We got ninety-eight votes, and I know which twenty didn't tell the truth."

Those ninety-eight were enough to keep him on the job and now his friends wanted blood to flow. They wanted people singled out and they wanted public punishment. Murphy didn't listen to them.

"If I had, it would have been chaos," he says. "We never would have healed."

Burruss, of course, was no longer speaker pro-tem and he also lost his chairmanship, so did two other verbal detractors. Others just fell in line, grabbing permanent seats on the Murphy bandwagon. But when the gesture was made and Burruss took the gavel that day, he outwardly rejoined the flock. The case was all but closed. Closure truly came when Burruss was elected majority leader. "He came to me and said he wanted to run for the job and I said I wouldn't work against him—but I wouldn't vote for him either. Al said some of my people had told him they'd help him if I wasn't going to be against him. I told him to go ahead," Murphy says.

In the years that followed, Burruss became one of Murphy's most solid backers. He again became a key player in the House. At the same time, he developed a close personal bond with the Speaker that went beyond politics.

On one of the final nights of the 1986 session, it was getting late. It was also getting late for Burruss, who would die of pancreatic cancer in a few months. Everyone knew he was ill. You could look at him and know. Murphy had retreated to his office for a quick break and Burruss asked if he could join him. His back was in horrible pain and he sat down on the floor, resting his back against the couch in Murphy's office, looking for a moment's relief. "Mr. Speaker, I want to tell you something," Burruss said. "There ain't nobody in this world that I have more respect for than you. You could have ostracized me when I ran against you. You didn't. You let me come back. You let me participate."

It was several years before another legislator challenged Murphy's position and this time it was a young legislator from Dublin who said he wanted to expand the circle of leadership and to modernize the way the House was run. DuBose Porter says he had neither the seniority nor the experience to be a committee chairman when he went after Murphy in 1993 but he thought it was a time for change.

Friends of Murphy think Porter was being pushed into that decision by Zell Miller since he was one of the governor's floor leaders. Porter says that was not the case, but rather that like so many other legislators he was just impatient. "We just needed to open it up more, to reflect the changes in Georgia," he says. "It is hard for people to elect a new legislator, send him or her to Atlanta, and just let him stay here for three, four, or five terms before he is effective. People expect more out of you. They expect you to accomplish something. I wanted to change that."

A legislative slush fund had been exposed around that same period and Porter believed voters identified that incident with the old way of doing business. He started talking to colleagues about that and how people connected such things to the small group that was in power. He began to talk about running for speaker and he might as well have bought air time. Information moves quickly at the capitol, especially if it's political. So the word was out, even before Porter wanted to be out. "It was like an explosion," Porter says.

He quickly resigned his position with the governor and went to work. As he began talking to people, few could believe he was really doing this. From the beginning, Porter says, he wanted to spell out their differences, not to personally attack Murphy. Just talking to some people wasn't easy. "There were a few people who were scared for anybody to know that I come up to talk to them, but really most folks were pretty nice about it."

Porter was pushing for the pre-filing of bills so legislators would have time to study them. He wanted better use of technology. He wanted things that would help the legislators better use their time. He even used new technology to spread his message, recording a video that he sent to every House Democrat.

The vote wasn't close.

Porter thinks it was worth the effort, claiming that most of the things he sought have been installed by Murphy. Now the daily calendar is on the House website so people around the state can keep up with legislation. Bills are now pre-filed so legislators will have advance knowledge of what is coming. More than anything, Porter believes the circle of leadership has been expanded.

"I think that race showed the Speaker that people were ready to be more involved, and he has allowed that," Porter says. "He's still as tough as ever, but he has a great ability to understand people and change. He has brought more people in. There's more diversity in the inner circle. He's brought in women and he has brought in more members of the Black Caucus. He understands that to maintain the power structure, that was necessary. Give him credit. He understood that and he did it."

Porter says he and Murphy never mention the race anymore, though some of his colleagues do. "Sometimes I'll have a project in the budget and I'll go into his office to talk about it and the people around the table will start puking it up, saying I get things because of that. I just tell them that they should have seen what I could have if I hadn't run."

As it was with Al Burruss, there was a time of retribution when DuBose Porter was a name seldom called. But before long, Porter was appointed a subcommittee chairman for the budget. Finally, he became chairman of the all-important Education Committee. Now, he chairs the University System Committee and Murphy tells people that Porter is one of his most efficient chairs.

So Murphy does seem to understand and he does often make declarations of Christian forgiveness. Nevertheless, much of his time as Speaker has been spent *feudin'*, *fussin'* and *fightin'* with somebody in Georgia politics. Be it Zell Miller. Be it Tom Perdue. Be it Pierre Howard. Be it Mike Bowers. Be it Tom Moreland. Be it DuBose Porter. Be it the press. Be it any number of state Republicans. He has never run from a good fight and even now, in the twilight of his years, he will challenge you—as Republican House member Mitchell Kaye learned not too many years ago.

Accomplishments or not, these conflicts will be part of his legacy. He helped build MARTA in Atlanta. They named the ballroom in the Georgia World Congress Center for him in appreciation for his efforts. He supported the Georgia Dome. He is building developmental highways all over the state. He has been part of improving the state's bond standing and keeping the budget in line. He has been a supporter of business and growth.

MURPHY AND MILLER. Miller and Murphy.

For three decades, feuding between Tom Murphy and Zell Miller was part of the fiber of state politics. It was a rivalry that will follow them to their graves. They were as interconnected as the coaches of two rival football teams. Like football fans who say "I'm for Georgia all season long—until they play Georgia Tech," these two had supporters who rooted for both of them until they went head to head. Their arena was the State Capitol. And as sure as Tech meets Georgia in early November, Murphy and Miller would go head to head every January.

Miller is now semi-retired to the college classroom at the University of Georgia, Emory University and Young Harris College. But, in the summer of 1999, the former governor had a phone call from Bremen, Georgia, a Mr. Murphy.

"He called and wanted me to speak to a Democratic Party meeting down there," Miller says. "I've *always* done what the Speaker asked me to do, so Shirley and I drove down there from Young Harris."

For some reason, Shirley Miller had always been their peacemaker. The Speaker went out of his way to say nice things about her, respectfully calling her "Miss Shirley." She got along well with him, too, telling people that he reminded her of her father, a former county sheriff in the mountains of North Carolina.

At the meeting in Haralson County, Murphy introduced the two-term governor, remembering clearly and honestly the sixteen years that one was speaker and one was lieutenant governor. And as usual, he mentioned the former First Lady. "If it hadn't have been for Miss Shirley there getting between us, the two of us would have killed each other several times." And there were times that folks wished she would have gotten out of the way.

Theirs was one of the most public feuds in capitol history, outdoing Carter versus Maddox because of its longevity. There were times it was humorous. But there were times when security guards should have confiscated each man's gavel. It first erupted over open meetings in the earliest days of Miller's first term as lieutenant governor in 1975 — even before he took his oath of office. It continued in 1989 as they squabbled over a state lottery and erupted again in 1997 when they fought over DUI legislation.

The Murphy-Miller relationship is well documented. It is a cross-stitch, endlessly weaving in and out of the two men's lives and careers. There is eight years difference in their ages, but their heritages are similar. Each was reared in a hard-core Democratic family, revering the memory of FDR. Each family was anti-Talmadge and said so. Each enjoyed a head-strong, undisciplined childhood. Each harbored a desire to coach. Each came from a family active in local politics, with parents on both sides serving as the mayor of their respective hometowns. Each family tree could be traced back to the Georgia General Assembly, Murphy's to the House, Miller's to the Senate. Each of them had a leadership role in the administration of Lester Maddox. Each is an obsessive baseball fan. Each one reveres traditional country music. Each one respects Georgia history. Each one cheers for Georgia Bulldog football. Each one was and is consumed by the process of politics, enjoying the chase as much as the finish line. The two men also share such adjectives as stubborn, complex, shy, insecure, and ill-tempered.

They were elected on the same day in November of 1960 and arrived at the state capitol on the same day in January of 1961. They joined a promising group of legislators, including three future governors—Senator Carl Sanders of Augusta, Representative George Busbee of Albany and Miller—two future House Speakers—George T. Smith of Cairo and Murphy—along with a number of other men who went on be federal and state officials. Even as the session began, it was an explosive year in the state and around that capitol but their paths crossed very seldom. Their allegiances were to separate bodies, which accounts for a lot of the fusses that were to follow.

Like his father, Miller took his oath in the Georgia Senate. In the scheme of Georgia politics, it had traditionally been seen as a lesser body. Under the old County Unit System, many of its seats were rotated from county to county so there was little time for anyone to build a personal power base. Ernest Vandiver was the governor in 1961 and it was under his administration that the House first became involved in the writing of the budget, shifting influence toward that side of the capitol and beginning the quiet move toward an independent House six years later.

Following his brother James and his cousin Harold, Murphy went into the House. He would soon begin to believe in the scripture that said all good bills begin in the House. As his mentor, he latched on to J. Roy McCracken, a lawyer from Jefferson County and a legislator since 1935. McCracken got few headlines, but he was a respected member of the House. Murphy was learning the old ways, the old values, never really thinking that one day he might lead that body into a far different era.

Murphy has never left his seat in the House, becoming Speaker after thirteen years. But a restless Miller only stayed in the Senate two terms. Over the years after he left the Senate, he twice ran unsuccessfully for Congress, worked in two state jobs and was appointed chairman of the Georgia Democratic Party by Governor Jimmy Carter. And on the same day that the Atlanta newspapers carried a number of headlined stories about Murphy being elected Speaker of the House in December of 1973, there was a less-ballyhooed article reporting that Zell Miller, an official with the State Pardon & Paroles Board, was resigning that post to run for lieutenant governor. Their heads were really about to bump.

Murphy had been Speaker only eleven months when Miller broke out ahead of a crowded field and became lieutenant governor. By then, both legislative bodies had gone through a metamorphosis. The Senate leadership was entrenched and graying and the House was becoming younger, but at the same time the Senate was considered the more liberal of the two. Locked and loaded, Miller hit the capitol running, proposing what he called a democratization of the Senate and promising that the proceedings of the Senate would become much more open, throwing a challenge at the House in the process.

Hearing of these plans, Murphy was condescending. "I was very sorry to hear that the lieutenant governor—who is a fine man and old friend of mine who came to the Senate the same year I came to the House—said that he would not appoint a conference committee unless they were pledged to have opening meetings...but maybe Miller is just inexperienced. I doubt that the lieutenant governor—and he's a distinguished gentleman and a very intelligent gentleman—I doubt that he has ever served on a conference committee on the budget."

As much as anything, there was a new kid on the playground, and the older kids were going to find out what he was made of. It was a rivalry between two men determined not to let the other one have the last word and the news media was delighted.

"We're an awful lot alike," Miller admits. "We both are quick to lose our temper and say things on the spur of the moment that we might not have said if we thought about it a little longer. When you put two people with hot tempers together, people who like to win, who as Dick Pettys says, 'go for the jugular,' that's what happens."

They quarreled over money. They smoked peace pipes. They promised to be good boys. They always knew how to rile the other, to push the other one's buttons, often resorting to childish name-calling. Murphy once referred to Miller as "the extinguished lieutenant governor" and at one inauguration ceremony needled him by saying he was "the past, present and future lieutenant governor." Miller, never short of stinging insults himself, once called the House "Murphy's Mausoleum."

Much of what was happening was no different than what happens in other states and between other state legislatures. When there are separate houses there are separate ideas, philosophies and styles. The national government and the historic competition between congressmen and senators in Washington is the best example of them all. Add the spice of two hot-headed leaders such as Tom Murphy and Zell Miller and you have a pot of chili that would make a Texan sweat.

They were making headlines all over the state, but Murphy seldom came out on top. Miller enjoyed the repartee with reporters. He spoke their language and the new lieutenant governor became the flag bearer for change while Murphy — on the job hardly a year — was the epitome of the country boys who had controlled state government for so long. So soon the war between the two leaders was all over the newspaper — from the front page to the editorial page. On the 6 o'clock news, they were always good for a biting byte, goading each other and the opposing body.

Veteran legislators remember those incidents well. "When we were working around spats between the speaker and Miller, I don't think we were affected too much," House

Majority Leader Larry Walker says. "Of course we laughed and joked about it at times. When there was tension, sometimes I hated to go over there to the Senate. At those times, we would laugh and say that in wartime it was the soldiers who got killed. The generals were up on top of the hill. We'd laugh and say we were the ones getting hurt."

"It was not a position I liked," says Roy Barnes, who as a Senator was often a courier between the two men. "I was loyal to Zell, but I could always talk to the Speaker, so I carried the messages back and forth. And then, when I became the governor's floor leader, the Speaker would try and kill the messenger."

Their personal rifts slowed down the legislative time clock, but observers generally agree that nothing vital to the state was ever affected. Some even maintain that Murphy's and Miller's fussing improved some of the legislation being considered. History is still answering some of those questions. But there is no dispute that both Murphy and Miller were taking on the role of lightning rods for their two bodies. To rally their troops, they needed a common enemy. While attention was being drawn to their individual differences, it allowed members of the House and Senate to carry out their business, creating legislation that vaulted Georgia several steps ahead of its neighbors.

Miller admits today that if there hadn't have been a Tom Murphy, he would have had to create one and that Murphy would have done the same. For sixteen years, they were perfect foils for one another. Miller proposing and suggesting. Murphy asking how he would pay for those programs. Miller in his cowboy boots speaking from the podium at Madison Square Garden. Murphy back home drinking coffee and talking to the same old boys at Garrett's Pharmacy in Bremen.

"Their differences were always overplayed," says Bill Lee, who retired in 1998 after forty-one years in the House. "There were some differences. I admit that. But if everyone agreed around here, it would be a bad situation."

During the years both were armed with gavels, no one would have trusted either with a hatchet, but in 1990 they buried the ones they had carried for so long. Zell Miller became governor of Georgia and on election night one of the first people to ride a private elevator to his suite at the Colony Square Hotel was Tom Murphy. It might have seemed to be a surprising move for Murphy, but Miller was now the governor and he was still the Speaker. For him, it was nothing more than simple respect and no one respected that office more than he. Besides, Haralson County had gone for Miller.

In a few days, Miller returned the gesture, personally going to Murphy's office for a face-to-face meeting. "I might get elected without your help," he told the Speaker, "but I can't run the state without you." Their shared stubbornness was history, replaced by growing respect, at first in the offices they held, then more outwardly with the other person.

For the two terms and eight years that Miller was governor, the two men co-existed well. After years of opposition to a state lottery, Murphy acquiesced to Georgia voters and to Miller and it passed through the House uneventfully. Near the end of Miller's second term, his years of work on strengthened DUI legislation finally came to fruition and that package of bills became law, despite personal pleas from Murphy who had never supported the measures.

"Zell was a better governor than he was a lieutenant governor," says Marcus Collins, echoing the sentiments of Bill Lee and some other Murphy cohorts. It was a begrudging, backdoor compliment at best.

Murphy's compliments go further than that. Remembering their long-running public debate over a state sales tax on grocery items, he says Miller was much more liberal on financial matters as lieutenant governor than he was when he became Georgia's chief executive.

"I guess before he didn't realize he was responsible for the money and as governor he became a little more conservative," Murphy says. "He's intelligent. He saw the handwriting on the wall if he didn't become a little more conservative. And he did."

Looking back on the give and take between the two of them and the two bodies they once represented, Miller says he admires the loyalty that House members always gave to Murphy—an admiration he probably didn't always feel. "Loyalty is important in legislative politics. You have to talk to all these different people and try to get them to be with you. They can't stand with you forever so you are always going to others and lining them up. And a person is not going to be loyal to you if you're not loyal to them. It's very much a two-way street. Those House members have always known that. That's why sometimes they follow him where their own personal politics would be better off if they didn't. And I can't say I don't respect him for that. I do."

Miller wasn't the only person to quarrel with Murphy. Former Department of Transportation director Tom Moreland was also a target. As with Miller, it exploded over taxes. Moreland favored an increase in gasoline taxes to pay for roads and Murphy always opposed him. They also fought bitterly over allowing fourteen-foot house trailers on Georgia highways, a fight Moreland eventually won. "And it liked to have run that industry all the way out of Georgia," Murphy says, still going after the last word.

During the administration of Joe Frank Harris, Murphy nearly was able to force Moreland out of his powerful position. With Murphy's support, Harris tried to engineer a secret meeting of the state's DOT board at a suburban Atlanta hotel at which time the governor was going to urge the board to fire the highway head. Moreland's supporters leaked word of the meeting to the news media and Harris did not follow through with his plans.

MURPHY ALSO WENT to war with Tom Perdue, who at the time was a key aide to Governor George Busbee. To Murphy and others, Perdue was meddling in matters beyond his position as a member of the governor's staff. That conflict boiled over in 1986 when Harris and Perdue—joined by another of Murphy's strongest adversaries, Attorney General Mike Bowers—turned their attention to the Georgia State Patrol, an agency that Murphy has always said was one of his pets.

Heading the patrol at that time was Hugh Hardison, a former Georgia Tech football player from Cedartown whose father was a friend of Murphy's father when both worked for the Central of Georgia Railroad. Tom Murphy had known Hardison all of his life. Allegations against Hardison revolved around an alleged ticket-fixing scandal that specifically involved officials of Callaway Gardens in Pine Mountain, Georgia. It had resulted in the public firing of Hardison.

The day after the firing and the issuance of a 500-page investigative report, Murphy met with reporters at the first news conference he had ever called in his twelve years as speaker. He handed out a blistering typewritten statement that covered four legal-sized pages. In plain words, it lashed out at Harris, Perdue, Bowers, the Georgia Bureau of Investigation and the Georgia Department of Public Safety board, making broad political threats and calling names.

When he finished, no one doubted where he stood.

"I think what happened yesterday was a tragic day in the history of Georgia. They've taken probably the finest public official in Georgia, one of the purest public officials in Georgia and removed him from public office. I deem it a little foolish for me to think that it would be a coincidence that one of the lead investigators of the GBI team investigating Colonel Hardison happens to be from the home town of Tom Perdue. I would deem it furthermore foolish for me to deem it coincidence that the major who is the Deputy Director who was placed there by Colonel Hardison at Mr. Perdue's direction is also from Mr. Perdue's hometown of Americus. I deem that too much coincidence, and I'll leave it to you to form your own conclusion about that."

Citing details of the case as seen by Hardison, Murphy got more vitriolic. "It appears to me what we have done in Georgia is that we have created a Gestapo in the form of the GBI for the Attorney General and Tom Perdue. It further appears to me that no city, county or state official is safe...Even if it comes out like Colonel Hardison, where you hadn't committed any crimes, they can destroy you. This I think is wrong."

Aiming directly at Bowers, he said the Attorney General had been the lawyer for the Department of Public Safety and Hardison and his administrative offices. He was also, Murphy said, the lawyer for the defendants and their prosecutor, and was a member of the Board of Public Safety that was trying the case. To Murphy, this was a blatant conflict of interest. But he didn't stop at the legal term.

"It appears to me that the Attorney General is representing himself as a member of the board. I have been a lawyer thirty-seven years and it has been a saying among us lawyers for thirty-seven years that any lawyer that represents himself or herself has a fool for a client. Well, now, don't misunderstand me. I'm not calling the Attorney General a fool. I'm just saying that's what us lawyers always said about each other."

Murphy then suggested that maybe the time had come for a private, non-political, Public Safety Board in Georgia and said he would entertain such a move from members of the House. He also admitted Hardison had erred in several ways but said four out of five men in the uniformed patrol still supported him. As for Harris, Murphy said he still considered the former House member a close friend.

"But I must admit that I am disappointed that he did not take a more personal part in the investigation and in the decision that was made. The only change in our relationship as far I am concerned is that in the past when there was an issue I've always been willing to give him the benefit of the doubt. I doubt I will be able to do that in the future. That will be the only change as far as I'm concerned. He may have a different feeling after this press conference, but that is my feeling about it."

When Murphy finished, reporters started firing questions.

Reporter: "What do you think Michael Bowers' motivation was?"

Murphy: "If you don't know son, you have no business sitting there with that pad."

Reporter: "Bowers directed the GBI. Do you see him having any role in it?"

Murphy: "I think he basically did what he was told to do. I think the report is slanted, what little I've read of it, it is slanted very badly."

Reporter: "Mr. Speaker, you talked about your relationship with the governor changing . . ."

Murphy: "I didn't say it was going to change now, I said I didn't anticipate there would be any difference in us, that he was still my friend, and I was still his friend. But in the future, I would not give him the benefit of the doubt that I have in the past. That's all I said."

Reporter: "I take that goes for the Attorney General as well?"

Murphy: "I have never given him the benefit of the doubt."

Reporter: "Did the governor let Mr. Perdue get out of hand?"

Murphy: "I have thought that for three years."

Murphy: "Thank you."

With that, the press conference ended.

Not that the peculiar connection between those men was over.

Verbal pot shots between Murphy and Bowers have never really ended. In 1997, as Murphy confronted Governor Miller over a bill involving Medicaid fraud, it was an opportunity to direct a barb at Bowers. Going to the well of the House, Murphy had a rolled-up a letter from the governor in his hand that quoted a decision made by Bowers. His face was flushed as he waved it at the members.

"I don't like Mike Bowers," he said. "He doesn't like me. We make no bones about it. But this letter from my friend, the governor...when it says I consort with thieves, my friends that hurts...."

As Attorney General, Bowers was often controversial, once ruling that an intern in his office could not be hired because she was an admitted lesbian. Other decisions by the outspoken Bowers also made headlines. He made political headlines when he announced he was resigning from the Democratic Party and becoming a Republican. He made them again in 1997 when he resigned his position to begin a campaign for the Republican gubernatorial nomination. Some editorial writers said flatly that Bowers might become the state's first Republican governor in modern times.

The Bowers campaign was picking up steam in the spring of 1998 when after weeks of whispers and allegations on a bitter website that suddenly appeared on the Internet, Bowers held a press conference and revealed that he had had a ten-year affair with a woman on his staff. His wife was at his side and Bowers said it was something she had known about for some time. He said he would not drop out of his combative campaign against Atlanta businessman Guy Millner, who had previously challenged Zell Miller in 1994.

Handling Millner's campaign was Tom Perdue, who once flirted with a congressional campaign before going on to work for Governor Joe Frank Harris. He left state politics to begin a banking career and resurfaced as a political consultant. His forte was personal politics, campaigns that were always on the attack. He made headlines in Alabama while working for then-Governor Fob James, firing most of his senior staff while the Republican chief executive was on a European trip. When James returned, Perdue was gone and some of the staff members were rehired.

When word of Bowers' personal indiscretions became public, Murphy says he was not surprised. Years before, when the illicit affair was just beginning, he says a number of capitol employees came to him and told him what was going on. Some of them were women who worked in the Attorney General's office. "Don't come to me," Murphy told them. "Go to the press."

But, he confesses, he was curious. Feigning an excuse after hearing about the former Playboy Bunny, Murphy went to the Attorney General's office personally so he could see what she looked like.

When asked why didn't he go public with the revelation himself, Murphy responded "Because I am many things, but I am not a gossip monger."

Neither Mike Bowers nor Tom Perdue was successful in 1998. Millner defeated Bowers in the Republican Primary, but despite the scandal still being discussed, the margin was still surprisingly slim. But in the general election, Roy Barnes gave Millner his third statewide political defeat in six years.

WHAT DOES MURPHY say about his adversaries? Regarding Bowers: "I didn't have much use for Mr. Bowers in the past and still don't. He is a hypocrite of the first order as far as I'm concerned."

Regarding Perdue: "I once called him a son-of-a-bitch. The truth isn't in him. I did say I wanted to whip his butt and all I can say is that his character hasn't changed."

The words between Tom Murphy and Zell Miller became much more civil than the darts Murphy continues to fling at Bowers and Perdue. In Miller's final term, though they bickered over politics, there were visits and phone calls between the two hard-line Democrats that were respectful and even affectionate.

It was the final night of the 1998 General Assembly. The business of making laws was winding down and so was the political career of Zell Bryan Miller. Everything that was happening was for the final time. Pictures were being made and so were memories. In a few minutes, he would be visiting the Senate and the House for the last time as governor. Emotions were high. So much had happened since the two old foes first came to that capitol in 1961 and sitting in the governor's office, he shared perhaps his most profound compliment of Tom Murphy. "I can't say I would have done things any different than he did if I had been the Speaker. Presiding over the House is harder than presiding over the Senate because you have so many more bodies," Miller says. "Do the multiplication. He had twice as many members as I did. I had to come up with twenty-nine votes to pass something. He had to come up with ninety-one. So yes, I would have probably presided very similar to him...but I don't know that I would have done it as effectively."

In a few minutes, joined by tearful staff members, he went back to where it began for him: visiting the Senate and speaking to the members from the podium where he once presided. He told them how much he loved that hall and that body.

Moving slowly through the crowds in the capitol rotunda, the governor waited outside heavy wooden doors that lead into the House Chambers. Doorkeeper Ward Edwards knocked, then entered. Finally, in a flourish, Edwards bowed, and announced the arrival of Zell Miller and his escorts in the House of Representatives.

Everybody in the House chamber was on their feet as the smiling governor started down the center aisle, reaching out to old friends as he walked. For him, the Senate would always be home. This hall had always been a battleground. Blood had been shed in this room. His blood and Tom Murphy's. But none of that mattered that night.

Waiting at the podium, Tom Murphy welcomed the governor and First Lady then introduced them to the cheering members. Miller recommended his job to anyone, and Roy Barnes, his ultimate successor, was out there in front of him that evening. He also recalled the fights they had had — "and you know how I love a good fight."

Zell Miller didn't talk long. He didn't have to, for these people knew what he was feeling. Everyone stood and cheered. Then, in a spontaneous gesture that sealed their years of fussing and feuding, Tom Murphy grabbed first Shirley Miller, then Zell Miller, and for only a moment the three shared a hug.

15

A SHEEP

IN WOLF'S

CLOTHING

SIX TIMES BEFORE Larry Walker had nominated Tom Murphy as Speaker of the House. Now he had been recognized by the clerk for a seventh and for five minutes the gentleman from Perry turned the chamber into a class on Georgia history. "I do this, realizing that possibly this is the last time I will have this privilege. Likewise, you should understand that perhaps this is the last time you will have the historic opportunity to vote for this great Georgian," Walker began.

It was 11 January 1999. Maybe this really would be the final time Tom Murphy stood for the job. He was coming up on his seventy-fifth birthday. He had health problems that go along with aging. He had held that lofty position nearly a quarter of a century, longer than anyone in the past and, likely as not, longer than anyone in the future. So Walker, an old-fashioned South Georgia orator, took the legislators and the gallery back to the second Monday in January 1973.

Only Walker and a few others were present in that same hall when the 1973 General Assembly was called to order. He reminded them that Jimmy Carter was governor, that George L. Smith was Speaker and that Tom Murphy was speaker pro-tem. He ran down an abbreviated list of who the House members were that day. He talked about the makeup of the body then: two women, thirteen African Americans and twelve Republicans. He recalled that George L. Smith died eleven months after that and that the House elected Tom Murphy of Haralson County as its new Speaker. He listed the governors who followed: George Busbee, Joe Frank Harris and Zell Miller, and pointed out that during all of their terms that Murphy remained as Speaker. "Not only has he served, he has given himself in a remarkably outstanding manner, being preeminent over others and striding over this legislature...this capitol...and this state like a giant colossus."

He talked about legislators of the past. "George L. Smith had a great political mind. Denny Groover was rapier quick and a master tactician. George Busbee was indefatigable. Wash Larson, Elliott Levitas and Bobby Hill were brilliant. Robin Harris, Papa Dent and Chappel Mathews demanded respect. Joe Frank Harris was honest and sincere. Bill Lee was a great judge of people. Sloppy Floyd and Marcus Collins understood the budget. But Tom Murphy was, and is, all of these things."

Then Walker, a veteran lawmaker himself in his mid-fifties, touched on what may be the foundation on which Tom Murphy has consciously or unconsciously built his personal and political life. In doing so, the Democratic Majority Leader talked about a book written by Tom Brokaw of NBC News. As a young reporter at WSB-TV in Atlanta, Brokaw once covered the Georgia state capitol and the Georgia House. His book, *The Greatest Generation*, spotlights the generation of Tom Murphy. "Speaker Murphy is seventy-four years of age. He was in the South Pacific fighting for our country on his twentieth birthday. He is of that generation of which Tom Brokaw says in his new book, 'I think this is the greatest generation any society has ever produced. I am in awe of them and I feel privileged to have been a witness to their lives and their sacrifices.' Mr. Speaker, I am in awe of you, and I thank you for allowing me to be your friend...allowing me to witness your life and your sacrifices...and allowing me once again to nominate you...and for giving me the opportunity to once again vote for you as our Speaker. January 11th, 1999. Georgia House members, I present to you for your consideration as our Speaker, the person whom I consider as possibly the greatest legislator to ever serve in this body, Tom Murphy of Haralson County."

In a seconding speech, Representative Jimmy Skipper of Americus called Murphy the "Energizer Bunny" who keeps going, going and going. He referred to critics who say he has had the job too long, that he is too powerful and that he is old-fashioned by reminding members who makes the House work and the state work and at the same time "looks after people who are many times less fortunate than ourselves."

He was not without opposition. Republican Minority Leader Bob Irvin was his opponent. He was depicted by a colleague as "new leadership," a "bridge-builder" and a man who would not "rely on force or intimidation." Irvin was in the House that elected Murphy and his listed occupation was "law school student." Representative Tom Campbell, a Republican from Roswell, nominated Irvin and said he would be capable of holding a position that Campbell compared to "herding cats."

Murphy won with a flourish, with members on their feet cheering boisterously as they did the previous twelve times. Many, as Larry Walker indicated in his nominating speech, thought this would likely be his final two year term— an assumption they had wrongly made several times before. As

Speaker, he has outlasted four governors and is working on his fifth. Scores of legislators have sat in those seats in front of him. He has buried some of his most loyal allies. He has had more than one heart attack and a stroke. The state has changed and so has the House. Yet, he still holds the gavel.

But even now, he remains that enigmatic country lawyer from Bremen. For decades, people have tried to explain, defend and understand this complex man. He has been called "Speaker of the Forgotten." He has been labeled a tyrant, a dictator, a bully, a "rustic King Arthur," a king-maker, a despot and a dinosaur. Reporters have rhapsodized about his cowboy hat and his cheap cigars. Friends say he "is the most misunderstood man in Georgia." All of these things, though often accurate, fail to define this self-drawn caricature who bellows at Republicans and weeps over children.

Walker was on the right track, for it begins with his generation. He was born in 1924 so he remembers the Depression, not as a historical event but a reality that brought people to his back door willing to work for a nickel so they could buy a loaf of bread. Other generations don't remember banks failing, small-town banks in which their own father owned shares. Other generations haven't seen flat-bed rail cars with families aboard them creeping through their town.

These things impacted Murphy and his politics.

His father was a railroad man, punching the clock for the Central of Georgia for forty-four years. His job was safe and steady while others struggled. Murphy wanted to follow the lead of his father and two older brothers on to the back of the powerful steam engines that came through Bremen. His father, however, preached the value of education wanting, like most parents of that generation, for their sons to have more than they did. He watched his mother work in the cotton patch, continuing to cut the grass at her house until days before she died.

These things impacted Murphy and his politics. It is more than remembering history. What helped shape him was watching how people dealt with these gut-wrenching setbacks. Many shareholders ignored their debts when the bank failed. Murphy's father mortgaged his house and paid everything he owed. Some people avoided eye-contact with people needing help. Murphy's father reached into his pocket for a nickel and gave it to a man who bought a loaf of unsliced bread. And he vividly recalls that the people who came to his family's back door were looking for work, not a handout. They had pride.

"Unfortunately, most folks have forgotten this," Murphy says. "Things have got so good. They spend money like it's going to continue forever. I guess I'm just tight." His children laugh about his spending habits—which are the same spending habits he wants the State of Georgia to use. Anyone who has dealt with him over the state budget would agree that he is genuinely tight.

It was the time of Franklin Delano Roosevelt and his Democratic Party, a political party that created jobs and compassionate programs to feed hungry people. He was people's friend. He talked to them in their living rooms. He assured them that things would be better, and they believed. He connected with them and, when war came, he led them. Georgians especially revered him since he spent so much time in the state, spending weeks at a time at his Little White House in Warm Springs. For a time, when E. D. Rivers was governor, the state even had a New Deal program of its own, although voters later refuted Rivers because he was never successful in paying for his programs. The Murphys were strong supporters of Ellis Arnall, who at one time in the 1940s was thought to be a possible vice presidential choice for Roosevelt.

This was the Democratic Party Uncle Bill Murphy talked about at the dinner table and this is the party to which Tom Murphy still clings. "He is more of a New Deal Democrat than I am—and I don't mean that in a bad way," Zell Miller has said. "He is very loyal to the ideals of the Democratic Party that came along with Roosevelt and Truman and beyond."

It wasn't just the economic memories that moved the television Brokaw to tell the story of so many people of that era. Brokaw makes a strong and emotional case that these men and women who came of age during the Depression years were forever transformed by their life-shattering experiences in World War II.

Murphy was in the uniform of a North Georgia College cadet on 7 December 1941, the day Pearl Harbor was bombed and the day America symbolically began to fight. He only had to look around him at the other young men on the parade field in Dahlonega, Georgia, to know their lives would never be the same. They knew where they were going and they would have it no other way. Ten days after he graduated in 1943, he was in the United States Navy. He was nineteen years old

In his 1998 book, Brokaw painted well a picture of what men and women such as Murphy—most of them still in their teens—faced as they went from cap and gown directly into uniform. "They answered the call to help save the world from the two most powerful and ruthless machines ever assembled, instruments of conquest in the hands of fascist maniacs. They faced great odds and a late start, but they did not protest. At a time in their lives when their days and nights should have been filled with innocent adventure, love and the lessons of the workaday world, they were fighting, often hand to hand, in the most primitive conditions possible," he wrote.

Murphy turned twenty and twenty-one on obscure islands in the South Pacific as a member of a Navy Seabee unit and was almost there to celebrate twenty-two. He was one of the fortunate ones, coming home with a single shrapnel wound, not bad enough for even a Purple Heart. Like so many others in that war, he talks very little of what he saw or did.

In writing about these soldiers coming home, Brokaw's words parallel the life of Tom Murphy, how he was mature beyond his years and tempered by what he had been through, how he soon married and started a family, how he "stayed true to (his) values of personal responsibility, duty, honor and faith." Then, how he joined thousands of others going to school on the GI Bill then started to work with the same passion and discipline he needed to survive the war.

Mike Murphy says one word captures his father. "It's duty," he says. "His duty as a father, as a husband, as a lawyer, as a friend, as the Speaker." He learned that from his parents. He was taught about it at North Georgia College. He lived it in the Navy. But the genesis for it all was the Primitive Baptist Church. His father was an elder— the title Primitive Baptists give their preachers. The family went to church on Saturdays and Sundays, far more than a free-spirited country boy really preferred.

"We're foot-washing Baptists," Murphy says, something he has often been teased about. But the Primitive Baptist Church is more than that sacrament. It is a doctrine created in the late 1700s by a hard-shelled group who believe in strict, traditional views. By 1832, the division among Baptists was so sharp that the Primitives withdrew from the fellowship.

The Primitive Baptist is not a denomination that believes in expensive buildings or towering steeples. Its church houses are usually simple. It does not reach out to others, believing that a person will find them if the Primitive Baptist Church is where they belong. Today, it struggles to survive as so many of its younger members have found other church homes. It remains close-knit and private, caring little about expansion or growth—only its core of beliefs.

It is a strict denomination that does not believe in the use of musical instruments in the church, does not believe in

Sunday Schools, does not believe in evangelism or missions and does not believe in schools of theology. It does believe in foot-washing, in the language of the King James translation of the Bible, in predestination, in unity, in law and obdience, in settling your differences, in having only men as the leaders of the church and, as Murphy often quotes, it believes in telling the truth and paying your debts.

According to Primitive Baptist doctrine, their beliefs do not "go beyond the word of God." In plain words, if it is not in the Bible, they do not practice it. Their beliefs were specified in the Black Rock Address in 1832, when they pulled away from the mainstream church. That white-paper explained their objections: "It is true that many things to which we object as departures from the order established by the great Head of the church, through the ministry of his apostles, are by others considered to be connected with the essence of religion, and absolutely necessary to the prosperity of Christ's kingdom. They attach great value to them because human wisdom suggests their importance. We allow the Head of the church to judge for us. We therefore esteem those things to be of no use to the cause of Christ, which he has not himself instituted."

Without delving deeply into theology, elements of Tom Murphy can be seen throughout this treatise. He is dogmatic. He is traditional. He believes in unity and in obeying the law. It is easy to see why he must have had trouble accepting the entry of women into roles of leadership. It is easy to see why he doesn't understand or accept the evangelical aspects of the Christian Right and the Christian Coalition or its political involvements. He believes in keeping his beliefs private and personal.

"You don't see Primitive Baptists out begging folks to join the church, It's a matter of your own belief, what makes you happy. Besides, we're all trying to get to the same place," Murphy says. "That's why I don't believe religion ought to be involved in politics. I just don't believe in proselytizing."

He doesn't campaign on Sundays. He doesn't allow his political ads to be aired on Sundays. He disdains the Christian Coalition that not only campaigns on Sundays but uses the pulpit. "If you want to campaign on Sunday, that's your business. But I'm not going to do it. I wasn't raised that way and I am not going to change. I refuse to go to a church for a political meeting. And lots of people go to church every Sunday just to be seen. I refuse to do that. I've got to live with myself. I found out a long, long time ago that I could hide from everybody in the world but myself and I ain't found no way yet. Lots of folks think I'm an outlaw, or that I don't go to church because I don't go to the big churches. But I'm usually in some church Sunday morning and most of the time we have two or three preachers. I love the singing where they don't have musical instruments. It's just pure singing. I wish I was good enough to be what a Primitive Baptist ought to be, but I know I'm not."

His friend and ally, Marcus Collins, remembers being at the capitol with Murphy when the Speaker said he needed to go to church. They looked in the phone book and found a small Primitive Baptist congregation in Atlanta and the two of them went. "We slipped in the back and sat quietly. The Speaker didn't say nothing to nobody. We just sat there and listened," Collins remembers. "Then, at the end of the service, they asked Brother Tom Murphy to pray. He didn't know them, but they knew him."

Though people may have teased him about being "a foot-washing Baptist," it is a ceremony that affects him greatly. "If that ceremony won't move you, you can't be moved," he says. It is a humbling, personal rite where one person washes another's feet. Not because they need cleaning but, again, because Jesus washed the feet of his disciples. Murphy tells of a Methodist minister who came to the House as its chaplain of the day. Murphy usually bounds into the chamber just at the appointed hour, but this Monday morning he was there early and he began to talk to the minister. "Since yesterday was the first Sunday, you probably had Communion."

"Yes sir, we did," the preacher said.

"Well, can I ask you a question preacher? As I read my book, it says after they took the bread and wine that Christ laid aside his garments and girded himself with a towel and commenced to wash the disciples' feet. He came to Simon Peter and Simon Peter said he wouldn't suffer him to be so and Christ said if I wash thy feet they have no part with me. My question to you, Preacher, is how do you all get around that."

The minister's answer still shocks him. "I've often wondered that myself."

These things impacted Murphy and his politics.

Another defining element to Tom Murphy is his relationship with his late brother James. When he came home from the Navy in 1946, he saw for the first time the seriousness of his brother's James illness. It was rheumatoid arthritis, and it was progressing rapidly. This information had been kept from him when he was in the Pacific. Now he saw James' twisted, weakened body.

Now, more than three decades since his brother's death, he still cries when he remembers him. "He was the smartest man I ever knew," he often says. "He was the best lawyer in this circuit," he adds. Whether or not James Murphy was really as smart as his brother says he was and whether or not he was that talented a lawyer doesn't matter. What is important is that Tom Murphy *believes* he was and, even more importantly, that his caring relationship with his older brother gave a purpose to his life that has forever changed and directed him.

This bull-headed, hot-headed man was slowly transformed. The temper wasn't taken away and neither was his naturally combative nature. But at least, James could point these things out to him when few others would dare.

"I got real cocky after I won that first political race. James called me down about it," says Murphy who saw his brother as his hero—a person he wanted to please, a person he wanted to emulate.

James was a lawyer so he became a lawyer. James needed someone to help him up the stairs, so his brother was there. James prayed for a cure or at best relief and his brother took him wherever there was hope. Like their father, James went into politics and finally so did his brother. It was a tender relationship that fate brought to a man who needed it.

"James was a teacher," says Clarence Vaughn, a law school classmate of the elder Murphy at the University of Georgia and later a member of the Georgia House with his younger brother. "He was bent over so he could hardly go, but he was a scholar, a very brilliant man."

He taught his brother in a variety of ways. "James played a big part in his life and in the political programs he has supported. He had a very profound impression on Tom Murphy," says Vaughn, now a Superior Court judge in Conyers.

People close to him talk about Murphy's softer side, as does Vaughn. "He is a very sensitive man. You wouldn't know it by talking to him on other issues, him being so overpowering. You wouldn't think he was that sentimental on things, but talk to him about supporting programs for the retarded or the handicapped."

Tragically, in recent years, Murphy has again been personally reminded of the heartache of his brother's arthritis through the illness of one of his sons-in-law. John Oxendine, the husband of his younger daughter Mary, was diagnosed in 1998 with amyotrophic lateral sclerosis, commonly known as Lou Gehrig's Disease. As the family has rallied around Mary and John, Murphy has become even more aware of the needs of people with handicaps.

This compassion has carried over to the House chamber. If a bill pertaining to the needs of handicapped people is on the floor, Murphy frequently takes the microphone in support of the measure, often telling the story of his brother James. He is just as apt to get involved if the legislation involves children. Older legislators still remember when former Representative Eleanor Richardson of Atlanta was pleading for state assistance at Grady Hospital's children's ward. Murphy went with her and upon seeing the needs became a champion of Richardson's cause, crying in the well of the House as he described what he had seen.

A living example of Murphy's tender heart is House post office manager Wiley Nixon. Nixon lives in Carrollton, just up the road from Bremen, and commutes to the capitol to take care of the members' mail. Though he is handicapped, he is one of the most valuable members of the House staff. It was Murphy who supported Nixon for the job many years ago. "Mr. Murphy is my friend," he says. "Say something nice about him, you hear?"

Murphy is also a favorite of the capitol maintenance staff. He goes out of his way to be their friend. "I don't know why folks aren't more nice. It doesn't take anything to speak and be friendly," Murphy says. Frequently, he is a loan officer to them. "I've loaned $100 here, $100 there for years—and never lost a dime." Admittedly, these gestures have a payback to him in other ways. Murphy will tell you that the capitol staff keeps him informed of anything that is happening under that golden dome.

People around Bremen have seen this side of Murphy more than people who only see him around the capitol in political settings. At home, he is the biggest fan Bremen High School's athletic teams have. He donates to the booster program. He still shows up at games, even after his own children and grandchildren are no longer participating. When his granddaughter was playing basketball, House members knew when she had a game because her grandfather would sneak away from Atlanta so he could quit politicking and start cheering. Good politics? Surely. But this is also a person who has been personally involved in a town since he was a boy riding his bicycle wherever he went.

Bremen native Robbie Rivers, the clerk of the House since 1992, was impressed with this side of Murphy when he was still in high school. He was in charge of the Monday morning chapel program and he asked Murphy, then just a member of the House, to be their speaker. He remembers very little about his formal remarks. What he remembers was the time they were together prior to Rivers introducing him to the assembly.

"We were out back of the gymnasium and he looked out toward the football field. There was this bank and he told me he remembered when they built that. 'I remember being out there raking and planting grass,'" he said. That has stuck in my mind all these thirty years. I can just see him out there with that big ground rake," Rivers says.

In recent years, many have noted the mellowing of the always blustery Speaker. That is understandable. This powerful man has not been without tragedy. His three older brothers are dead. Agnes Murphy—he always calls her "Mama"—died in November of 1982. "We had thirty-seven years, three months and a few days before the Lord took her," he says. His four children have had more than their share of illness and injury. Now he is going to the funerals of too many friends and relatives—giving a touching eulogy for a first cousin of his in the summer of 1999.

In June 1998, Murphy stood at the graveside of one of his favorite legislative friends, Elmore Thrash. He was eighty-three, eight years older than Murphy. A diminutive fellow from Lowndes County, Thrash was as much a capitol fixture as any of the statues or portraits that decorate the historic building—even after surviving a debilitating stroke. He had been around the Georgia House more on than off since 1927. He served as messenger of the House for forty-three years. More than anything, he was Tom Murphy's friend.

Elmore Thrash could talk to the powerful Speaker as though he was Thrash's little brother who had gotten in trouble at school. When Murphy went astray, Thrash would tell him so. Mo Thrash says his father and the Speaker were like brothers. To the younger Thrash, Tom Murphy has a heart of gold.

During the annual craziness that is the General Assembly, Elmore Thrash was always near the Speaker's elbow. In the morning, if he didn't think Murphy was up, he would call and say something profane to get him out of bed. If Murphy needed to speak to someone, Thrash would go and get them. Outwardly, it looked as if Thrash was taking care of Murphy and his cohorts, but there were times when it was really the other way around. If the group was going too fast for Thrash, they slowed down. If they didn't see him, they looked for him. They needed him and Elmore Thrash needed the House.

More than fifteen years ago, Elmore Thrash didn't think anyone needed him. He was in a hospital in Augusta. He was getting older and he was getting sicker. And he didn't think he could stop drinking. Checking up on his friend frequently, Murphy decided to sidestep the doctors. He went to Augusta to offer his own encouragement. It went something like this: "Elmore, get your ass out of here. The session is coming up and I can't do without you." When Tom Murphy gives orders, people respond. So did his friend, pulling his life together in every way. "He gave him the will to live," Mo Thrash says.

When Elmore Thrash died, he received a state funeral. There was a State Patrol honor guard. There were helicopters hovering over tiny Gay, Georgia. There were 130 State Patrol. Governors came. Legislators people had forgotten showed up for Elmore. Lobbyists, members of the capitol staff, and other people who had had so much fun being around this loyal old man, attended his funeral.

Governor Zell Miller delivered the eulogy. "He taught us how to laugh at ourselves and not to take ourselves so seriously and how to grow old with grace and optimism. I never knew anyone who grew old with more style and flair...I'll think of him frequently as I grow older. He showed me and you how it should be done."

Tom Murphy cried like a baby.

FOR SOME, IT is difficult to connect the man at the graveside with the man at the podium, the man who can put you down with a stare or slice you with words. But they are cut from the same cloth. Every side of this complex country lawyer was shaped and honed by the same forces. His problem is that he only shows the softer side when he chooses—sometimes using the blustery side to mask his own feelings of doubt. After all of these years of being the Tom Murphy whom editorial writers rant about, it may be difficult for even him to step out of this familiar character.

Murphy refuses to use the term middle-class because he doesn't believe in class. He prefers to refer to people based on their income. Like his old friend Lester Maddox, he is most comfortable with these little people. That's why he continues to practice law. That's why the lobby to his law office is usually busy. It keeps him in touch. Good for his politics. Good for his practice. Good for him.

"He is misunderstood and he is under appreciated, but he is good at satisfying people's needs," former press aide Jet Toney says. "All people have to do is ask. Unlike so many other politicians, Tom Murphy is a minister. He doesn't minister to their politics. He ministers to their needs."

These are not things you see about Murphy because these are seldom things he shows. And he is who he is because of where he has been and what he has seen—partly because he is a member of the generation that Tom Brokaw writes about, partly because of the times he carried his brother from the car to his home, partly because of the strictness of the Primitive Baptist Church. Only in recent times has he begun to let others see glimpses of the man instead of the gavel.

Terry Coleman says he has always wanted to write a book about the Speaker. In fact, he shuffled around on his desk in the Appropriations Chairman's office and found a card on which he had written the title he would use. To Coleman, these five words say it all about the Tom Murphy he knows: *"A Sheep in Wolf's Clothing"*

Not bad. Not bad at all.

16

MAN

OF THE

HOUSE

WHITLOW WYATT WAS a pitcher when baseball teams rode trains and the Dodgers got their mail in Brooklyn. He was a hero to the folks in Haralson County old enough to remember him on the mound instead of his farm near Buchanan. He was also a friend of Tom Murphy's. Used to send him $100 every time he qualified for another term.

But it was his big league baseball career that made Murphy keep one of Wyatt's blue Dodger caps under a plastic shield in his office in Bremen. Wyatt's style of pitching was like Murphy's way of running the Georgia House, so Murphy—the old catcher—always enjoyed hearing Wyatt talk about his days in Brooklyn.

"He pitched in the World Series against the New York Yankees. He didn't like to see batters dig in too much. Not even Joe DiMaggio. He pitched him tight and DiMaggio started out to the mound. Before DiMaggio got to the mound, Mickey Owen, the catcher, tackled him. Whit said he didn't care. He already had the ball back."

Whitlow Wyatt, also one of the greatest managers in the history of the minor league Atlanta Crackers, died during the baseball season of 1999. And not only did he and Murphy enjoy giving opponents a hard one under the chin every now and then, they shared another piece of philosophy. "Old Whit was quite a fellow. He said he never did understand relief pitching. He started twenty-four games in 1941 and finished twenty-one of them. He didn't understand these young pitchers. They don't finish."

Tom Murphy also believes in finishing things. That's why after nearly twenty-six years, he is still the Speaker of the Georgia House. He doesn't throw the high hard one as often as he once did. But then, folks quit digging in against him long ago. Years and circumstances have mellowed him, though it still wouldn't be wise to dig your spikes in on him unless you're ready to get the back of your uniform dirty. The Murphy who presides in 2000 isn't the Murphy who unexpectedly became Speaker in 1974. But neither is the world.

"He's kind of like an alligator that has been able to survive the evolutionary changes pretty much intact," Terry Coleman says. "But he still has a pretty strong bite and his jaws are mighty strong. He exerts his authority when it's necessary and when it isn't, he doesn't."

Today, Murphy still is prickly, proud and political. With a few changes, of course. He keeps his temper and his blood pressure under better control. He doesn't work as many hours as he once did. He gives up the gavel to younger members, giving him time to wander the floor and visit, but not so far away that he cannot rescue them if they get in trouble. He shows sides of his personality he once kept hidden under the brim of his Stetson. He even talks about the day when there will be another Speaker of the House.

But observers agree, there will never be another Tom Murphy.

"He's the only stable touchstone," says Roy Barnes.

"He's one leg of the stool," says Calvin Smyre.

"He has managed that store so well," says Bill Lee.

"He is the glue that keeps this state together," says Butch Parrish.

"He has defined the character of Georgia," says Tom Baxter.

"He has put his own imprint on that House," says Zell Miller.

"He will be the benchmark," says Chuck Clay.

"Tom Murphy is the tradition," says Milo Dakin.

"He's the most stable force in state government," says Hermann Talmadge.

"He's the common thread in Georgia politics," says Jet Toney.

Since 1961, he has been answering the roll call as a member of the House. Long enough for a personal reminder when the 1999 session began. Elections had been held. House members new and old were to be given the oath of office. And, according to state law, a member of the state judiciary was there to give them the historic oath. He was a new judge with a new robe and an old name.

Giving the oath that morning was Judge Mike Murphy of the Superior Court in the Tallapoosa Judicial Circuit. He was brief. And he was his father's son. "Before I administer the oath, I want each one of you to understand what a honor this is for me to be standing here. You know, in a way, I've grown up in this House. I was twelve-years-old when my father was first elected at age thirty-six in 1960. As bad as I hate to say it, I'm fifty-one years old today as he is going into his twentieth term. My mother was here for eleven of those terms and I wish she was here today. I always wanted to make a speech. I always dreamed about it when I was a young fellow.... This is my one and only opportunity and I always dreamed I'd be making speeches from the well of this House. But as things turned out, this is my one chance. And I really have but one point I want to make to you and I'll be quite brief. I want to share something that happened to me when our chief judge was considering retiring. It was mentioned to me about becoming a judge. I can tell you that the thought never crossed my mind about being a judge. I had a phone call from a lawyer in a nearby town who called me up and said, 'Mike, you must be flattered that people would think enough of you to ask you to consider this position.' I thought to myself, you should know me better than that. I'm not flattered. I'm humbled. There is a world of difference between being flattered and humbled. I understand the responsibilities of my office and what I hope is that you will remember that. Now that the elections are over and you are about to be sworn in, I want you to remember that after you take your oath. When you go home at night, my prayer for each of us is that when you look in that mirror for the last time and turn out the lights and go to bed, that you can say to yourself that I did what was right for all of the people of Georgia to the best of my ability." Then with one hand raised and the other on the Bible, he swore in the duly elected members of the 1999-2000 House. One of them was his father.

The appearance of this fifty-one year old judge was a physical reminder of how long Tom Murphy had served—as if House members need a reminder of those twenty plus years. They're older, too. They know that Murphy's time as their leader is growing short. "Whoever the next speaker is, it will be a tough place," says Governor Roy Barnes, a former House member. "That's the great unknown, but that person will have to have some of the traits of Tom Murphy to make it over the short term. They will need that unique ability to bring in and co-op the sinners. That's really been the secret of his success when you get down to it. That will be tough for someone just winning as speaker to master...and really the key to their success is whether they'll be able to master that."

Zell Miller says Murphy's personal imprints will make it difficult for the person who succeeds him. "There will never be another one like him. There will never be another Tom Murphy in Georgia history, because the House has changed so much. And he has put his imprint on that House, his own personal imprint, so strongly that whenever he is gone, it is just going to completely change. Nobody else will ever have that kind of power for that extended time ever again."

Jim Wooten confesses that his outlook on Murphy has changed dramatically. "I have come to see him differently in recent years as I begin to look at the world after him," he says. "This is a House on the verge of chaos."

A look no farther away than Alabama shows what Wooten may be envisioning. Alabama's government has been at a political standstill because of disruptions between the governor and the two governing bodies as well as serious conflicts between Democrats and Republicans.

Marcus Collins believes Murphy will be missed more than some people realize. "I've got enough sense to know that times marches on. I know his time is limited and I know it won't break when he's gone. But I'm going to tell you this. Five years after he's gone, people are going to say, 'Why did we let him leave?'"

Speculation of his successor has circulated for many years. Assuming Democrats maintain control of the House, Terry Coleman and Larry Walker would be the first names mentioned. Among capitol insiders, they are called "the young princes." These two veteran House members long have been seen as the leading candidates since veteran Speaker Pro-Tem Jack Connell of Augusta is too old to be thought of as a successor. Coleman, as chairman of the Appropriations Committee, has to be considered the favorite since knowledge of the budget process will be so vital to the person who takes over the position.

Walker has been a victim of circumstance. He has in the past considered runs for governor and Congress but decided against both moves. Now he could be passed over for this position.

No one can forecast how the race for speaker will come together, but Coleman and Walker could cancel one another out. Both have revolved in the same circles in the House. And, depending on the popularity and strength of Murphy at that time, the two of them might be bypassed because of their obvious ties to the Speaker. Both are from Middle Georgia—Coleman from Eastman and Walker from Perry—and that could split the South Georgia votes. Observers also note that until 1998 when Mark Taylor of Albany and Cathy Cox of Bainbridge were elected lieutenant governor and secretary of state, South Georgia candidates had been faring poorly in statewide elections. How that would translate into votes within the House is unknown. Should Coleman and Walker falter, the door would be open to anyone, but rising leaders such as Jimmy Skipper of Americus, Calvin Smyre of Columbus, and Dubose Porter of Dublin would be among the names at the top of the next tier of possibilities.

Should Republicans gain control before Murphy retires, Minority Leader Bob Irvin of Atlanta would be the likely choice among current Republicans since he has been the GOP's choice to run against Murphy the past two terms.

Sometimes, the ones who are waiting for their time appear to be getting exasperated, as Dick Pettys notes. "Murphy's generation, his peers, they're almost all gone. He relies on his lieutenants but they are younger, almost his children or even his grandsons. I sometimes see in him a little impatience, a paternalistic impatience. And on their side, I can almost see a son's exasperation, a son chafing under paternal discipline."

Whoever the next Speaker of the Georgia House is, he or she also will face the same challenges football coaches meet when they are hired to replace a legend. Seldom does that person succeed. Too much is expected of them. Comparisons are drawn to their predecessor. Roadblocks are quietly put in their way. Support wanes, since so much of the support was there because the longtime coach was so popular. Similar things also will be hurdles for the person who succeeds Tom Murphy, meaning the next Speaker will be considered by many as a caretaker, assuming that another candidate soon will emerge.

But Tom Murphy also faced such obstacles and such comments in 1973 when his candidacy first was mentioned. How, everyone wondered, could anyone replace George L. Smith? He was a giant. He was irreplaceable. Now the name of George L. Smith is mentioned among only a few.

When he makes his decision to again be just a country lawyer, Murphy will leave behind a political legacy unparalleled by a single Georgia legislator. His fingerprints will be found on most of the important legislation that has come out of the General Assembly for the past forty years. He is a rural legislator who helped build the Atlanta of today.

When MARTA needed help, there was Murphy, then the Speaker Pro-Tem. It was one of the first times since the demise of the County Unit System that a rural legislator had come to the aide of urban Atlanta. It was also a departure from the legislature's love of asphalt. "We're pouring millions and millions of dollars down those rat-holes we call expressways and they're obsolete before we finish them," he told the House. His speech was fiery enough for his seatmate Jim Parrish to change his vote. "You son-of-a-bitch," he snapped at Murphy. "You didn't convince them. You shamed them."

Murphy also supported the original construction for the World Congress Center, improvements for Grady Hospital, and the building of the Georgia Dome. This was made easier by the fact that since Atlanta is the capital city, legislators from all over Georgia experience its problems every year. This is in contrast to other states whose capital cities are not their urban centers.

Zell Miller says Murphy was among the first to recognize the extraordinary needs of Atlanta. "He knows that you have to have this economic engine that is Atlanta in order to have the revenue that is needed to run the state. That is a very important part of this man from rural Georgia—and about as rural as you can get—that he has often times been the champion of these projects in Atlanta."

At the same time, Murphy has been instrumental in the construction of the Agriculture Center in Perry, the Carpet Center in Dalton, the Trade Center in Savannah and the RiverCenter for the Performing Arts in Columbus. "It's time we did things for the rest of Georgia," he said. The *Atlanta Journal-Constitution* slammed him editorially for these things but it didn't bother him. "That's all right," he said. "I'm a tough old bird."

Jim Wooten believes state finances should be Murphy's legacy. "I think the one area that he will never get the credit that he is due is that he and his generation, and the people who believe the way he does, have made it possible for this generation of legislators to have as much money to spend as they do. This state moved forward and has achieved absolutely sound fiscal condition in part because these people hated debt. They were afraid of it. They saw what debt had done in the Depression, that you lose the farm if you can't make the payments. They were frugal. They didn't borrow excessively. They didn't grant exemptions to the tax law. The younger legislators are spending the resources that Tom Murphy provided us."

These are the concrete pieces of legislation. Many say his legacy should include the legislation that did not pass. Through his influence, the Georgia House has never been bogged down in protracted debates over emotional issues such as gun control, abortion or prayer in schools. Governors and lieutenant governors have depended on him to protect the state against the hot-button issues as well as other items that would be considered simply bad legislation.

AS HIS PERSONAL powers have grown, Tom Murphy has been able to build the strength of the House and the entire General Assembly. To his old friend Judge Clarence Vaughn, this is the way the framers of Georgia's government intended it to be. "He has been in charge of the legislative division and has kept it separate from the other branches of government exactly as our founding fathers wanted it to be," says Vaughn, now a Superior Court judge in Rockdale County. "He wasn't particularly behind the scenes because he is too outspoken for that, but he has been a shadow part of the cabinet of every governor we've had in the past thirty years."

His own party has also depended upon him. Hard-core Democrats see him as the state's most loyal party member. It has also depended upon him to be a sentinel for party problems, using his loyalty and his fearless reputation. In 1984, when former Labor Commissioner Sam Caldwell and members of his staff were facing indictments, party regulars wanted Caldwell to resign. Only no one wanted to deliver the message. Caldwell had been a state department head more than twenty years and was closely aligned with the followers of Senator Herman Talmadge. Murphy took the assignment.

Steve Anthony and Jet Toney from the Speaker's staff were dispatched to Caldwell's office while Murphy went to get his car. The two messengers told the commissioner that Murphy wanted to see him—right then. They walked with him to the sidewalk outside the labor department building and stayed with him until Murphy drove up. The two Democrats rode around town for quite awhile. During the trip, Caldwell was given the symbolic kiss of death from the party. "It's over, Sam," Murphy told him. Caldwell resigned.

But Murphy is more than a party hatchet man, though his reputation always precedes him. That must have been on the mind of Representative Chuck Sims one night when the phone rang at his home. He was wrestling in the floor with his sons so his young daughter answered the phone. She laughed and talked for a long time before finally handing the phone to her father.

"It's Mr. Murphy," she said.

Sims was nervous. What did the Speaker want with him at home? What have I done? And why did his little girl talk to him so long? He quickly asked her what was said.

"It's just Mr. Murphy," she explained.

Hearing the story, Murphy saw nothing unusual about the little girl's extended conversation with him. "Kids know people who love them," he said.

There is the paradox. A big-time Democrat with a hatchet is the same man that takes time enough to patter with a little girl on the phone. But that will always be the paradox of Tom Murphy. As the sun begins to set on his tenure, the memories of those years will be just as enigmatic as the man.

Tom Baxter says Murphy has defined the state's character. "Georgia is uniquely Southern but not quite like the other Southern states. Somebody once told me that you will never find anyone from Georgia who got suckered on anything. They're never willing to admit they've been 'hornswaggled.' And I don't think anyone ever did sucker Tom Murphy. There is something in that character — hard nosed, cigar chewing, poker playing, the mean rawboned guy with the heart of gold. These are defining traits, even in the Georgia we see today."

To Herman Talmadge, Murphy is one of the few contemporary politicians with old-fashioned courage. "Practically all of them today are just like a kite in the breeze. They drift which ever way the breeze is blowing," the former governor and US Senator says. "Tom has the courage of his convictions. He will give you a yes and a no. He means what he says and he says what he means. He has guts — which is the most scarce commodity among politicians there is. We have a lot of people that are well educated. We have a lot of politicians who are intelligent. But we have practically none with any courage. I often wonder what would have happened to this state had Murphy not been in the leadership of the House."

Republican Congressman Johnny Isakson says Murphy's personal power will overshadow his good deeds. "His assimilation of power and his ability to keep it through dynamic changes is incredible," he says. "It's sad that the things he did for little people won't be written about — and I'm not talking about political favors."

When will he step aside? Perhaps Tom Murphy isn't even sure. He openly said he would not run again in 1998, but he did, saying veteran colleagues told him they wouldn't run if he stepped aside. Now, some of his closest friends are saying he plans one more run for Speaker in 2000. Friends say when he does go, he will go on his own terms. What this indecision will mean to his ability to lead and manage the House isn't clear. What it will mean to the Democratic Party depends on factors beyond the House. What it will mean to the younger members who want to move into the leadership roles in the future will have to be observed.

After nearly three decades, it is still interesting to watch Murphy himself. During the 1999 session, members and other observers said he was the most relaxed and content they had seen him in years, while at the same time he had regained all of his mental sharpness after his light stroke in 1998. People in the pressroom laughed during one debate when Murphy had given up the gavel to one of his lieutenants and was strolling around the chamber. Dick Pettys of the Associated Press was busily taking notes when he was surprised to look up and see Murphy — his nose pressed against the glass that separates media from member. Murphy just laughed and continued on his way.

Governor Roy Barnes sees all of this as a peculiar way for Murphy "to plan his own funeral." For him, it is hard to watch, though remarkable, he says. "I've watched him and

I've listened to him. He has taken the people he knows are the people who will be considered as the next speaker and he is putting them up there at the podium to let the members see how they perform. This goes back to that paternalistic side he has. Remember, he feels he is the protector of a family...and the protector of an institution. Subconsciously in my view, he has come to the conclusion that his great final act in protecting the House is to allow some orderly transition. And the way he has decided to do that is to allow all of those princes-in-waiting to have their time up there and for others to be able to make a better choice. I don't know if he planned that, but it is a remarkable thing to behold."

TOM MURPHY HAS mellowed. But so have the people around him, even his most strident dissidents. He wants only to be remembered as a man who told the truth, and maybe that is enough. He claims only to be "Baptist and a Democrat," although he frequently repeats a phrase that has become his mantra: "Everybody knows I'm an ultra-conservative on fiscal matters. But when it comes to old folks, little children, and the mentally ill, I am a bleeding heart liberal and I don't care who knows it. There are still folks we have to look after and I've always tried to do that."

Knowing those people still need help—more specifically, his help—he may want to stay for another inning, for like Whit Wyatt he despises relief pitchers.

Bill Bulger, who gave up presiding over the senate in Massachusetts to be a college president, said he stayed in politics "as long as the party was fun." He said he planned to leave when it became tedious or dull. "It would be good to go quickly and with a certain grace. I should hate to linger in the doorway like an awkward guest, one who could not bring himself to say his thanks, bid a cheerful farewell and be about his way."

When the party's no longer fun for Tom Murphy, one would hope that he accepts it and is able to leave with grace and that his farewell will be that cheerful. Right now the party is still fun. Murphy revealed in early November 1999 that he intends to stay around for one more term. At least. He and other democrats want him to preside over the all-important re-apportionment in 2000. So for now, he will swing that big gavel as he always has and bark out the run-together phrases he can recite in his sleep.

"There's a certain awe you feel on occasion just watching him work—hearing that auctioneer's cadence or watching him close a session sine die," Dick Pettys says. "There is a theatrical majesty about it. He's artful. There's just something there. Even after how many years of watching, there are times I am awestruck by it."

And so is the rest of Georgia.

APPENDIX 1

SPEAKERS OF THE GEORGIA HOUSE

1777	Noble Wimberly Jones, Chatham
1778	James Whitfield, Chatham
1780	William Glascock, Richmond
1781	Nathan Brownson, Liberty and John Jones, Burke
1782	William Gibbons, Sr., Camden; Samuel Saltus, Liberty; Joseph Clay, Chatham; and James Habersham, Chatham
1783	John Houston, Chatham; Noble Wimberly Jones; and William Gibbons Sr., Sr., Chatham
1784	James Habersham, Chatham
1785	Joseph Habersham, Chatham
1786-1787	William Gibbons Sr.
1788	Nathan Brownson, Effingham
1789	John Powell, Burke
1789-1790	Seaborn Jones, Richmond
1791-1793	William Gibbons, Chatham
1794-1795	Thomas Napier, Richmond
1796	Thomas Stevens, Liberty
1797-1801	David Meriwether, Wilkes
1802-1806	Abraham Jackson, Burke
1806-1810	Benjamin Whitaker, Jefferson
1811	Robert Iverson, Putnam
1812-1818	Benjamin Whitaker, Jefferson
1819 1820	David Adams, Jasper
1821	David Witt, Jackson
1821	David Adams, Jasper
1822	Allen Daniel, Madison
1823	David Adams, Jasper
1824-1825	John Abercrombie, Hancock
1825	Thomas W. Murray, Lincoln
1826-1828	Irby Hudson, Putnam
1829	Warren Jourdan, Jones
1830-1832	Asbury Hull, Clarke
1833-1834	Thomas Glascock, Richmond
1835-1839	Joseph Day, Jones
1840	Charles Jenkins, Richmond

1841-1842	William Wofford, Habersham
1843-1847	Charles Jenkins, Richmond
1849-1850	John W. Anderson, Chatham
1851-1852	James A. Meriwether, Putnam
1853-1854	John E. Ward, Chatham
1855-1856	William H. Stiles, Chatham
1857-1858	John W.H. Underwood, Floyd
1859	Isiah Tucker Irvin, Wilkes
1860	Charles J. Williams, Muscogee
1861-1863	Warren Akin, Cass
1863-1866	Thomas Hardeman, Bibb
1868-1870	Robert L. McWhorter, Greene
1871	James M. Smith, Muscogee
1872-1873	Joseph B. Cumming, Richmond
1873-1874	Augustus O. Bacon, Bibb
1875-1876	Thomas Hardeman, Bibb
1877-1881	Louis F. Garrard, Muscogee
1884-1887	William A. Little, Muscogee
1888-1889	Alexander S. Clay, Cobb
1890-1891	Clark Howell, Fulton
1892-1893	William Y. Atkinson, Coweta
1894-1895	William H. Fleming, Richmond
1896-1897	Hudson A. Jenkins, Putnam
1898-1901	John D. Little, Muscogee
1902-1904	Newton A. Morris, Cobb
1905-1908	John M. Slaton, Fulton
1909-1912	John N. Holder, Jackson
1913-1917	William H. Burwell, Hancock
1917-1920	John N. Holder, Jackson
1921-1926	William Cecil Neill, Muscogee
1927-1931	Richard Brevard Russell Jr., Barrow
1931	Arlie Daniel Tucker, Berrien
1933-1935	Eurith Dickerson Rivers, Lanier
1937-1940	Roy Harris, Richmond
1941-1942	Randall Evans Jr., McDuffie
1943-1946	Roy Harris, Richmond
1947-1954	Fred Hand, Mitchell
1955-1958	Marvin Moate, Hancock
1959-1962	George L. Smith, Emanuel
1963-1966	George T. Smith, Grady
1967-1973	George L. Smith, Emanuel
1974-1999	Thomas B. Murphy, Haralson

APPENDIX 2

Georgia Governors Tom Murphy has served:

* Ernest Vandiver	1959-1963
* Carl Sanders	1963-1967
* Lester Maddox	1967-1971
# Jimmy Carter	1971-1975
George Busbee	1975-1983
Joe Frank Harris	1983-1991
Zell Miller	1991-1999
Roy Barnes	1999-Present

- As a member of the House
- # Became Speaker in 1974

APPENDIX 3

Family History:

GREAT GRAND-PARENTS:
James Harvey Murphy and Sabra Denman Murphy
Thomas B. Jones and Celia S. Jones

GRAND-PARENTS:
Bailey Murchison Murphy and Martha Sewell Murphy
John Thomas Jones and Helen Hogan Jones

PARENTS:
William Harvey Murphy and Leta Jones Murphy

SIBLINGS:
Brothers: William Earl Murphy, Eugene Hogan Murphy, James Rutherford Murphy (three sisters died at birth)

MARRIED:
Agnes Bennett (d. November 28, 1982)
Bremen, Georgia
July 22, 1946

CHILDREN:
Michael Louis Murphy, February 15, 1947
Martha Louise Long (Dennis), May, 18, 1949
Lynn McAdams (Kenny), December 6, 1950
Mary June Oxendine (John), June 1, 1956

GRAND-CHILDREN:
David Bailey McBrayer, 1967
Matthew Chad Long, 1971
Holly Michelle Long, 1974
Lauren Murphy, 1975
Lyndsey-Michael McAdams, 1986

GREAT GRAND-CHILD:
D.J. McBrayer (1997)

APPENDIX 4

Tom Murphy: Brief Chronology

BORN:
Thomas Bailey Murphy
March 10, 1924
Bremen, Georgia

EDUCATION:
Bremen High School (1941)
North Georgia College (1943)
University of Georgia Law School (1946)

MILITARY:
United States Navy (1943-1946)

RELIGION:
Primitive Baptist

PUBLIC SERVICE:
Bremen Board of Education (1948-1965)
Chairman, Bremen Board of Education (1960-1965)
Georgia House of Representatives (1960-Present)
Administrative Floor Leader for Gov. Lester Maddox (1967-1970)
Speaker Pro-Tem of House (1970-1973)
Speaker of the House (1974-Present)

ORGANIZATIONS:
President, Bremen PTA; First President Bremen Rotary Club;
American Legion; Moose Club; Fraternal Order of Police; Peace
Officers Association; Blue Key National Honor Society; Georgia
Sheriffs Association; Georgia Veterans of Foreign Wars (Lifetime
Member) and the Gridiron Secret Society; Chairman, Council of
State Governments.

BIBLIOGRAPHY

Books

Bartley, Numan V. *The New South, 1945-1980: The Story of the South's Modernization*. Baton Rouge, LA: Louisiana State University Press, 1995.

Black, Earl, and Merle Black. *Politics and Society in the South*. Cambridge, MA: Harvard University Press, 1987.

Bowles, Billy and Remer Tyson. *They Love a Man in the Country: Saints and Sinners in the South*. Atlanta, GA: Peachtree Publishers, Ltd., 1989.

Bremen, Georgia Centennial Edition, 1883-1983. Bremen, GA: Gateway Printing Company, 1983.

Brokaw, Tom. *The Greatest Generation*. New York: Random House, 1998.

Bulger, William M. *While the Music Lasts: My Life in Politics*. Boston, MA: Houghton Houghton Mifflin Company, 1996.

Caldwell, Sam. *The Caldwell Conspiracy*. Lakemont, GA: Copple House, 1987.

Carter, Dan T. *From George Wallace to Newt Gingrich: Race in the Conservative Counterrevolution 1963-1994*. Baton Rouge, LA: Louisiana State University Press, 1996.

Clarke, Harold G. *Remembering Forward*. Macon, GA: Mercer University Press, 1995.

Clowse, Barbara Barksdale. *Ralph McGill, A Biography*. Macon, GA: Mercer University Press, 1998.

Cook, James F. Carl Sanders: *Spokesman of the New South*. Macon, GA: Mercer University Press, 1993.

Cook, James F. *The Governors of Georgia, 1754-1995: Revised and expanded*. Macon, GA: Mercer University Press, 1995.

Fleischmann, Arnold, and Caroll Pierannunzi. *Politics in Georgia*. Athens, GA: The University of Georgia Press, 1997.

Gingrich, Newt. *To Renew America*. New York: Harper Collins Publishers, 1995.

Godbold, Edwin C. *Dillingent in His Business: Warren Sewell*. Atlanta, GA: Warren and Ava Sewell Foundation, 1985.

Goodwin, Doris Kearns. *Lyndon Johnson and The American Dream*. New York: St. Martin's Press, 1991.

Halberstam, David. *The Fifties*. New York: Fawcett Columbine, 1993.

Haralson County History Book. Dallas, Texas: Taylor Publishing Company, 1983.

Harris, Joe Frank. *Personal Reflections on a Public Life: The Autobiography of Georgia's 78th Governor*. Macon, GA: Mercer University Press, 1998.

Henderson, Harold P., and Gary L. Roberts. *Georgia Governors in an Age of Change: from Ellis Arnall to George Busbee*. Athens, GA: The University of Georgia Press, 1991.

Hepburn, Lawrence R., editor. *Contemporary Georgia*. Athens GA: Carl Vinson Institute of Government, The University of Georgia, 1987..

Hyatt, Richard. Zell: *The Governor Who Gave Georgia HOPE*. Macon, GA: Mercer University Press, 1997.

Kearns, Doris. *Lyndon Johnson and The American Dream*. Kytle, New York: Signet's New American Library, 1976.

Kytle, Clavin, and James A. Mackay. *Who Runs Georgia?: A contemporary account of the 1947 crisis that set the stage for Georgia's politcal transformation*. Athens, GA: The University of Georgia Press, 1998.

Mills, James R. *A Disorderly House: The Brown-Unruh Years in Sacramento*. Berkeley CA: Heyday Books, 1987.

Murphy, Reg, and Hal Gulliver. *The Southern Strategy*. New York: Charles Scribner's Sons, 1971.

Newman, Lois Owens. *Haralson County, Georgia — A History*. Roswell, GA: Carroll County Genealogical Society, W.H. Wolfe Associates Historical Publications, 1994.

Shipp, Bill. *The Ape-Slayer and Other Snapshots*. Macon, GA: Mercer University Press, 1997.

Short, Bob. *Everything's Pickrick: The Biography of Lester Maddox*. Macon, GA: Mercer University Press, 1999.

Spritzer, Lorraine Nelson, and Jean B. Bergmark. *Grace Towns Hamilton and the Politics of Southern Change: An African American woman's struggle for racial equality*. Athens, GA: The University of Georgia Press, 1997.

Magazines

American Journalism Review, Adelphi, MD.
Atlanta Journal-Constitution Sunday Magazine. Atlanta, GA.
Atlanta Magazine. Atlanta, GA.
Georgia Historical Quarterly, Athens, GA.
Georgia Journal, Athens, GA.
Georgia Magazine, Tucker, GA.
Georgia Trend, Atlanta, GA.

Newspapers

The Atlanta Constitution, Atlanta, Georgia.
The Atlanta Journal, Atlanta, GA.
The Atlanta Journal-Constitution, Atlanta, GA.
The Bremen Gateway, Bremen, GA.
The Columbus Enquirer, Columbus, GA.
The Columbus Ledger, Columbus, GA.
The Columbus Ledger-Enquirer, Columbus, GA.
The Macon Telegraph, Macon, GA.

Personal Interviews

Allen, Rick, Atlanta, 1996

Barnes, Roy, Atlanta, March 21, 1999

Baxter, Tom, (Telephone) August 25, 1999

Blanchard, Jim, Columbus, GA., April 29, 1998

Buck, Tom, Atlanta, January 22, 1998

Bullock, Charles (Telephone) August 12, 1999

Chambliss, Tommy, Atlanta, February 16, 1998

Clay, Chuck, (Telephone) September 7, 1999

Coleman, Terry, Atlanta, March 19, 1998

Collins, Marcus, Atlanta, January 15, 1998

Dakin, Milo, (Telephone) August 9, 1999

Edwards, Ward, Atlanta, January 15, 1998

Holcomb, Bryce, Atlanta, March 19, 1998

Holladay, Mac, Atlanta, March 6, 1998

Houston, Jim, Atlanta and Columbus, GA., 1998, 1999

Irvin, Tommy, Atlanta, February 16, 1998

Isakson, Johnny, (Telephone) September 13, 1999

Jamieson, Jeanette, (Telephone) September 7, 1999

Kaye, Mitchell, Atlanta, March, 6, 1998

Lee, Bill, Atlanta, January 16, 1998

Long, Martha Murphy, Bremen, GA., April 30, 1998

McDonald, Bubba, Atlanta, February, 1998

Maddox, Lester, Atlanta, March 1998

McAdams, Lynn Murphy, Bremen, GA., April 30, 1998

McGahee, Nelson, Columbus, GA., August 11, 1999

McWherter, Ned, (Telephone) September 9, 1999

Miller, Zell, Atlanta and Young Harris, GA., 1996, 1997, 1998 1999

Murphy, Harold, (Telephone) September 4, 1999

Murphy, Carol, Bremen, GA., April 30, 1998

Murphy, Mike, Bremen, GA., April 30, 1998

Murphy, Tom, Atlanta and Bremen, GA., 1997, 1998, 1999

Oxendine, Mary Murphy, (Telephone) September 29, 1999

Parrish, Butch, Atlanta, February 16, 1998

Pettys, Dick, Atlanta, March 11, 1999

Porter, DuBose, Atlanta, March 4, 1998

Rivers, Robbie, Atlanta, August 18, 1999

Rowan, Bobby, Atlanta, February 16, 1998

Shipp, Bill, Atlanta, 1996

Sims, Chuck, Atlanta, February 16, 1998

Smyre, Calvin, Atlanta, January 16, 1998

Steely, Mel, Carrollton, GA., May 6, 1998

Talmadge, Herman (Interview with Jet Toney) Lovejoy, GA., 1990

Taylor, Mark, (Telephone) September 1, 1999

Thompson, Albert, (Telephone) September 7, 1999

Thrash, Elmore, Atlanta, February 16, 1998

Thrash, Mo, Atlanta, March 11, 1999

Toney, Jet, Atlanta, March 4, 1998

Towery, Matt, (Telephone) May 12, 1998

Vaughn, Clarence, (Telephone) September 11, 1999

Walker, Larry, Atlanta, March 4, 1998

White, Otis, Atlanta, March 6, 1998

Wooten, Jim, Atlanta, March 5, 1998

Video Tapes

Georgia Heritage Project, State University of West Georgia, Carrollton, GA (Three interviews conducted in Bremen and Atlanta by Mel Steeley, 1997)

ACKNOWLEDGMENTS

_____

SUMMER OF 1997. Bremen, Georgia. We were there to get acquainted, to make Tom Murphy more comfortable about having a book written on his life. Three of us gathered in a meeting room at his law office. There was no microphone, no tape recorder, no list of probing questions. Just a legal pad and a pen to jot down pertinent names and phone numbers.

After a few minutes of small-talk, the speaker said there wasn't much to say, that he didn't know why anybody would want to do a book on him. Then, as he reared back in his chair and started telling tales, I scrambled for my pad. He giggled as he talked about he and Carl McPherson getting into scrapes as young boys. He remembered the Great Depression, World War II and the everlasting memory of seeing his brother James in a wheelchair for the first time. He talked about the Georgia House, Republicans, old friends and a few old enemies. Quickly, he jumped to the question that was on my mind and also on the mind of Cecil Staton, the publisher of Mercer University Press.

"I should tell you right now," Murphy said. "I ain't gonna run again."

That got our attention. Then he talked about being tired, about how politics wasn't as much fun as it used to be. "And I don't why you all want to do a book about me, anyway. Nobody's gonna read it."

He changed his mind about running again and I think this book will change his mind about having a newspaper reporter peek into his life and about being the subject of a book. Talking about himself and his accomplishments doesn't come easy for Tom Murphy. You learn as much by watching as you by listening. As his Republican colleague Johnny Isakson says, "The Speaker says more by saying nothing." But that morning in his office, he was in a playful mood and as I scrambled to take down the high spots, he replayed his life. There was a twinkle in his eye and his voice as he told his personal war stories.

Without knowing it, Tom Murphy was loosely describing the outline of this book. The rest of my time has been spent putting the meat back on those bones. The resulting story is his story with my words, my observations and my conclusions. It is also a concluding chapter on Georgia politics as we aging natives know it, for Thomas Bailey Murphy is the last of a down-home breed. For someone weaned on colorful larger-than-life political figures, their passage from the Southern scene is reason to mourn. The self-important breed that follows has been assembled on a button-down assembly line that is turning out a generation of politician that makes a writer want to sell his keyboard and spend his lifetime watching reruns on the Home Shopping Network.

As a Georgia boy who saw his first face-to-face governor while listening to Ben Fortson tell tales to his third-grade class at the state capitol, I've been blessed. As a reporter in Atlanta and Columbus, I have written about those characters of the past. Sometimes while they were on top. Too often while they were laying in state. For me, writing about these colorful but fading characters has been a gift.

Thanks to Mercer University Press, I have been able to record the stories of first Zell Miller and now Tom Murphy. Writing about them has underscored to me their intertwining impact on their state. I hope that after reading these books a person will have a deeper understanding of who they are and why they are. And while you're on their journeys, I trust you will learn more about Georgia, her history and her politics.

But don't consider this book an academic history on the politics or the career of Tom Murphy. Nor is it a definitive look into his historic performance as Speaker of the Georgia House. Such assignments will fall to the trained historians who come later. I did not seek to defend or attack, just to explain why Murphy is the towering figure who has been a common link between so many people and events and to reveal where the foundation of his political beliefs were laid.

Such an effort can't be done in a vacuum. Help is required in massive quantities. My support came from a number of directions, much of it starting in Bremen, Georgia. The Murphy family—Mike, Martha, Lynn, Mary and Carol—opened their doors to a stranger and in typical blunt fashion threw out their opinions and told their stories. Murphy's other family, his loyal staff at the state capitol, wanted this book done right so they offered needed support and a long list of private phone numbers. And in their own way, each of the 180 men and women in the Georgia House helped make this work possible.

On an individual level, thanks to Marcus Collins for his cheese toast, his solicited and unsolicited insight, and for finding clean coffee cups for a newcomer at his early-morning breakfasts. Thanks to my colleagues in the capitol press room, particularly Dick Pettys of the Associated Press, whose decades of covering the capitol ought to get him a better parking space than the governor. I'm glad I got to meet Elmore Thrash, a man I won't forget. And a special thanks to Joy Dunn who helped organize the stacks of research.

Even with a good story to tell, a writer is only as good as his research. I offer special thanks to the library staffs at Columbus State University, Georgia State University, Mercer University, the Washington Library in Macon, the Sewell Library in Bremen, and, most of all, the helpful people at the State University of West Georgia where Dr. Mel Steeley made available the university's valued files of historic video tapes.

Two times—both in extraordinary conditions—I have worked with the people of Mercer University Press. They are friends as much as they are publishers. Quietly, they are putting together a catalogue of biographies on Georgians you ought to know and read. Words of thanks to Cecil P. Staton, Jr., Marc A. Jolley, Kevin Manus, and Amelia Barclay. Special gratitude to Johnny Mitchell, Senior Vice President of Public and Governmental Affairs for Mercer University, who graciously lets the members of the General Assembly think *they* are making the laws.

But without Tom Murphy there would have been no story. In early 1999, a reporter asked the speaker about the book I was writing about him. "I don't give a damn what he writes," Murphy cracked. But he has and he does. He is a complex man with a simple story who has been a footnote to most of the history that has been made in his state for the past four decades.

I'm glad I got to go along for the ride.

RICHARD HYATT
Columbus, GA
September, 1999

INDEX